DAMN RIGHT!

BEHIND THE SCENES WITH BERKSHIRE HATHAWAY BILLIONAIRE CHARLIE MUNGER

Janet Lowe

JOHN WILEY & SONS, INC.

New York • Chichester • Weinheim • Brisbane • Singapore • Toronto

Published by John Wiley & Sons, Inc.
Published simultaneously in Canada.

This publication is designed to provide accurate and authoritative information in regard to the subject matter covered. It is sold with the understanding that the publisher is not engaged in rendering professional services. If professional advice or other expert assistance is required, the services of a competent professional person should be sought.

Library of Congress Cataloging-in-Publication Data:

Lowe, Janet.
   Damn right! : behind the scenes with Berkshire Hathaway billionaire Charlie Munger / Janet Lowe
      p. cm.
   "Charles T. Munger speeches": p. .
   Includes bibliographical references and index.
   ISBN 13: 978-0-471-44691-0
   1. Munger, Charles T., 1924-   2. Capitalists and financiers—United States—Biography. 3. Berkshire Hathaway Inc.—History. I. Title: Behind the scenes with Berkshire Hathaway billionaire Charlie Munger. II. Title: Berkshire Hathaway billionaire Charlie Munger. III. Title.

HG172.M84 L69 2000
332.6′092—dc21
[B]

                                                            00-043745

FOREWORD

L ate in the summer of 1991, I appeared before a house subcommittee chaired by Congressman Ed Markey to answer questions about the Salomon scandal. The hearing room was piled high with TV and print reporters, and I was more than a little nervous when Chairman Markey led off with his first question. He wanted to know whether the reprehensible behavior that had occurred at Salomon was characteristic of Wall Street or rather, as he put it, *"sui generis."*

Normally I would have panicked at the introduction of such a strange-sounding term: In high school, I barely made it through elementary Spanish and never came close to Latin. But, I had no trouble with *sui generis*. After all, I knew a walking, talking example: Charlie Munger, my long-time friend and partner.

Charlie truly is one of a kind. I recognized that in 1959, when I first met him, and I have been discovering unique qualities in him ever since. Anyone who has had even the briefest contact with Charlie would tell you the same. But usually they would be thinking of his, shall we say, behavioral style. Miss Manners clearly would need to do a lot of work on Charlie before she could grant him a diploma.

To me, however, what makes Charlie special is his character. It's true that his mind is breathtaking: He's as bright as any person I've ever met and, at 76, still has a memory I would kill for. He was born, though, with these abilities. It's how he has elected to use them that makes me regard him so highly.

In 41 years, I have never seen Charlie try to take advantage of anyone, nor have I seen him claim the least bit of credit for anything that he didn't do. In fact, I've witnessed exactly the opposite: He has knowingly let me and others have the better end of a deal, and he has also always shouldered more than his share of the blame when things go wrong and accepted less than his share of credit when the reverse has been true. He is generous in the deepest sense and never lets ego interfere with rationality. Unlike most individuals, who hunger for the world's approval, Charlie judges himself entirely by an inner scorecard—and he is a tough grader.

On business matters, Charlie and I agree a very high percentage of the time. On social issues, however, we sometimes see things differently. But despite the fact that we both cherish our strong opinions, we have never in our entire friendship had an argument nor found disagreement a reason to be disagreeable. It's very difficult to imagine Charlie on a corner in a Salvation Army uniform—no, make that *impossible* to imagine—but he seems to have embraced the charity's creed of "hate the sin but not the sinner."

And, speaking of sin, Charlie even brings rationality to that subject. He concludes, of course, that sins such as lust, gluttony, and sloth are to be avoided. Nevertheless, he understands transgressions in these areas, since they often produce instant, albeit fleeting, pleasure. Envy, however, strikes him as the silliest of the Seven Deadly Sins, since it produces nothing pleasant at all. To the contrary, it simply makes the practitioner feel miserable.

I've had an enormous amount of fun in my business life—and far more than if I had not partnered up with Charlie. With his "Mungerisms" he has been highly entertaining, and he has also shaped my thinking in a major way. Though many would label Charlie a businessman or philanthropist, I would opt for teacher. And Berkshire clearly is a much more valuable and admirable company because of what he has taught us.

No discussion of Charlie would be complete without a mention of the beneficial, indeed transforming effect of his wife, Nancy. As a front-row observer of both people, I can assure you that Charlie would have achieved far less had he not had Nancy's help. She may not have entirely succeeded as a Miss Manners instructor—though she tried, oh how she tried—but she has nourished Charlie in a manner that has in turn enabled him to nourish the causes and institutions in which he believes. Nancy is truly extraordinary. What Charlie has contributed to the world—and his contributions have been huge—should be credited not only to him but to her as well.

WARREN E. BUFFETT

Omaha, Nebraska

PREFACE

The thousands of shareholders who attend the Berkshire Hathaway annual meeting in Omaha, Nebraska, each spring go to see Warren Buffett, but they also are fascinated by the man who sits beside him on the stage and helps the Oracle of Omaha answer questions. They call it the *Warren and Charlie Show*. It usually goes this way: Buffett answers the question, giving it as much or as little time as he sees fit. At the end, he turns to his longtime partner Charles Munger and asks, "Charlie, do you have anything to add?" Charlie sits there looking as if he'd already been chiseled into Mount Rushmore, and gives a brusque reply. "Nothing to add." He and Buffett play their little jokes each year to an audience that enjoys going right along with them. The meeting does have a deeper element though. Buffett gives serious thought to the questions. And occasionally, something will come over Munger and he delivers a little lecture, based on his long life and abundant experience. When he does speak, Munger has the audience's undivided attention.

He has messages that he thinks are important: Deal ethically with others; face reality; learn from the mistakes of others, and so forth. He delivers those sermonettes with missionary zeal.

"Daddy is very conscious of the fact that he represents social values that are not all that common in the business world," said his first daughter Molly Munger.

Munger isn't as wealthy as Buffett, partly because his life is organized differently. He isn't the showman Buffett is, though he can be enormously entertaining. Thanks to these two factors, the Munger family has long enjoyed the privilege of being billionaires without the inconveniences of fame.

I told Munger about this book project when I saw him at the Berkshire Hathaway meeting in May 1997, and said I would attend the Wesco Financial Corporation meeting later the same month and hoped we could talk more about the project at that time. Munger didn't say much except that he didn't think the book would sell many copies. My husband, a friend, and I did attend the Wesco meeting and when it was over, Munger rose and in a loud voice asked, "Is Janet Lowe here?" The assembled audience of several hundred people craned their necks searching for the culprit, and a few who know me pointed in my direction. I timidly stood, "Yes, Mr. Munger." He rose from his chair and declared, "Follow me," and turned and marched out a back door. I waved goodbye to my husband and friend, not sure when I would see them again. Munger silently led the way up the elevator and to a private office where he told me that the Munger family didn't want a biography of him. They could see their cherished privacy slipping away. Being a fundamentally shy person who doesn't enjoy confrontation, I did not find this meeting easy. But I explained that I had signed a contract and would need to deliver the book, even if he did not cooperate. I said, however, that I believed the book would be much better if he did. "All right then," Munger barked. "You can start by reading these books." He handed over a long list of his favorites, including Richard Dawkins' *The Selfish Gene*. Later, Munger told me that he went through phases, at first opposing the book, then trying to minimize the damage, and in the end, working right beside me, trying to make the events of his life as understandable as possible. It clearly wasn't always easy for him, especially when I pressed for details about the death of his son and the misguided surgery that left Charlie blind in one eye.

Nevertheless, Munger sat for long interviews at his home in Santa Barbara, his office in Los Angeles, and twice at his sister's home in Omaha. The Mungers invited my husband and me to their vacation retreat in Northern Minnesota, where I spent several days interviewing family and neighbors, but also went hiking, boating, fishing, and hanging out with the Mungers.

I have been researching and writing this book for three years. Although some of the research builds on work done earlier on value investor Benjamin Graham and his star pupil Buffett, that material could only serve as background. Munger's photograph has appeared on the cover of *Forbes* and he has been profiled in a couple of newspapers, but there is very little written about him. More than 75 percent of the research in this book is original. I've done 44 interviews with 33 different persons. I attended eight Berkshire shareholder meetings and five Wesco Financial Corporation annual meetings, where Munger is alone on the stage and doesn't hold back anything. I worked with transcripts of about a half dozen speeches that Munger gave in various places, including one for his class reunion at Harvard Law School.

Although he became involved in the project, Charlie tried to resist the temptation to direct the book, other than to say often that he hoped it would emphasize the lessons he's learned during his 76 years of life. He would like others to benefit from his errors and successes. Indeed, the lessons of his life are not so much in the telling as in the living. The way he and his wife raised eight children through all kinds of adversity—how Munger constantly strove to maximize his talents and his financial situation, the responsibility he feels to be a connected, contributing citizen—all that is something of a saga. While writing this book, I often burst out laughing, but there were times I winced in pain or felt sorrow. Life threw Charlie about everything it had.

While Munger is a one-of-a-kind, he also is typical of the fusion of West Coast culture with Midwestern values, which took place primarily in the first half of the twentieth century. If Buffett shows that it is possible to be an alpha male investor and live and work in Omaha, a city not known as a financial center, Munger shows that despite some commonly held assumptions, valuable, innovative financial, and cultural ideas can and do flow from west to east.

Munger often lectures on big ideas that can change your life, but in those speeches he does not give detailed instructions on what to do. He hands his listeners a map with which they can find the treasure of wisdom, and like any good treasure map, it's so simple that it is deceptive. You don't get the treasure until you figure out what the instructions mean and follow them to the end.

Acknowledgments

So many people have helped make this book possible. Most important, of course, have been Charles T. Munger, his wife Nancy, and seven of their eight children, Hal and David Borthwick, Molly, Wendy, Charles Junior, Emilie, and Barry Munger. The spouses of the Munger children also have been supportive, helpful, and interesting to know. Doerthe Obert, Charlie's secretary has been wonderful, as was Buffett's assistant Debbie Bosanek. Carol J. Loomis, an editor at *Fortune* magazine and an old friend of Buffett and Munger, has been extremely generous with her time and ideas. At the back of this book is a list of the people interviewed, and rather than name all of those people here as well, let me thank them as a group. It goes without saying, but must be said, that Warren Buffett's cooperation opened rows of doors.

My literary agent Alice Fried Martell has been essential to the writing of this book, as has the editorial staff at John Wiley & Sons. Publisher Joan

O'Neil, editor Debra Englander, Robin Goldstein, Mary Todd, Peter Knapp, and Meredith McGinnis. My work would be impossible without the help of Phyllis Kinney, Jolene Crowley, and most of all my husband and helpmate, Austin Lynas. Thanks to everyone.

JANET LOWE

Del Mar, California

CONTENTS

CHAPTER ONE

AN EXTRAORDINARY COMBINATION OF MINDS

I've been associated with Warren (Buffett) so long, I thought I'd be just a footnote.[1]

Charles T. Munger, when he was first named to the
Forbes magazine list of richest Americans in 1993

"**M**y CLOSEST AFFILIATION WITH CHARLIE MUNGER is a strange one," said Katharine Graham, retired publisher of the *Washington Post.* "At first I consulted him because I found myself in charge of not only a company, but in charge of children's and grandchildren's trusts, and with no experience. I asked Warren's advice, and he did what he very typically does. 'This is what I think, but talk to my partner Charlie. He agrees with my position in most things.' "

"So I went to talk to Charlie in Los Angeles in his office. I thought he was interesting and rather brilliant, of course. I took out a yellow legal pad and started taking notes. This made Warren laugh. To this day he teases me about how I took notes of Charlie's words of wisdom."

After Warren Buffett, the billionaire financier from Omaha, set up a meeting between Graham and Munger, she said, "Charlie and I had a lively, long correspondence. It was too strange."

Graham kept a file folder of the letters and reviewed it when preparing her Pulitzer prize-winning autobiography, *Personal History.* "I looked over the correspondence which was the main, very close contact I had. I can't make out from it why we started writing. This went on for about 10 years, both of us riding bicycles without using our hands, showing off to each other, making jokes."

Graham, who in her shy, retiring way, always worried that her best efforts weren't good enough, finally realized that for the most part, "He was reassuring me that I was doing better than I thought."

"The thing that strikes me is how strongly alike Warren and Charlie sound. The voice, the manner, and the humor," said Graham. "They play off each other and tease each other. And they do make, to my mind, a most extraordinary combination of minds."

"I HEARD ABOUT CHARLIE MUNGER IN 1957," explained Buffett, who years later would become America's wealthiest citizen. "I was managing money on a very small scale, in Omaha, about $300,000. Dorothy Davis was the wife of Edwin Davis, the most prominent doctor in town. I knew about them and they knew about my family. I went over to their apartment, Mrs. Davis was very sharp. I explained how I ran money. Dr. Davis paid no attention. When I was done, they conferred—then agreed to invest $100,000. I said to Dr. Davis, 'You weren't paying any attention. Why did you put money in?' He said, 'You remind me of Charlie Munger.' I said I didn't know Charlie Munger but I like him already."

When Munger was growing up in Omaha in the 1920s and 1930s, the Davis family were both neighbors and close friends. The doctor was a little unusual, but "a very talented odd fellow. And certainly the Buffett investment worked out very well for the Davis family," said Charlie. The money the Davises placed with Warren represented most of their net worth.

"Eddie Davis *was* a little odd and he got odder as he got older," concurred Buffett. "He finally got a little senile. Later, when he was adding to his investment with me, he started making the checks out to Charlie Munger. I told Eddie, 'I don't mind you confusing the two of us under many circumstances, but make the checks out to Warren Buffett.'"

Two years after Buffett first heard Charlie's name, the two men met. "In 1959, when Charlie's dad died, he came back to help settle up. The Davises arranged a dinner. We hit it off immediately," said Buffett.

The Davises that Warren now referred to were not the doctor and his wife, but rather the Davis children, who had been Charlie's childhood playmates. Both Davis boys, Eddie and Neil, became doctors and by then the daughter, Willa Davis, was married to Omaha businessman Lee Seemann. It was Neil who arranged dinner at the old Omaha Club. The party included Willa and Lee Seemann, Joan and Neil Davis, Charlie and Warren. "It was electric in a really nice way," recalled Willa.

Munger had heard other people mention Warren as well, but he did not have particularly high expectations about meeting him. "I knew everyone in the Buffett family except Warren," said Charlie. Munger noticed a few things about the bespectacled young man right away. "He had a crew cut. Warren was working out of a sunporch at his house, and his dietary habits were toward Pepsi, salted nuts, and no vegetables."[2] Charlie, who considers himself fairly tolerant about such matters said, "Even I get surprised watching Warren eat breakfast."

His minimal expectations of the meeting were unjustified. Munger, who is reserved in his judgments, was floored. "I would have to say that I recognized almost instantly what a remarkable person Warren is."[3]

Charlie began asking questions immediately about what Buffett did for a living and how he did it and was fascinated by what he heard. The following evening another mutual friend, Dick Holland, invited both to dinner. Warren, who was then 29, and Charlie, 35 years old, again fell into deep conversation. Charlie was so wrapped up in what he was saying that when he raised his glass to sip his drink, he held his other hand up to stop anyone else from interrupting the conversation.

The timing was propitious for the two to meet. Charlie's beloved father had died, and Buffett's mentor, Benjamin Graham, had retired from investing and moved from New York to Los Angeles. As Graham became less interested in investment problems, Warren felt the loss. He needed a new sounding board. It may be precisely because Munger was so similar to Graham in his thought processes—honest, realistic, profoundly curious, and unfettered by conventional thinking—that he captured Buffett's attention in the first place.

"I think Charlie is a lot more like Ben Graham than Charlie knows," explained Louis Simpson, co-chairman of GEICO and the man believed to stand second in line should Buffett or Munger become unable to run Berkshire Hathaway. "Charlie takes the academic approach, but also has interests in a lot of different things. In his reading, his tastes are eclectic."

Buffett, who is known for his single-minded focus on investing, agreed that Munger is like Graham in his wide range of interests. "Charlie's mind has a greater span than I do. He has read more biographies, hundreds per year. He soaks them up and remembers [them]."

By the time Fidel Castro seized power in Cuba and the youthful John F. Kennedy was elected U.S. president, Buffett and Munger had become "mental partners," a relationship that involved no contract or titles—at least in the beginning.

It was more like a "brother act" than a business arrangement, Buffett said. Based on mutual trust and confidence, it grew discussion by discussion, meeting by meeting, deal by deal.[4]

Though Charlie had lived only blocks from the Buffett home in Omaha and had worked in the Buffett family store as a teenager, the six years difference in their ages kept them in separate circles. Yet it was the common threads that allowed the two to make an immediate connection.

"If you think of Charlie and Warren as boys, they were very similar," observed Munger's oldest daughter, Molly. "Similar parents, values, same town. One of those alone would make a friendship."

Munger and Buffett had something else in common. "Like Warren, I had a considerable passion to get rich," said Charlie, who early on earned his living as a lawyer. "Not because I wanted Ferraris—I wanted the independence. I desperately wanted it. I thought it was undignified to have to send invoices to other people. I don't know where I got that notion from, but I had it."[5]

CHARLES T. MUNGER IS VICE CHAIRMAN and the second-largest shareholder in one of the world's most renowned holding companies, Berkshire Hathaway Inc. He also is head of the Daily Journal Corporation, the largest-circulation legal newspaper group in California and of Wesco Financial Corporation, an 80 percent-owned subsidiary of Berkshire. Additionally, Munger is an indefatigable participant in the philanthropic life of Los Angeles. When his image appeared on the cover of a 1996 issue of *Forbes* magazine, the general public began to realize Munger was more than Warren Buffett's straight man at the Berkshire Hathaway annual meetings.

One of the most elusive, intriguing, and independent business leaders in America, the 76-year-old Munger said it was his goal to stay just below the wealth-level required to be named to the *Forbes* richest Americans list. It would help him stand just outside the limelight. The strategy didn't work.

In 1998, Munger's fortune was calculated at more than $1.2 billion. On the richest Americans list, Munger ranked just below the family heirs to the Levi Strauss fortune. He ranked just above Michael Eisner, head of the Walt Disney Company; hotel heir William Barron Hilton, and most surprisingly, higher than Silicon Valley computer nabob Steven Jobs.[6]

Like Warren Buffett, Munger inherited no wealth. He built his fortune on the sheer power of his will and his business acumen.

"While no real money came down, my family gave me a good education and a marvelous example of how people should behave, and in the end that was more valuable than money," explained Munger. "Being surrounded by right values from the beginning is an immense treasure. Warren had that. It even has a financial advantage. People touted Warren partly because he was a Buffett and people trusted the Buffetts."

According to the worldwide rumor mill powered by members of Buffett's cultish fan club, Munger may be the wizard behind the Berkshire Hathaway throne. Howard Buffett, Warren's eldest son, has said that his father is the second smartest man he knows. He says Charles Munger is the first.[7] Certainly Warren Buffett, in his wry way, builds on Munger's mystique: "Charlie does the talking," Buffett claimed at one of Berkshire Hathaway's annual meetings. "I just move my lips."

One year, Buffett fielded a question from a shareholder, then passed the query on to Munger, who gave the expected reply, "I've got nothing to add." Buffett, who teases Munger unmercifully, chuckled. "Sometimes he *subtracts.*"[8]

Warren and Charlie put on an entertaining show at the Berkshire Hathaway annual meetings. They also do a conscientious job of portraying the business and investment philosophy of one of America's most talked about but least understood corporations. Yet Buffett is indisputably the star of the event and his personality takes the spotlight. Charlie Munger has perfected his role as the curmudgeonly sidekick, and in fact seems to enjoy the straight-man role.

"But that guy you see sitting next to Warren, that isn't Charlie. That's just the image he's cultivated," explained Munger's stepson, Los Angeles attorney Hal Borthwick. "It's true, probably, he doesn't have a lot to add and he wants to get on with it. I think he works better in small groups than he does in large crowds, but at the end of the day, that isn't the real Charlie Munger that's sitting up there."

Who is the real Charles T. Munger?

To Borthwick he is a dedicated step-father, a mentor and someone who has made life a real adventure.

To *Forbes* magazine, Munger is the foil that makes Buffett's down-home image believable. His "tough style approach makes possible Buffett's Mr. Nice Guy."[9]

To the former top managers of Salomon Brothers Inc., he was a hard-nosed board member who recognized a deception early and insisted that government regulators and the public be given a full and contrite explanation of an episode involving U.S. Treasury bond trading misdeeds, even if Salomon's lucrative bond trading business was put at risk.

To the small but prestigious Los Angeles law firm, Munger, Tolles & Olson, Munger is a powerful client magnet who attracted oil companies, public utilities, and other corporations. Many decades ago, Munger brought in a small and loosely connected group of companies that in time became the Berkshire Hathaway of today.

To those who support women's rights, Munger is a hero—the catalyst who years ago sparked the movement to legalize abortion in the United States.

For those who oppose abortion rights, Munger is a powerful nemesis, one who deserves to be picketed now and then.

To Roger M. Grace, Los Angeles gadfly publisher of *The Metropolitan-News,* Munger is a billionaire bully intent on using his Daily Journal Corporation to monopolize the California legal publishing market.[10]

To his bridge partners, including Buffett, *Fortune* magazine editor Carol Loomis, Los Angeles billionaire Otis Booth, Microsoft founder Bill Gates, and the late comedian George Burns, he's a good bridge player who would be even better if he didn't occasionally verge into aberrant behavior. His partners sometimes have a little trouble understanding why he makes certain bids or plays certain cards, though usually he is following some simple logic of his own.

To boat owners and builders, Munger is a guy who is intrigued by new and offbeat ideas for watercraft, and who just might be persuaded to back a project. "My dad is a pushover for anyone with a wild idea for a boat," said his eldest daughter Molly.

To James Sinegal, chief executive officer of Costco, the warehouse retailing chain on whose board Munger sits, Munger is one of the best-connected businessmen in the country. When he met Charlie to ask him to serve on Costco's board of directors, the two had lunch at the prestigious downtown Los Angeles business club, the California Club. "There was a big lunch crowd," recalled Sinegal. "I think all 400 of them knew Charlie."

Later at Munger's first Costco board meeting in 1997, Sinegal started to introduce him to another director, prominent political activist Jill Ruckleshaus. It turned out that Munger and Ruckleshaus had met long ago. "You're never shocked by whom Charlie knows," said Sinegal.

Among Munger's friends are Bill Gates, Nathan Mhyrvold (once the futuristic idea man at Microsoft), General Electric chairman Jack Welch, former U.S. Trade Representative Carla Anderson Hills, Los Angeles Mayor Richard Riordan, and many governors, senators, and presidents.

As similar as they seem, Buffett and Munger also are quite different—opposites in some ways. Whereas Buffett specializes in simple language, folksy stories, and allegory, Munger grants nothing to small words. If he can use a big word when a small one will do, he spends the syllables.

Munger thrives on complex ideas and detailed analysis. While Buffett is uninterested in clothes, Munger is a natty dresser. Buffett lives in the first house he ever bought and has done only limited remodeling over the years. Munger loves architecture and owns seven homes in all. And finally, Munger is a staunch Republican, while Buffett calls himself "mostly a Democrat."

Munger's personal life has been difficult and at times even tragic, and money did not come to him as easily as it seemed to come to Buffett. Yet, as with other great partnerships, such as those involving Microsoft founders Bill Gates and Paul Allen; Sony Corporation's Akio Morita and Masaru Ibuka; or Buffett's early mentor Ben Graham and his partner Jerry Newman—there is a synergy, even a magic in the relationship. Each man is talented on his own, each would have attained great wealth and lived an interesting life separately. But both have gaps in their personalities or skills that are filled in by the other. The two fare much better as a duo than either could do independently. As Munger often says, you can get "lollapalooza" results when you bring together the right combination of factors.

Buffett had formal training in business and finance, but not in law. Munger had been a corporate lawyer and, though he had experience in operating businesses, he still had a lot to learn about being a professional investor.

"You know the cliche that opposites attract?" Munger said. "Well, opposites don't attract. Everybody engaged in complicated work needs colleagues. Just the discipline of having to put your thoughts in order with somebody else is a very useful thing."[11]

In Munger, Buffett found someone who shared his values and goals and to whom he could talk on a sophisticated level.

One of the greatest similarities between the two men is their sense of humor. Like many Midwesterners, they have learned to deal with discomfort, stress, surprise, and even grief by making jokes. Humor breaks the tension, provides psychological protection, and allows them to assert dominance over their circumstances.[12]

Munger brought more than comradeship to the mix. Though Buffett had inherited a group of former Graham-Newman investors and was busily recruiting money from Nebraskans, Munger spread the word about Buffett's skills in California, bringing millions more dollars into his investment pool. To a large extent, Berkshire's early success was due to the acquisition of Blue Chip Stamps, See's Candy, and other California companies, most of which were discovered by Munger and his circle of West Coast investors.

Just as Munger looked on in amusement at Buffet parochial food preferences, Buffet came to understand Munger's unusual personality. In 1967, in one of their early ventures, Munger and Buffett went to New York to buy a small company called Associated Cotton Shops. Buffett recalls walking along a street in Manhattan with Charlie, talking about the business deal. Suddenly Buffett looked around and discovered he was talking to himself. Charlie was gone. Later Buffett learned that Munger remembered he had to catch a plane, and just walked off.

Despite Munger's ungraceful abruptness, said Buffett, "He is a sensational friend. The niceties are not there. None of the superficial acts, but all of the real ones. We've never had an argument. We've disagreed at times and we've done a lot of things together, but there's never been one time we've been mad or irritated or anything. If you talk about ideas, he's not going to get emotional about it. But if he has superior facts or reasoning, he won't back off. We both think the other one is worth listening to."

HIS OWN LIFE, insists Munger, is "not a big story—long dull stretches are possible. To finish first you have to first finish. Don't get in a position where you go back to go. What's interesting is that some guy whose grandfather was a lawyer and a judge—hurriedly going to Harvard Law with a wave of veterans—I was willing to go into so many different businesses. I was constantly going right into the other fellow's business and doing better than the other fellow did. The reason it was possible? Self-education—developing mental discipline, big ideas that really work."

Munger's life story reveals a number of large, though perhaps loosely organized, ideas that served him well: Live within your income and save so that you can invest. Learn what you need to learn. As Buffett likes to say, "if it's trite, it's right."

Warren Buffett often counsels college students to develop early the right habits of thought and behavior, since most of the time, people act on habit. This goes hand in hand with another big idea promoted by Munger—always act as honorably as possible. "How you behave in one place," he says, "will help in surprising ways later."

CHAPTER TWO

THE LAKE—
A PLACE THAT
DEFINES MUNGER

*There are a lot of things in life way more important than
money. All that said, some people do get confused. I play golf
with a man who says, "What good is health? You can't buy
money with it."*[1]

Charlie Munger

I t IS THE LAST SUMMER OF the twentieth century and Charles and Nancy
Munger clamber from the motorboat onto the dock at their Star Island
house, greeting a chattering gaggle of children and grandchildren. A
flaxen-haired three-year-old says "Hi Grandad, hi Grandad," and when
Charlotte fails to get Charlie's attention, she simply takes his hand and
quietly walks beside him. Minutes later Charlie begins talking to the little
girl, as if he'd known all along that she was there. Charlotte glows, clearly
pleased that her strategy paid off. This is a big family, and competing for
the attention of the patriarch is a common occurrence.

Daughter-in-law Sarah calls from the kitchen, "Charlie, Warren
called. Call him back."

"Okay," shouts Charlie, but instead of going to the telephone, he
gives directions to his sons and to the houseman, Felipe Velasquez, as to
where various pieces of luggage (including an unwieldy bag of fishing
rods) are to be deposited.

Felipe holds up a sturdy, plastic bait box that had been checked as
luggage on the Munger's three-leg flight from visiting friends in Maine to
Bemidji, the nearest airport to the Munger family lake houses in Northern
Minnesota. "Look," Felipe grins with delight. "Not dented!" The box

holds a collection of newfangled lures that Charlie Munger, a certified billionaire, ordered from a television fishing show.

When the fuss and flutter of his arrival at the Cass Lake retreat settles, Charlie goes to the only telephone in the house, which hangs on the wall in the kitchen. There a gang of adult children (led by Sarah who is a professional chef) is preparing dinner for the thirty family members and friends on hand. A preteen granddaughter, Mary Margot, solemnly peels carrots, alert for any mention of a fishing trip. Mary is smitten with fishing and is restless to check out the lake with her grandfather.

Charlie glances around the kitchen, as if calculating the odds of carrying on a reasonably private conversation with his pal and business partner, the second richest man in the world, the Sage of Securities, Warren Buffett. Nancy Munger comes to her husband's rescue. "It's a walk-around phone Charlie. Just take it wherever you want and dial the number." As if unconvinced that the phone has enough range to work outside or from an upstairs bedroom, Charlie goes just around the corner into the living room and punches in the telephone number that he knows by heart. Pandemonium continues in the rest of the house as Charlie plops down in a lumpy upholstered chair to chat with Warren.

"Mumble, mumble, mumble."

Silence.

"Mumble, mumble."

Silence.

"So it's the price that bothers you?" asks Charlie.

Silence.

"If you wait, I think you'll get your price."

Silence. "Okay." Click.

Though Charlie Munger's story begins in Omaha, Nebraska, on January 1, 1924, he clearly considers Star Island home. It is the place where he has knotted a rope between his past, present, and future. The summer cottage has brought the family together during sad times, extremely busy times, and especially later as the children grew up, scattered around the world, and created families of their own. Charlie's grandparents vacationed there, his parents vacationed there, and over the years, this collection of cabins on the small island in the middle of Cass Lake, Minnesota, has become the family seat for Munger's eight children, fifteen grandchildren, and an assortment of aunts, uncles, nieces, nephews, and cousins.

The Munger family that gathers at the island each summer is an amalgamation of his, hers, and theirs. Charlie has two daughters from his first marriage—Molly and Wendy. His wife Nancy has two sons from her first marriage—Hal and David Borthwick. Charlie and Nancy have four children together—Charles Jr., Emilie, Barry, and Philip. All are married with children now, except Philip, who is a graduate student in New York City.

"We all think the island is central to the family," said Wendy Munger. Star Island is the sort of community that is difficult to form in today's hectic urban centers. "If you've got a hole in the roof," said Wendy, "the neighbors come help fix it. If your boat breaks down, they help. It's very communal. There is a connection to your neighbors, a lot of sharing of everything."

The island is a place of precious memories to the Munger children because their work-absorbed, ambitious father made a ritual of spending time with them there each summer.

"That's where we saw the most of him," said Wendy.

The island is aptly named. Its shape resembles that of a star that has fallen from the sky and splattered to earth. The dense evergreen forest starts directly in back of the houses and the clear water of Cass Lake laps up just 40 feet from the front door of Munger's eastern shore cottages. Lake Windigo, a body of water completely contained within the island, is less than a 15-minute hike from any of the cottages.

There are no roads on the island, and to get around, residents use a system of hiking trails dividing uncut woods. The only way to reach Star Island from the mainland is by private boat. Most of the island is now controlled by the U.S. Forest Service, but the longtime residents who own the several dozen cottages perched along the edges, feel it is theirs.

Munger's grandparents discovered Star Island in 1932. Cass Lake was a two-day drive from their home in Lincoln, Nebraska, but to the Mungers, the trip into the Northern Minnesota wilderness was worth the effort. They came upon the snug resort community in their desperation to escape the stifling 90-degree heat, 90 percent humidity that settles over Nebraska in the summers. Home air conditioning was almost unknown, and any Midwesterner who could afford to do so fled to the cooler north.

After the solitary hotel on the island burned, the only accommodations left were an American-plan lodge (which later was acquired by the U.S. Park Service and demolished) and a sprinkling of primitive cabins around the shoreline. At first, the Munger family rented one of the cabins. Charlie's grandparents were a stalwart couple. Federal Judge Thomas C. Munger and his wife believed that roughing it with no electricity, no toilets, no telephones, no nearby stores, was good for their family. It built character. Electricity didn't come to the island until 1951 and telephones weren't available until the 1980s.

"I think I was 13 when the bathroom went in," recalled Wendy Munger. "Before that, we had outdoor toilets and a couple of sinks."

The original Munger cabin was built around 1908. Charlie's father bought it in the 1940s from Dr. Tommy Thompson, a Lincoln orthopedist. Dr. Thompson's droll comments on life still hang on some walls.

"My dad paid $5,600 for this house in 1946," explained Charlie. "My grandmother had just died and he inherited some money. Before that he didn't have anything extra."

An avid outdoorsman, Al Munger was delighted to own his own lake house. But Charlie's mother Florence, always called Toody, had to muster up her courage to make the annual trip to Minnesota.

"It was Dad's love. Father was a passionate fisherman, a duck hunter, loved dogs," recalled Charlie's sister, Carol Estabrook. As for Toody, "She was allergic. She was not an outdoor lady at all."

Although the short boat ride from the mainland marina to the family dock was an ordeal for her, Toody Munger set the standard for all grandmothers.

"Here was this woman who couldn't swim, and yet she came every summer to an island out of love for her children and grandchildren," recalled Wendy. Once she was safely on the island, Toody Munger's sense of humor returned.

"At Cass Lake," said Charlie's childhood friend Willa Davis Seemann, "just before dinner we had to straighten things. 'I want this cottage artistic by sunset,' Toody would say. She was clever and fun."

Allergies and insecurity on water weren't Toody's only problems with the island. She was terrified of mice, and there were plenty of rodents to be found in a cabin in the woods that was unoccupied much of the year. The Mungers have never been able to get rid of the mice completely, even though the house has been remodeled several times. Even at home in Omaha, Toody Munger had to confront her aversion to rodents, thanks to her only son, Charlie.

Charlie recalled that when he was a small boy, he and his mother would go out walking together. One day he saw a dead rat by the side of the road. "I'd already sensed her aversion to rodents, so I picked it up and said, 'Mother, what's this?' and waved it in front of her. She turned and ran down the road and I ran after her, still holding the rat."

"It was the only time she took out after me with a coat hanger," Charlie said.

Later Charlie became enamored with raising hamsters in the basement. It was a popular hobby at the time, and Charlie began trading his pets with other hamster farmers, usually children like him. The Omaha Cavy Club met downtown in the county courthouse, and Charlie was always riding off to meetings on his bicycle.

"The idea was getting a bigger buck, or a hamster with unusual coloration, or something like that," explained Munger. At one point he owned about 35 hamsters and when one of them died, he wanted to keep it in the refrigerator.

Carol Munger Estabrook said that her brother sometimes forgot to feed the hamsters or would come home from school late. The little creatures "squeaked like crazy and could be heard all over the house. Finally they got to smelling so bad mother made Charlie get rid of them."

Munger and his two sisters inherited the Minnesota cabin from their parents, but Charlie's sister Mary, who has since died, sold her share to buy her own island cabin down the beach. Now, Charlie, his wife Nancy, and his surviving sister Carol, each own one-third of the property.

"We like the island life," observed Nancy Munger. "There are generations of people there. We're into the fifth and sixth generation of friends."

John Ruckmick, a Star Island neighbor who lives most of the year in Evergreen, Colorado, has spent 72 summers on the island. His parents vacationed there in the late 1920s when his mother was pregnant with him, and John started coming to Star Island the very next year. Ruckmick figures he was between five and seven years old when he first met Charlie. The two boys played together when island families gathered for picnics. "He exhibited his character early," said Ruckmick, laughing at the memory. "He was assertive!"

Returning to the island each year once he grew up was not easy for Charlie, especially after he moved to California in the mid-1940s and spent the next two decades raising a large family and trying to establish a financial foothold.

"We started going to the island when I was around three or four," remembered Molly. "In the early days, sometimes we would fly to Omaha and then drive up to the island. Wendy flew with my mother because she was young enough to sit in my mother's lap. Once I went on a train with Teddy and Daddy. It took a long time. I had red sandals."

When there was a little more cash, the family flew from California to Minneapolis then got to the lake the best way they could figure out. "We sure took some weird flights to save money," said Wendy. "We split up. The older kids went on a Greyhound bus. It was a dramatic sign that times had changed when we all started to fly from Minneapolis to Bemidji—a big shift."

To Charles Munger, Jr., summers at the lake were a time when the family had their father's full attention. "Up here we went fishing. We were always making fires. The rest of the year we didn't see him much."

Now, said Wendy, "we all try to be there together, usually seven of the eight children, or at least six of the eight. It is crucial to our well-being," "We all want to be there at the exact same week. We had to buy up property on the shore to make room."

When the Munger clan gathers there in late July or in August, there can be nearly three dozen people living in the assortment of Munger cottages. Because it is difficult to store enough food for that many people in the small kitchens, the Munger children take turns boating across Cass Lake for daily shopping excursions. The food bill invariably runs more than $300 per day. The family takes delight in finding fresh lake fish or a reliable supply of locally-harvested wild rice, or in bringing home 100 ears of fresh corn, bought from a farm truck parked along the road.

As nearby cottages came up for sale, Charlie bought them—starting with the house dubbed "Munger West." Later third and fourth cottages farther along the shore were acquired. In 1999, the Munger children communicated by telephone, fax, and e-mail to plan, build, and furnish a "great room," which allows family and friends to gather in one place for meals and games.

The original main house, "Munger East," has doubled in size since Charlie's father bought it. A guest house equipped for use by a disabled person later was built with ramps and other devices to accommodate Charlie's sister Mary, who in the late 1980s succumbed to Parkinson's disease. Eventually a boathouse with an apartment over the top was added, then a tennis court, and in 1999, a more substantial dock that Charlie designed himself.

A sign over the front door of the main house reads "Anglers' Rest," a name taken from one of Charlie's favorite books by P.G. Wodehouse, demonstrating Charlie's devotion to both Wodehouse and fishing. Before the house was remodeled, the upstairs walls, more partitions than anything, didn't go all the way to the ceiling. Molly lay in bed at night hearing her father in his own bedroom chuckling as he read stories about Wodehouse's zany character, Bertie Wooster.

The Mungers may be on vacation at Star Island, but they don't forget the companies that made all this comfort possible. Much of the furniture that wasn't originally in the cabins was purchased from a Berkshire-owned furniture store in Omaha, The Nebraska Furniture Mart, and shipped to the lake. It was floated out to the island on a barge owned by

Munger. Gillette toiletries are stocked in the bathrooms and the refrigerators are loaded with Coca-Cola, both companies in which Berkshire has substantial ownership.

With the extra cottages came more docks and boats. There are now thirteen boats, including fishing dinghies, two Mark Twains, a Stingray, and a catamaran sailboat. The Star Island boats, said Molly Munger, are a constant source of vexation, since family members live thousands of miles away most of the year and the boats are untended and in "various stages of disrepair."

The upkeep on the houses is especially daunting, since Charlie and Nancy also own homes in the Hancock Park district of Los Angeles, in Santa Barbara, Newport Beach (California), and in Hawaii. A local businesswoman, Ann Cramer, has for 25 years supervised the Munger property in Minnesota, taking a hand in overseeing what seems like never-ending construction and remodeling projects.

For Charlie, the childhood memories are essential to who he is, but even without the memories, he might keep coming back for the fishing. By any measure, Munger is a fervent and determined angler.

"Charlie would fish in a rain barrel," said King Williams, a friend of Munger's who is captain of a huge sailboat that Munger built and keeps in Santa Barbara.

Cass Lake is one of a series of lakes that stretch north, and each lake has nooks and backwaters where, according to local lore, bass, muskie, and possibly walleye are most likely to bite. On the eightieth birthday of a Star Island neighbor, J.D. Ramsey of Des Moines, Iowa, Munger chided his friend about his fishing habits, which sound like Munger's own:

> "I have seen a lot of peculiar fishermen in my life who, like me, are willing to suffer to fish in promising water," Munger wrote in a tongue-in-cheek tribute to Ramsey. "But only J.D., wearing the hair-shirt that duty requires in his unflagging conception, sees the whole point of fishing as the welcome opportunity to carry small boats through swamps and otherwise suffer in reaching fishing that is selected partly for its difficult access and partly for the difficulty of encountering any fish."[2]

Barry Munger explained that just as his father is a patient investor, he also is an extremely patient fisherman. "He tries to find the best technique day in and day out and will stick with that lure, or whatever, even if others on the boat are having better success with something else. At one time he was dedicated to a chartreuse jig, day in and day out. I guess it works, but if I'm out on a day when the fish aren't taking that, I will try every color in the tackle box."

Charlie and his son Barry on Star Island.

Munger's attitude about fishing is revealed in the story he once told when musing on the gullibility of many investors:

> This fishing tackle manufacturer I knew had all these flashy green and pur-
> ple lures. I asked, "Do fish take these?" "Charlie," he said, "I don't sell these
> lures to fish."[3]

DAVID BORTHWICK, MUNGER'S STEPSON, said it was at Star Island that he realized Buffett played an exceptional role in their lives. "In 1963 or 1964, Warren came up and stayed a few days in August. Normally father would have dispatched Hal [David's older brother] to pick someone up. Father went himself. That was a clue that this was an important guest."

But it was Buffett's second visit to Star Island that has become legend among Buffett followers. It was the occasion on which Munger nearly drowned his business partner.

"I went up with Rick Guerin," said Buffett. "His wife had died. He had a boy. We thought it would be a good idea if they got away."

John P. "Rick" Guerin, Jr., was at the time chairman of the Los Angeles-based brokerage firm Mitchum, Jones and Templeton. He also served as chairman of the New America Fund, in which Munger was a major shareholder. Guerin is a street-smart, physical fitness buff who wears dark glasses, open-collared silk shirts, looks suspiciously like he works in the film industry, and in fact he now owns his own film company. The most unlikely member of the stolidly conventional Munger-Buffett circle, Guerin nevertheless, has been a longtime business associate.

Guerin said his first wife Ann used to call Charlie and Warren and (Los Angeles attorney) Chuck Rickershauser his master group. Ann committed suicide in 1980. "It was obviously traumatic," said Guerin. "Warren and I were talking about it a few days later and about the effect of the death of a loved one on a child. Patrick was eight years old."

Warren suggested to Rick that the three of them join Charlie and his family, who were on their annual pilgrimage to Cass Lake. Guerin was welcomed by Munger, who himself had suffered a tragic and untimely death in the family.

"We hung out," recalled Guerin. "We played bridge."

And naturally, Munger took his pals fishing.

"Charlie insisted on driving the boat. I offered, but he insisted," said Guerin. There are several different versions of what happened next, but generally, the story goes this way:

> "It was a calm day. We were out a mile or so," said Buffett. "Rick and I were talking away."
>
> In an effort to reach a better casting position, Munger put the boat's motor in reverse.
>
> "Suddenly," said Guerin. "I looked down and I'm in the water. We were going backward and water was flowing over the gunnel."
>
> Guerin yelled at Charlie, who replied, "I'll take care of that." Charlie then put on full power, but still in reverse. The boat sank. Both Guerin and

Buffett were underwater for a few moments before they popped up side by side. "Warren's eyes were as big as his glasses," said Guerin.

The borrowed boat, explained Charlie, was not designed so as to keep the water from rushing in when the boat was going backward. Buffett is athletic, but he is not a highly skilled swimmer.

"I had to help Warren. The story has been a little stretched," admitted Guerin. "We *know* Warren was going to live with or without me. I've often said since, if he were in real trouble, I'd have made a deal before I helped him get a life preserver. *I'd* have been chairman of Berkshire Hathaway!"

That mishap, concluded Guerin, is why Charlie's friends sometimes call him Admiral Munger. Despite the misadventure, Guerin says that the time he spent at Cass Lake that summer was an invaluable first step in his recovery from grief. He says it showed him that Munger and Buffett were more than just business associates.

"Warren gave me the greatest gift he could possibly give: Three days of his time. And Charlie gave that, too. We try to be realistic and smart and logical all the time, but there is another side to it."

The way Buffett reacted to the boating accident was typical of the business relationship between him and Munger. "Even when I took him fishing in Minnesota and upset the boat and we had to swim to shore, he didn't scream at me," said Munger.[4]

One of Munger's children noted, however, that the ill-fated fishing trip was the last time Buffett ever joined the family at Cass Lake.

Munger said there was another reason Buffett never returned: "After dunking him in the lake, we tried to cheer him up by making him watch a bunch of high school students perform Moliere in a Bemidji tent." Moliere, even if delivered professionally, is not Buffett's style.

CHAPTER THREE

THE NEBRASKANS

An increased percentage of people come from Nebraska. Some people say they are from Nebraska when they aren't, for status reasons.

Warren Buffett, 1997 Berkshire Hathaway annual meeting

HUNDREDS OF THOUSAND OF PIONEERS, heading west to the Oregon and Mormon Trails, passed through Nebraska in the nineteenth century. Omaha was a gateway to the vast, rich lands beyond the Missouri River, and the ruts left by the wagon trains are visible in Nebraska farm fields more than 150 years later. Omaha was so rough and primitive back then that one of Charlie Munger's grandmothers for a while refused to live there; it was too far from the sophistication of her native Iowa.

"Mother's parents moved to a job in Omaha, "said Carol Munger Estabrook, "but our grandmother insisted on living in Council Bluffs, Iowa. It's now full of casinos and strip joints. But back then, Nebraska was considered more of a frontier than Iowa."

Omaha has improved, but living in Nebraska still is a character-building experience. Temperatures can hit more than 100 degrees Fahrenheit in the summer and plummet to 40 below zero in the winter. Two big rivers, the Platte and the Missouri merge in Omaha, and melting snows can produce early spring floods.

There are many Nebraskans of notable character, including the creator of modern rodeo, Buffalo Bill Cody; novelist Willa Cather; former U.S. President Gerald B. Ford; entertainers Henry Fonda, Johnny Carson, Marlon Brando, Nick Nolte, and Fred Astaire; and civil rights activist Malcolm X.[1]

Munger says he owes a lot to Omaha, the community in which he was raised. He paraphrases an old saying, "they can take the boy out of Omaha but not Omaha out of the boy."

19

"Charlie tries to make the point that he is the way he is because he grew up in Omaha," said Munger's daughter Wendy. "But Warren says he doesn't think so. There weren't any others like Charlie in Omaha."

The first child and only son of Omaha lawyer Alfred C. Munger and his wife Florence (Toody), Charlie came into the world during the "Roaring Twenties," four years after the Volstead Act brought the prohibition of alcoholic beverages to America and four years before penicillin was discovered.

Calvin Coolidge was president, replacing Warren G. Harding who had died in office a year earlier of a heart attack. Perhaps worried that the same fate would befall him, Coolidge took a two- to three-hour nap each day. His restful habits didn't seem to hurt the nation's economy, which was in the midst of a great business boom. Coolidge once declared, "The business of America is business," and indeed, from 1921 to 1929, the gross national product soared from $74 billion to $104.4 billion. The buying power of a skilled laborer swelled 50 percent during that period. Bricklayers' wives began wearing silk stockings and the bricklayers themselves bought touring cars.[2]

Al Munger had moved the roughly 50 miles from Lincoln to Omaha because it would have been problematic to practice law in his hometown where his father was the only federal judge and a dominant force in the community. Charlie's father practiced law in the same building in downtown Omaha from 1915 to 1959, taking time out to serve as an assistant attorney general and to fulfill his obligations in World War I.

The Munger family history stretched way back in America, reaching to an ancestor who was among the earliest British settlers in New England. The Munger name derives from the German word *monger,* a person who sells some commodity, such as fish or iron. At some early point, the Mungers moved from Germany to England and thereafter were increasingly Anglicized.

The first Munger arrived in America in 1637; Nicholas was a 16-year-old freeman from the county of Surrey, England. He settled in Guilford, Connecticut, where the family farm proved boggy and unproductive, so the Mungers moved from one disappointing farmstead to another, hoping to improve their fortunes. Over time, the family migrated West, with some landing in the Territory of Nebraska.

"Among us not many great, not many mighty, but most belonging to the reliable 'middle class,' the strength of a nation," wrote a Munger family historian. "Some few have cast considerable luster on the family name. Among these I class the sturdy pioneer, those who fought in the Colonial Wars, the Revolution, and in the War for the Union, aren't they worthy?"[3]

One of these Nebraska Mungers became a teacher and married a school marm. Teachers earned a pittance in the early days of this country and the family was extremely poor. Nonetheless, one of their two sons became a doctor and the other, Charlie's grandfather, became a lawyer and later a judge.

Charlie's grandfather, Judge T.C. Munger, was influenced all his life by his early poverty. He would frequently recall being sent to the butcher with a nickel to buy the parts of the animal others would not eat. He had to leave college after one year for lack of funds and thereafter educated himself, using books and self-discipline. Even so, he rose to a position of influence, all the while holding to the beliefs and characteristics of his pioneer forbears. Judge Munger was determined to move the family as far as possible from the hard-scrabble life his parents had experienced. "He wanted not to be poor," recalled Charlie. "Self-sufficiency and hard work would be his salvation. My grandparents thought Robinson Crusoe was a great moral work. They forced their children to read it, and my grandmother read it to me. That generation admired the conquering of nature through discipline."

Molly Munger, who takes a great interest in family lore, explained that "Judge was anti-gambling, anti-saloon. Financially conservative. Underspending his income. Making money by lending money to the good German farmer, the good German butcher. As a judge he was a progressive. It was a big deal to be a federal judge. There weren't many back then."

Indeed, in 1907 Judge Munger's name made a headline in the Lincoln newspaper. "Bar president takes train to D.C. to visit President." In 1939, the Omaha World Herald printed a feature article about Judge Munger, who was celebrating both the fifty-fourth anniversary of his admission to the bar and the beginning of his thirty-third year as a United States District judge. Judge Munger, who was 77 at the time the article was published, was then the second-oldest federal judge in service. He was appointed to the bench in 1907 by President Theodore Roosevelt, after having served in the state legislature and as county attorney of Lancaster County.

"Back in the harness after a vacation in Mexico, Judge Munger is not unduly elated by this anniversary, and is digging into his work as usual. The routine cases he ordinarily hears will be interrupted with a more exciting job when he goes to Hastings to preside in a kidnaping trial Monday."[4]

According to the *Omaha World-Herald*, "He firmly believes that work is the best way to keep young." His bright blue eyes snap when he says, "I call myself a member of the present generation because I feel that way, and let it go at that."[5]

Among Judge Munger's most memorable cases was a train robbery that took place west of Omaha shortly after he took the bench and the prosecution of a group of Nebraskans accused of staking fraudulent homesteads.

"He has a reputation for giving juries more thorough instructions than any other judge in the middle west." the writer noted.[6]

Certainly the standards were high in the Munger and Russell families—Charlie's two sets of grandparents. The Mungers were Presbyterians and pillars of the church; the Russells were New England style Emersonian Unitarians and a little more irregular in church attendance.

Carol Estabrook says that despite Toody Munger's free-thinking family history, she tried to instill religion in her children. "We were brought up under strict ethical standards, in the Unitarian Church. Dad seldom went. Mother dragged us until we wouldn't go any more." "Ultimately," said Estabrook, "our ethical training came from our parents, our grandfather."

"I had four aunts, my only blood aunts, every single one a Phi Beta Kappa," explained Charlie. "On my mother's side the religion was that of New England style intellectuals, but their religious organization is now a left-wing political movement and the Russell descendants are Unitarians no more."

The *Washington Post*'s Katharine Graham said she once received a letter from Charlie in which he told about the moral rectitude of his Aunt "Oofie," his father's older sister. "Oofie" was taught by her father, the Judge, never to flinch and always do her duty well. Indeed, she became "Oofie" instead of "Ruth" because at a young age she mastered the delivery of long and complex bedtime prayers. After hearing these prayers, her younger brother Al, who had trouble pronouncing consonants, would then say "Dear God, mine's just like Oofie's."

As an adult, Aunt Oofie was so dutiful that after her husband died, she viewed his autopsy.

Her nephew Charlie adored Oofie, partly because her standards were so extreme that she amused him. But even Charlie was floored by Oofie's reaction to Judge Munger's sudden death at age 80. Just before he died, Oofie noticed that her father had made a mistake in arithmetic. She said to Charlie: "It was God's grace to take Judge, knowing he wouldn't have wanted to stay on and make errors."

From the Russells and the Mungers, Charlie inherited both intellectual and physical hardiness. In addition to the Judge's longevity, Charlie's great-grandfather on his mother's side lived to age 87 and his wife lived to be 82.

Florence Russell Munger's maternal grandparents, the Inghams, were among the first citizens of Algona, Iowa. Captain Ingham brought his young wife to Iowa, and the couple lived at first in a "sodhouse," which was nothing more than a cave. The captain loved to relate stories about his pioneer days, whereas his wife would only say: "They were mean, hard days and I don't like to think about them."

Much later, Captain Ingham came to operate the most prosperous bank in Algona and accumulated tracts of farm land. He became affluent enough so that when the industrialist Andrew Carnegie offered to pay half the cost of a town library, Ingham, at the insistence of his wife, put up the other half.

A fisherman, his 150-pound tarpon was carefully preserved by a taxidermist and hung in the basement of Algona's library, no doubt, a condition of his gift. He also had been a dedicated hunter, but when he accidentally killed his beloved hunting dog Frank, he gave up hunting forever.

"A strong personality," said Charlie. "He'd fought in the Indian wars, thus becoming Captain Ingham. Every year the cousins used to come to Algona—his many grandchildren and live there, a lot like Star Island. Mother and her sisters came. They stayed and lived in his house all summer, year after year."

Captain Ingham impressed his grandchildren by rapidly making "magic squares," wherein all straight lines of big numbers added to the same sum, no matter what the direction of the line. Captain Ingham shared this mathematical addiction with Benjamin Franklin and said he made the squares "to rest my mind."

Captain Ingham's son Harvey became a crusading newspaper editor and a meticulous recorder of family history. Toody Munger was particularly fond of one sentence in her Uncle Harvey's description of the Inghams: "There was plenty of plain living and high thinking in the old house."

Nellie Ingham, one of Captain Ingham's daughters married Charlie Russell. She was Charlie's grandmother.

Toody Russell's' family had been affluent much longer than the Mungers had been, and yet they were politically left of the Mungers. They called themselves "Wilsonian Democrats." The Inghams side of the family originally came from the Seneca Falls area of New York state which was famous for it's early anti-slavery, pro-women's suffrage attitudes, and the Inghams pushed similar ideas in Iowa. Despite the Mungers' more conservative ways, they respected Toody's family.

"Toody was the real deal," said Molly Munger. "They thought she was an elegant girl from a lovely family. Beautiful, very funny, smart in a quick, witty way. A happy person who laughed a lot. Educated at Smith College, she had a college-educated great uncle at the time of the Civil

War. Her grandmother's mother, Caroline Rice, had a prosperous life in upstate New York. She was connected. She grew up in a mansion. Horse and carriage, long clothes. Very unlike the Mungers."

In turn, Toody's family approved of her choice of a husband. When pretty, charming Florence announced that she would be marrying Al Munger, who stood 5 feet, 5½ inches tall and wore thick glasses, her grandmother Russell observed, "Whoever would have thought she had the sense?"

For years after his father died, Charlie carried Al Munger's briefcase to work. He had it engraved "Alfred C. Munger 1891-1959. Charles T. Munger 1924-." He no doubt liked the briefcase, but it also served as homage to a loyal and supportive father. Although Al Munger was by any measure a successful and respected attorney, "I think it's fair to say Al never achieved the height his son did," said Molly. "His greatest achievement was Charlie—a prodigy—a lively, energetic, funny little boy. Grampa Al just threw himself into his son. He adored him and they were very close. My father sort of wore my grandfather's colors. My father was very anxious to make his father proud of him."

"Al Munger," said Charlie, "was one of the happiest men who ever lived and achieved exactly what he wished to achieve, no more or less. He faced all troubles with less fuss than either his father or his son, each of whom spent considerable time foreseeing troubles that never happened. He had exactly the marriage and family life that was his highest hope. He had pals he loved and who loved him, including one-in-ten-thousand types like Ed Davis and Grant McFayden. He owned the best hunting dog in Nebraska, which meant a lot to him. I don't see my father as less successful in the sense that really matters. He was just differently aimed and lived in a time when lawyers made less money."

Warren Buffett said that Al and Charlie had none of the tension or jealousy that sometimes muddies a father-son relationship. "Charlie once said that if he'd come home at midnight and said, 'Dad, you've got to help me bury this body in the basement,' his father would have gotten up and helped him bury the body. Then the next morning, he would have gone to work on convincing Charlie he'd done something wrong."

Al Munger always took an interest in his son's hobbies. Then, as Charlie would outgrow them, or lose interest, or go on to some new stage in life, his father would carry the hobbies on. Al subscribed to the *American Rifleman* magazine until his death because Charlie had first subscribed when he was captain of his high school rifle team. Charlie had joined the rifle team because it seemed the only way he could earn a sports letter. "I hoped to impress the girls with my sports letter, prominently

worn on my sweater," said Charlie. "And I did turn heads, but the reason
was the girls wondered how a spindly little guy like me could have won a
sports letter."

Long before his son took up shooting, Al Munger was a fisherman
and duck hunter. "He loved everything about the out-of-doors," noted
Charlie. "To him, heaven was finding a farmstand."

Al liked catfish and would often drive into the predominantly black
neighborhood of Omaha where people kept concrete tanks full of live catfish in their basements.

"You picked out what you wanted," recalled Charlie. "My father also
loved ethnic shops, bakeries. He had a special butcher he went to."

Though he could not be described as a lavish spender, Al Munger sa-
vored just the perfect thing, whatever it was he needed. Al had learned
the joy of artful living from his mother. She shopped for the very best coffee beans, then took great pleasure each morning in grinding them for
fresh coffee. It was a Tao philosophy, Midwestern style. In the *Tao Te
Ching,* Lao-Tse urged seekers to regard the small as important and to make
much of the little. "The little obsessions," Charlie called them.

WHEN AL AND TOODY MUNGER WERE FIRST MARRIED, they lived in a home
on the North side of Dodge Avenue just a block from Toody's parents.
Charlie's father built the little house at 420 41st Street in 1925. A few
years later, after the Russells passed away, the Mungers moved to the
South side of Dodge Avenue, a long, broad thoroughfare that splits
Omaha in two and today is lined by miles of shopping centers. Their
next home was at 105 South 55th Street, a double-gabled brick house
in the Happy Hollow, University of Nebraska area not far from where
Buffett lives today. This is a neighborhood notable for its mature trees,
and today, its older homes. In the spring, trails of crocus, tulips, and daf-
fodils rim the sidewalks and driveways and bring patches of purple, yellow, and red to lawns awakening from winter dormancy.

At the time they moved to the 55th Street house, which they purchased from Omaha pioneer Peter Kiewit, the home was on the western
fringe of town. Yet Omaha was small enough that, despite its expanding
borders and the cultural and ethnic mix, most people felt part of a single
community.

"In my early boyhood, we lived around Germans in Omaha and there
were several German language newspapers. Omaha was very ethnic,"
Munger recalled. "It was not like the Latinos do today—[back then] they
assimilated. There was a big Italian neighborhood, Irish, Bohemians, a

packing house district. A lot of pronounced ethnicity. It was a very good town to grow up in, and a good time. There were better behavior standards in school and everywhere else."

Carol Estabrook agreed, somewhat.

"In the early days in Omaha, there was a sense of stability, belonging, you were comfortable, but terribly insular," she said. "We were way too unaware of things we should have been more aware of. It was the center of our universe."

Though the Munger children were sheltered from such things, there was a resurgence of racism in America, and in 1925 the Ku Klux Klan staged a 40,000-man parade down Pennsylvania Avenue in Washington, DC. Shortly before Charlie was born, there had been a mob lynching in Omaha. The labor movement was on the rise and attempts to unionize or picket a workplace sometimes turned brutal.[7] Those harsh events did not touch the Munger children.

"In that day and age, there was no crime at all," said Carol Estabrook. "No drugs. We'd play outside in the evenings, games like capture the flag, kick the can. Our neighbors put an ice-skating rink in their yard. We went to the movies on Saturday."

By the 1930s, Omaha's exquisite Orpheum Theater had changed from a vaudeville house to a talking-movie theater. "You had to pay as much as a quarter to see a first-run movie there," said Charlie. "I loved all the adventure movies, the Kipling movies, the horror movies, Frankenstein and Dracula. The first movie I remember really well was the original *King Kong*. I went to it all by myself. I couldn't have been more than eight. I think everyone in my generation who could afford it went to the movies. I loved comedies, loved to laugh. John Anderson, my friend, had a big, booming laugh. Once, in the Orpheum we laughed so hard that the rest of the people in the theater started laughing just because we were."

In 1977, Berkshire Hathaway moved its annual meeting to the Aksarben (Nebraska spelled backwards) fair grounds—familiar territory for Munger. "I used to come here as a boy for the circus. Now we have a circus of our own."

CHARLIE, MARY, AND CAROL MUNGER all attended Dundee Elementary School and later moved up to Central High School, which is housed in the stately former territorial capital building. Central High was considered one of the 25 top college preparatory schools in the country. Susan Buffett and the Buffett children went through the same schools, though Warren did

Young Charlie in knickers in Omaha.

not. When his father became a congressman, Buffett finished elementary school and attended high school in the Washington, DC area.

Buffett says he still gets letters from people who went to school with Charlie. "Miss Kiewit was one of his elementary school teachers." She was the sister of the well-known Omaha contractor Peter Kiewit, who later became the first citizen of Nebraska. Miss Kiewit played the organ at the First Presbyterian Church and was a member of Eastern Star. She had taught for 42 years when she retired from the Omaha school system in 1970. "They had great teachers because, for other jobs, there was prejudice against women then," said Buffett. Such talented women later passed over teaching for jobs in other professions.

The teachers of Omaha, and especially Miss Kiewit, emphasized "thought" problems at which Munger always excelled. They also required the children to serve as crossing guards and do other chores. "Teachers were very well-behaved people," said Munger, "good moral exemplars in the old-fashioned sense. There was discipline. The moral teaching was good."

Charlie was a star student, but he also was one of the most challenging to deal with.

"Charlie was so lively that you could hardly miss him," said Estabrook. "He was up to something all the time. Occasionally he got in a scrape with his teachers. He was too independent minded to bow down to meet certain teachers' expectations. Our children are the same way. We think it's the way to be."

Charlie also liked to tease and play tricks.

"Mother used to say, 'Charlie is both smart and smartie,'" said Willa Davis Seemann. Mrs. Davis did her best to improve young Munger. When he was visiting the Davis' and misbehaved, Charlie got his legs switched right along with the Davis children.

The classroom, said Munger, was only one part of his early education. "I met the towering intellectuals in books, not in the classroom, which is natural. I can't remember when I first read Ben Franklin. I had Thomas Jefferson over my bed at seven or eight. My family was into all that stuff, getting ahead through discipline, knowledge, and self-control."

Charlie, Mary, and Carol received several books each year as Christmas gifts. "We had them read by Christmas night." said Carol. "We were very bookish people. Dad loved mysteries, Dickens and Shakespeare, biographies. Mother belonged to a book club which read everything that was current. I remember staying at the Davies and reading medical books. That's what the Davises had and what you read."

Despite the family's love of reading, Charlie had trouble learning to read until his mother took it upon herself to teach him phonics. Whatever held him back quickly disappeared, and he was soon skipped ahead in school.

"My parents used to say, 'there were no dumb Mungers,'" recalled Willa Seemann.

Small and slight of build all through high school, Munger grew to his full stature of nearly 6 feet late. He was not particularly athletic, but spent this time with books, hobbies, friends, and people he liked.

"He was always gregarious, friendly, social. He was interested in science, almost anything—he had a curious mind. Both parents had a big influence, but in different ways," explained Estabrook. "I think he related to Dad in the business and law sense. Mother was sociable. Of course, the Davis family was part of everybody's lives. They lived two or three blocks away."

The Munger and Davis families spent a lot of time together. Charlie was between the ages of the Davis boys, Eddie and Neil. Charlie's sister Mary was Willa's closest girlfriend.

"Anytime anything went wrong at the Munger house, they called mother," said Willa. "Once Toody fell through the French doors. Back then they didn't have stretchers, so they took down a door and carried her out. Mother was a nervous eater, so she went to the kitchen and got a sausage and an apple and ate them going to the hospital."

Like his parents, Charlie was fond of all the Davises. "Dr. Ed Davis was my father's best friend, and I did something unusual for a person as young as I was—five, eight, twelve, fourteen—I became a friend of my father's friend. I got along very well with Ed Davis. We understood one another."[8]

Charlie became so interested in Ed Davis and his work that "I watched movies of his main operations and familiarized myself with surgical outcome statistics in his field."

THE PROSPERITY ENJOYED BY SO MANY AMERICANS in the 1920s came to an abrupt end in the 1930s. By the time Charlie was six years old, the world was in a Great Depression that lasted until after he graduated from high school. The frightening era erupted on Black Friday, October 29, 1929. Between October and mid-November of that year, stocks lost more than 40 percent of their total valuation, a drop of $30 billion on paper at least. The effect was devastating to the more than 1.5 million Americans who dabbled in the stock market, often on borrowed money. One investor, presented with a margin account bill from her broker wailed, "How can I loose $100,000. I never had $100,000."[9]

After Black Friday, the market rallied a few times, but finally floundered. Matters were made worse when a series of natural disasters deluged the United States—floods, droughts, plagues, and dust storms. More than 40 million Americans descended into dire poverty.[10]

Though Munger was unaware of it, something else happened in Omaha in 1929 that would influence his life. Warren Buffett tells the story this way:

> I'm quite fond of 1929, since that's when it all began for me. My dad was a stock salesman at the time, and after the Crash came, in the fall, he was afraid to call anyone—all those people who'd been burned. So he just stayed home in the afternoons. And there wasn't television then. Soooo . . . I was conceived on or about November 30, 1929, and I've forever had a kind of warm feeling about the Crash.[11]

Warren was born nine months later on August 30, 1930.

Times were so bad that every day hobos knocked on the back doors in Omaha's better neighborhoods, offering to sweep the driveway or do some other chore for a sandwich. "It was amazing how poor people were in the 1930s," said Munger. "One summer it took family pull to get me a summertime job at 40 cents per hour. And all through the depression you could get all you could eat at Henshaw's Cafeteria, including meat and dessert, for 25 cents."

But, said Munger, he learned some of his most important life lessons during that time: "I had the example in early life of family members who behaved well under stress. It must have been very hard for Grandfather Munger to cure family financial distress that wouldn't have happened if the suffering family members had been more like the Judge. But he came through anyway."

Both sets of grandparents did what they could to help their children through the lean years.

"When the 1930s came Grandfather Russell, was down to very modest circumstances, his wholesale dry goods business having foundered," Charlie said. "Uncle Ed was in real estate, and was stone cold broke and owed money. Grampa Russell cut his house in half and moved in his daughter and Ed—even as their oldest child died slowly of meningitis leaving medical and hospital bills that took years to pay."

On the Munger side of the family, one of Charlie's uncles owned a small bank in Stromsburg, Nebraska. Farmers defaulted on loans, and the bank wasn't sound enough to reopen after Roosevelt's bank holiday in 1933. "Uncle Tom needed about $35,000 worth of good assets to replace $35,000 of crap. Grampa Munger had $35,000 in good mortgages and put them into his son-in-law's bank in exchange for the crap. It was a big risk. It represented about half of his assets and there were no pensions for judge's widows at that time. At the end of the bank holiday, Uncle Tom's bank re-opened, and, eventually, over many years, much of the Judge's investment was recovered as bad assets became merely mediocre assets."

One of Munger's aunts had married a musician over the Judge's objection. Judge Munger gave him money to go to pharmacy school, then lent him money to buy a well-located, but bankrupt pharmacy that prospered. Both the Mungers and the Russells stuck together and pulled through. Despite the problems the rest of the family had, Al Munger was relatively secure.

"My father was never again so rich in real income as he was in 1936. It was his peak of lawyering. We didn't live in a big house and have a chauffeur, but we were very comfortable—by the standards of the day."

Al Munger's prosperity in the mid-1930s was partly due to a law case Al handled on behalf of a tiny soap company. Al argued that one of the New Deal's tax laws was unconstitutional, and the case somehow got accepted for review by the U.S. Supreme Court. On the outcome swung a huge sum of money for Colgate Palmolive Peet and a small sum for Al's client. Colgate paid Al generously for allowing Colgate's famous New York lawyer to argue the case, which the New York lawyer then lost. "I could have lost it just as well for less," said Al.

Despite his family's relative prosperity in the 1930s, Charlie took jobs when he could: "I first encountered the Buffetts when I worked at the family grocery store. The hours were long, the pay low, opinions cast in iron, and foolishness zero."[12]

Buffett & Son was started in 1869 by Warren's great-grandfather, Sidney Buffett. When Charlie worked there, it was owned by Warren's grandfather Ernest. The Buffett sense of humor apparently is hereditary. Ernest's brother was named Frank.

Originally located on 13th Street, the store later moved to the western edge of Omaha, 5015 Underwood Avenue, six or seven blocks from Munger's home.

"It was a credit and delivery store," explained Buffett. "It had a mezzanine where my grandfather would sit. Basically he was the boss. He'd give orders. Uncle Fred, Ernest's son, did all the work."

The store had squeaky wooden floors, rotating fans, and floor-to-ceiling wooden shelves. When a customer wanted a can from a higher shelf, a young clerk moved a sliding ladder to the right place and retrieved the item. Grocery boys unpacked and shelved cases of food, cleaned out the produce bins, carried grocery bags to the homes of Omaha matrons, and swept floors. Charlie "slaved" in the store on Saturdays. "You were just goddam busy from the first hour of morning until night," he explained.[13]

If Warren's older cousin, Bill Buffett, arrived late, he was greeted by the portly, white-haired Grampa Ernest, standing above on the mezzanine with watch in hand, "Billy, what time is it?"

Ernest Buffett was a strict employer and he held strong political views. "He paid $2 for 12 hours of uninterrupted work. Social Security had just been enacted, and he used to require each boy to bring two pennies to the store to pay his contribution to the system," said Charlie.[14]

At the end of the day, Charlie handed Ernest his two pennies and in return received two dollar bills, plus a lecture on the evils of socialism.

For Munger, "The Buffett family store provided a very desirable introduction to business. It required hard, accurate work over long hours, which caused many of the young workers, including me (and later Ernest's grandson Warren), to look for an easier career and to be cheerful upon finding disadvantages therein."[15]

Warren's Uncle Fred Buffett, who once was voted the most popular man in Omaha, took over running the store in 1946 when Ernest died. As late as the 1960s, Buffett's grocery still accepted phone-in orders and made home deliveries. When Fred finally closed the business in 1969, it had been operating for 100 years, run by three generations of Buffetts. The building remains in the Dundee area surrounded by a cluster of antique shops.

BY THE TIME CHARLIE MUNGER was nine years old, Franklin Roosevelt had been elected president, the New Deal had been introduced, and Prohibition had been repealed. When Charlie was 14, Orson Welles terrified the United States with his overly realistic radio broadcast "War of the Worlds." Munger was 15 when Hitler's Nazi army invaded Poland. The whole world was experiencing dramatic change that would carry Charlie away from his home in Nebraska.

CHAPTER FOUR

SURVIVING THE WARS

He's a poker player, likes to keep things to himself. Even when we were children, he'd say, "We'll see. We'll see," more than any other comment. If you ask him a question he doesn't want to answer, he just pretends he doesn't hear.

Molly Munger

TWO OF THE MUNGER GRANDCHILDREN, Charles Lowell and Nathaniel (ages ranging from seven-ish to ten-ish), and a mob of kids from neighboring cabins clamor up and down the stairs of the main Star Island house to a third-floor loft, where they have set up a fort and have formed a secret club.

On this sunny, languorous August day at the Munger compound on Cass Lake, they play a game that children have played for centuries, making up elaborate rules, planning raids on imagined enemies, and seizing territory. Their chatter has a recurring theme. One youngster bursts out, "I've got an idea!" No sooner does the gang discuss and agree on the plan, than young Nathaniel Munger pipes up, "I've got a better idea." Back to the drawing board. Nathaniel always has a better idea.

To improve the fortification and deter intruders, the children pile a chair and suitcases at the top of three flights of stairs. All is well until Nathaniel decides to make a reconnaissance trip to the first floor. Suddenly, with an alarming clatter, the chair, the suitcases, and Nathaniel all tumble down.

Charlie Munger Senior glances up from his book and listens to the bawling Nathaniel and the thunder of feet as the other children run to gawk and as adults rush to survey the damage. Miraculously, Nathaniel has no broken bones, not even a bruise that anyone can locate. Once he is the center of attention, Nathaniel's crying stops. The family reports to

Grandad that no damage was done. Charlie continues to read. "I didn't think so," he mutters. By the end of the day, Nathaniel is boasting to his pals that he fell all the way down the stairs and didn't even get hurt.

THE 1940s BROUGHT TURMOIL AND CHANGE both to America and the Munger household. Some of that change was to be expected because Al and Toody's children were growing up. As rumblings of war were heard from across the oceans, first Charlie, then Mary, and finally Carol left for college. In the middle of those natural transitions, a dreaded inevitability occurred—the United States was dragged into World War II.

Charlie was 17 when he left, in 1941, to enroll in the University of Michigan where he majored in mathematics—and never after, except for visits, returned fo Omaha. Mary Munger chose Scripps College in Pasadena, but Carol followed in her father's footsteps and went east to Radcliffe, nominally the women's college at Harvard at the time.

At Ann Arbor the students, including Charlie and his roommate, Nebraskan John Angle, listened to Bing Crosby records, watched young Bette Davis at the movies, and explored new academic vistas. Charlie was introduced to physics. "To me, it was a total eye-opener," he said. Although Munger only took an introductory level class, it was the physicists approach to problem solving that made a lifelong impression on him.

"The tradition of always looking for the answer in the most fundamental way available—that is a great tradition, and it saves a lot of time in this world. And, of course, the problems are hard enough that you have to learn to have what some people call assiduity. Well, I've always liked that word—because to me it means that you sit down on your ass until you've solved your problem."

Munger says that if he were running the world, anyone who qualified to do so would be required to take physics, simply because it teaches a person how to think.

"I am in no sense a working scientist or a working amateur scientist," Munger concedes, "but I have a very deep appreciation of science and I find the methods used are useful outside of science."

But he was not to have a long period of tranquil studies at the University of Michigan. Instead, the prospect of war was troubling the minds of most Americans. The political temperature was rising in Europe, then, early in Charlie's first year of college, on December 7, 1941, there came the surprise attack on the U.S. Naval fleet at Pearl Harbor. The imperative of World War II forced many young men out of college and into military service, and Charlie was no exception. He stayed at the University of

Michigan through the end of 1942, then, a few days after his nineteenth birthday, joined up.

When Charlie enlisted, the war was well underway in Europe, Africa, and the Pacific. Because he had been a member of the Reserve Officer Training Corps (ROTC) in high school and college—a total of six years— Munger was bored with marching. He decided against going into the infantry and to his everlasting good fortune joined the Army Air Corps.

Charlie's mother was frantic about the safety of her only son, although Carol Estabrook said Toody Munger tried to hide her fear. Surely Al Munger suffered similar anxieties, but to compensate, he threw himself into the war effort at home. Consequently, World War II became an exciting time for Charlie's father. He cultivated a huge victory garden, recruiting a nephew to work in it with him. Then he found a partner, a priest who was a professor at a local Jesuit college and who had some land in the country. Together they raised pigs so that they could have bacon and other pork cuts, which were scarce because so much meat was being shipped overseas to feed the troops. About the time their pigs matured, though, rationing ended and pork products again became available at reasonable prices.

"It was very expensive bacon," chuckled Charlie. "I think my father did it mostly because he liked raising pigs."

When he first joined the military, Munger was an ordinary soldier, and his training gave him time to think about his future. "As a private in the Army in Utah in a tent, in the mud and snow—very unpleasant conditions—I remember talking to someone. I said I wanted a lot of children, a house with lots of books, enough money to have freedom."

After Munger took the Army General Classification Test, he found out that a score of 120 qualified a soldier to be commissioned as an officer. Charlie did much better than that, scoring 149. He soon was promoted to Second Lieutenant.[1]

He was first dispatched to the University of New Mexico in Albuquerque, and then to a distinguished private college of science and engineering, the California Institute of Technology in Pasadena, California, to train as a meteorologist. In plainer language, he would be a weather forecaster. Charlie took one look around Pasadena and knew he liked his new surroundings.

Pasadena was a graceful old town, full of Spanish colonial-style mansions and shaded by billowing purple jacarandas and fragrant eucalyptus and pepper trees. It had been settled a hundred years earlier by Midwesterners who built impressive churches and cultural institutions like the ones they enjoyed back home. Smog wasn't yet the problem it would become, and on most days, the San Gabriel Mountains seemed so close that you could reach out and touch them. To the west stretched the energetic, exotic metropolis of Los Angeles.

"Southern California was quite different. It looked like a bigger, more interesting place than Omaha, a city that I love," he said.

Munger's three roommates at Caltech also impressed him favorably. One roommate, Henry Magnin, was the son of an influential Reform Jewish rabbi. The second was the son of a music professor famous for teaching prodigies, and another was from a family of well-known scientists and inventors. "They were all Californians. Interesting guys with interesting families," recalled Charlie.

Following his weatherman training, Munger was dispatched to Alaska, which was cold and dark, but, according to his own account, not particularly dangerous. Charlie noted that his experience contrasted starkly with the dangers to which others were exposed. U.S. casualties in World War II totaled 292,000 dead, 672,000 wounded, and 140,000 taken prisoner or declared missing.

The war interrupted his education, but it did not have the deeply formative influence on him that it had on others, said Charlie. "I don't think I knew well 15 people who died in World War II. It wasn't like a whole generation of young men died, as the Europeans did in World War I or Americans in the Civil War. I never got near military action. I was stationed in Nome. I couldn't have gotten farther from action."

Just as Munger had avoided the poverty and degradation of the Depression, he was spared from the battlefield by serving in a vital noncombat job. Nevertheless, his years in the military allowed him to refine what later became an important skill—card playing.

"Playing poker in the Army and as a young lawyer honed my business skills," said Charlie. "What you have to learn is to fold early when the odds are against you, or if you have a big edge, back it heavily because you don't get a big edge often. Opportunity comes, but it doesn't come often, so seize it when it does come."

Munger's deployment to Caltech coincidentally overlapped with his sister Mary's enrollment at nearby Scripps College. She introduced Charlie to one of her classmates, a girl named Nancy Huggins, whose family owned a shoe store that catered to the well-heeled residents of Pasadena. The whole nation was in the throes of wartime angst, and young love, under the threat of long or even permanent separation, became highly romanticized. The combination of youth, war, and romance led to predictable consequences.

"The first Nancy goes to Scripps College—is a lively, pretty girl, from the lively, attractive Huggins clan," explained Molly. "Willful, indulged.

She rooms with a much calmer, steadier, bookish girl from Omaha. She has a brother who started [to college] in Michigan. He was sent to Caltech. And they utterly rushed into marriage—he was 21, she 19—no idea of what they were doing, both people of high spirits. Young people in the middle of a war. They made severe mistakes."

It took several years before it would become apparent that Munger's marriage was a misjudgment. In the meantime, the Mungers did what many young, postwar couples did. They sought additional education on the GI Bill and started a family.

Though Munger had by now attended several universities and taken advanced courses, he had not earned a college diploma. That did not deter this ambitious 22-year-old. Even before he was discharged from the military in 1946, Charlie, like his father, applied to the nation's oldest and perhaps most distinguished law school, Harvard. Charlie was following a family tradition, but law also seemed the best career choice for him, given his skills, or lack thereof, in certain areas.

"The Army gave two tests," he explained. "An IQ test and a mechanical aptitude test. I got a radically high score on IQ and a much lower score for mechanical aptitude. That confirmed what I already knew. My spatial talents were not up to my general level of talents. If I'd have gone into surgery when I was young, I wouldn't have been an outstanding surgeon. My father's best friend, Dr. Davis, was a famous surgeon. I could tell he had this vast mechanical ability that I lacked."

As for his original college major—mathematics—well, Charlie performed admirably in the math classes he'd taken, but he knew he wasn't as talented as his best teachers. He recalled watching his Caltech thermodynamics professor, Homer Joe Stewart, stride into the classroom and spend hours writing very complex equations on the blackboard as fast as his fingers could move, spouting rapid-fire explanations as he went. Charlie realized he never could be as good as that, and for a professor at a prestigious university, it is necessary to be like Homer Joe Stewart. To go into a calling where he would not be exceptional was not in Charlie's thinking.

Despite the fact that Al Munger had graduated from Harvard Law, Charlie was not welcomed with open arms. "I was admitted over the objection of Dean Warren Abner Seavy through the intervention of family friend Roscoe Pound," Munger said.

A Nebraska native, Pound was the retired dean of Harvard Law School. Charlie knew from family stories that Pound was a polymathic supergenius who, as dean, seldom convened faculty meetings because he figured he could make better decisions by himself. When Munger, faced with rejection, asked to confer with Pound, Seavy warned Charlie that the

Dean would agree that he should finish college before going to law school. Munger replied, "We'll see."

When Charlie called upon him to plead his case, Pound reviewed the transcripts of the work Munger already had completed. After reaching a favorable conclusion, Pound contacted the new law school dean and saw to it that Munger was admitted.[2]

Harvard's flexibility proved sound. By the end of Charlie's first year he won a $400 Sears prize for placing second in his class. Nonetheless, in retrospect, Charlie considered himself prepared enough for Harvard Law, but inadequately prepared for life.

"I came to Harvard Law School very poorly educated, with desultory work habits and no college degree."[3]

At the 75th anniversary celebration of See's Candy, Munger and Buffett spent nearly an hour taking questions from the audience. One See's employee asked the two men what their most important school experiences were.

"I hurried through school," said Munger. "I don't think I'm a fair example [of an ideal education], and I don't think you are either, Warren. I learn better sort of plowing through written material by myself. I've done a lot of that in my life. I frequently like the eminent dead better than the live teachers."[4]

Buffett confessed that his main objective in college was "getting out." He was impatient to get on with life and start his career as an investor, though Buffett said that attending graduate school at Columbia University and studying under the legendary investor Benjamin Graham was one of the most important things he did.[5]

Charles Munger once described himself as having a black belt in chutzpah, and probably that trait helped him rise to the challenge.[6] He had grown up in the households of a judge and a business lawyer, and had been exposed to lawyerly thinking all of his life. He also was opinionated, almost to the point of arrogance. When a professor called upon him to answer a question that Munger was not prepared for, he responded, "I haven't read the case, but if you give me the facts, I'll give you the law."[7]

Munger later came to realize that conversational gambits of that type were foolish and impeded his progress in life. Remembering the incident, Munger says he doesn't know why he behaved so badly, but he thinks it may have been partly due to hereditary factors that he has subdued but not conquered. He has admitted, in fact, that he apparently was behind the door when humility was handed out.

One of Charlie's Harvard Law classmates, Henry Gross, became a successful investment counselor in Los Angeles, and defended Munger when an acquaintance remarked that prosperity was making Charlie pompous. "Nonsense," said Gross. "I knew him when he was young and poor; he was always pompous."

Munger can be highly self-assured and sometimes reactive, but what saves him is that his opinions aren't set in stone. James Sinegal, president and chief executive officer for Costco, said Charlie doesn't "have an agenda. If you don't buy off on his viewpoint, he doesn't pout. He's prepared to move on with the conversation."

While at Harvard, Charlie again had a sister nearby: Carol arrived to study at Radcliffe. "I babysat their first child (Teddy). I fed him his Pablum dry—I was so unfamiliar with babies," said Carol. "He ate it, too. It didn't kill him."

Molly, the Munger's first daughter, was born in Massachusetts and was brought home from the hospital to cramped student quarters. "I used to move her crib into the bathtub each night. It was a small crib and fit well," said Charlie.

At Harvard Charlie was as sociable as he had been in elementary and high school back in Omaha. He circulated widely among different types of people. Walter Oberer, who later became dean of the law school at the University of Utah, worked with Munger on the *Harvard Law Review.* On one occasion, they spent many days in the lower parts of the Widener Library checking citations in a turgid article written by a European scholar. "After about four days Oberer said that our situation reminded him of a time when he was working as a pick-up day laborer inside box cars in 120-degree heat alongside a tramp who needed money for food. Finally, the tramp threw down a grain sack and walked off saying, 'Fuck this shit. I didn't kill anybody.' Nonetheless, Oberer stayed the course to the end at the *Harvard Law Review.* But after a while, I imitated the tramp."

Munger completed law school in 1948, along with Kingman Brewster who became the president of Yale University, Ed Rothschild, who founded the law firm of Rothschild, Stevens and Barry in Chicago and Joseph Flom, who went on to become a famous lawyer in New York. Charlie was one of 12 in the 335-member class to graduate magna cum laude.

He talked to his father about returning to Omaha to practice law, but despite the connections that Charlie might enjoy there, Al Munger advised against it. Apparently Al felt that Omaha was too small a pond for Charlie. Even though Omaha was an affluent small city, headquarters to the Union-Pacific Railroad, several agricultural corporations, and numerous insurance companies, Charlie would not be challenged by the practice that he could build there.

Besides that, Charlie was enchanted by Pasadena and taken with the Californians he'd met. Charlie, Nancy, and their growing family would head back West.

Al Munger approved, even though his personal experiences in California had been discouraging. He had visited Los Angeles right after the end of World War I, with a view to possibly relocating there. However, appalled by the lack of water and greenery, he had declared "There's no future in this town." He returned to Nebraska, only to have his son grow up and make the opposite decision.

Even Munger's own children think it was odd, in some ways, that Charlie would end up such an integral part of the most nontraditional city in the United States.

"Charlie loves Mark Twain and Ben Franklin. He's Midwestern," observed Barry. "He's definitely not very coastal. But LA was a big growing megalopolis and his business life intersected with that. He didn't move there because he liked to surf. He is a guardian of the mountain."

Nevertheless, Charlie has a taste for adventure when it comes to homes and friends. To Charlie, Los Angeles was a rational choice.

"I am not one who usually hates where I am," said Munger. "I liked Albuquerque. I liked Nashville, Tennessee, where I spent some months during the war. I liked Boston, and thought of staying there. But Boston in 1948 was terribly interbred—intermarried. It was a hard town in which to get ahead. In Los Angeles, I would go ahead faster."

He was right. The growth was amazing. With city limits that encompass 467 square miles, Los Angeles by the end of the twentieth century was home to more than 3.5 million people. And that's only within the city limits. Los Angeles County has 80 incorporated cities and 10 million residents.

Despite Munger's conservative, Midwestern ways, longtime friend Otis Booth said, "Charlie did not seem to stand out. Los Angeles is full of all kinds of people, and particularly in the early years was peopled by Midwesterners."

That Southern California was his wife's home may not even have been a consideration: "I don't remember discussing it with her," said Charlie.

On the other hand, said Molly Munger, Charlie was intrigued by his wife's entrepreneurial in-laws and didn't mind living near them. "My father always liked my Huggins relatives. He had respect and admiration for what they accomplished with the shoe store. He liked their lifestyle and high spirits. They were successful and positive. He talked about what a good business they had and what a good job they'd done."

Nancy Huggins, like Charlie himself, was descended from an old New England family, but the Huggins were a different clan from the Mungers. Her great-grandmother, Molly said, was "very smart and hard-working," the first girl in her high school to study algebra. She married shoe salesman Fred Huggins, Molly's great-grandfather, in Pasadena in 1890. At the time, Pasadena was a popular resort for Midwestern million-aires, including the Wrigley chewing gum heirs. The Huggins opened their own store, with her keeping books and Fred selling shoes. Later they branched out to Santa Barbara and Palm Springs. Their main store, on Pasadena's South Lake Avenue was later sold, but Nancy Huggins, an only child, inherited the stock that was issued in the sale. "The stock we took has continued to be valuable," said Molly.

In addition to their business acumen, the Huggins had a flair for liv-ing. "They were hard-drinking, kick up your heels types and married very well," said Molly. "They married up. Their mother bought the sons one tuxedo. They rotated it to go to fancy parties."

Charlie returned to this lively environment and was admitted to the California Bar in 1949. He joined the Los Angeles law firm of Wright & Garrett, which later became Musick, Peeler & Garrett. The firm had a re-spected name in the legal community, but was relatively small com-pared to others in the city. Charlie started out at a salary of $275 a month. He felt fairly affluent at the time, having accumulated $1,500 in savings.[8]

Once he was settled in California, Munger went about making con-nections with the same type of people he would have associated with had he stayed in Omaha.

For the most part, he stuck close to the law community. Charlie con-nected with old California families and with Midwesterners seeking to replicate their culture under more favorable weather conditions. Gradu-ally he joined social groups that would help further his connections—the classic downtown men's club, the California Club; the Los Angeles Coun-try Club and the Beach Club.

CHARLIE'S PARENTS HAD PROTECTED HIM from the sorrows of the Great De-pression. With luck he landed far from the battlefields of World War II. But his luck gave out. In the 1950s, the decade considered most felicitous for America, Munger walked unsuspectingly into the darkest experiences of his life.

"I think I must have been very young [when my parents split]," said Wendy Munger. "I don't remember his living in the house, but remember him picking us up on weekends. A divorce is a terrible thing. Teddy died at nine, I was five, Molly seven."

Because she was older, Molly remembers much of what happened when her parents divorced in 1953. Charlie and the first Nancy had married young and now, "They fought, yelled at each other. It was abundantly clear they weren't happy," explained Molly. And when it was obvious the Mungers could no longer live together, "They handled themselves in a way that was exemplary. They said all the right things. We're not happy with each other. We need to be apart. We love you guys. It won't affect our relationship with you."

Although she was just a preschooler when her parents' marriage broke up, Wendy Munger felt sure of one thing. "The divorce wasn't his doing, but I don't know [why they separated]," said Wendy. "A less well-suited pair hardly exists on this earth. They were just babies when they married."

As is the case with so many families, the children didn't fully understand what caused the irreconcilable differences between their parents, one a serious young lawyer and the other a free spirit, but they quickly grasped the consequences of the decision to end the marriage.

"He lost everything in the divorce," Molly continued. Her mother stayed in the house in South Pasadena, but despite his absence, Charlie went to great lengths to help the children realize that he was still their father and responsible for their well-being.

"When the divorce happened, Teddy said, I'm going to live with Daddy," Molly recalled. "He didn't."

Though he was in California, far from those roots, Munger got through that time by following the rules he learned in Omaha. "He was living in dreadful bachelor digs at the University Club," said Molly. "But there was not slippage. Every Saturday he was there. Every Saturday he was cheerful. He took us to the zoo, pony rides, took us to see his friends. Divorce in the 1950s was not a normal thing. We were very, very conscious of having a traumatized life compared to what else was going on. He drove this awful car—a yellow Pontiac. He always had great style, expressed it in his clothes but the car made it look as if he had not two pennies to say hello to each other. This yellow Pontiac had a cheap repaint job. I remember going up to the car in the University Club garage, and I said, 'Daddy, this car is just awful, a mess. Why do you drive it?' 'To discourage gold diggers,' he replied."

Charlie and the first Nancy had been separated a short time when they were told that their son Teddy was gravely ill with leukemia, a disease that had taken the life of Teddy's maternal grandfather. Charlie was stunned by the news. It went against everything that he'd experienced, everything that he'd dreamed. "He knew how to have a boy, be a loving father, and he was going to do it all over again," said Molly, but with Teddy, at least, that wasn't to be.

When Teddy Munger became ill, Charlie and his wife sought the best medical help they could find. The child had a blood disorder that allowed almost no chance of remission. Today, a child with leukemia has an excellent chance of full recovery.

"This would be in the early 1950s, you see," said Hal Borthwick. "They didn't really have anything that they could do for leukemia. Nothing. No bone marrow therapy—forget it. Even now, it is not an easy thing, but there are a lot more options. But in those days you just literally sat and watched your kid die by inches."

First the divorce, then Teddy's illness affected all areas of Munger's life. "In those days there was no medical insurance," said Munger. "I just paid all the expenses. You'd have a bonding experience in the leukemia ward. Parents and grandparents were having the same experience. They were all going to lose. In those days it was 100 percent. I've often wondered how professionals are able to steel themselves when dealing time after time with children facing mortality rates so high."

His friend Rick Guerin described the 29-year-old Charlie's grief: "He said when his son was in the bed and slowly dying, he'd go in and hold him for a while, then go out walking the streets of Pasadena crying."

But Munger tried to live a normal life. After the divorce, a law partner introduced him to a young divorcee, Nancy Barry Borthwick. She also had two young children, and Charlie and the second Nancy began taking their youngsters on outings together. At first the entourage included Teddy.

"I knew he was very sick, and I knew he was dying," recalls Hal Borthwick. Hal was about Teddy's age, and met the boy when Charlie and Nancy took the children to a private beach club on the Pacific Coast Highway. The club was affectionately called The Filthy Fifties, so named by a rival club because of the number of members. The second Nancy's family had been members for years.

"I do remember being down there one day with Teddy, and it was fairly near the end," recalled Hal. "I asked if he wanted to go play and he said, 'No, I really can't. I'm just too tired.' He was—you know . . . you could tell . . . What nine-year-old boy doesn't want to play at the beach? He was just too tired."

In 1955, one year after the diagnosis, Teddy Munger died. "I can't imagine any experience in life worse than losing a child inch by inch," said Munger. "By the time he died my weight was down 10 to 15 pounds from normal."

Hal Borthwick said that for the other children the end had a surreal feeling to it. "I don't have any recollection of going to the funeral or anything like that. I don't even know if Molly and Wendy went to it. In fact, I don't even know if there was a funeral. Teddy just sort of disappeared." There was a small religious service for Teddy but because Nancy and her sons weren't family yet, they did not attend.

Though the adults knew what was coming, Teddy's death also shocked his younger sisters. "We didn't know at all he was going to die," said Wendy. After he did. "We each kind of held our breath when we got to nine years old and released it when we got to ten. It was a silly kid thing to do, but I didn't like it when my kids were nine either."

With Charlie living at his club and Teddy gone, the once cozy three-bedroom, two-bath house Munger had built on Edgewood Drive in South Pasadena became a lonely place situated on a quiet street surrounded by gracious homes and majestic trees, it is only a block from Wendy's present home. Even after so many years, it looks like a sad little house to Molly and Wendy when they drive by.

"Molly and I lived in that house until 1957, then mother remarried," said Wendy Munger.

Charlie's first wife married radiologist Robert Freeman, one of the doctors who tended to Teddy Munger during his illness. Molly and Wendy felt that their mother's remarriage definitely improved their lives. They moved from the modest Edgewood Drive house to a much grander home on Madeline Street. Next door was the Westridge School for Girls, where Molly and Wendy soon enrolled. Now, they lived in a "big house, with an attic, basement, many rooms. It was a wonderful thing for a nine-year-old," said Molly. "Daddy had married, was producing babies. Our step-brother Hal was a very special person. Just a hoot. I knew he had great relative potential. He was just my age, reactive, an idea-a-minute type kid. My stepfather was more grandfatherly. He had his own children who were older than we were and a building medical practice. He doted on us. Daddy would come and get me. I very shortly thought it was a happy outcome to a bad situation. It was fine."

Dr. Freeman, the son of a local Presbyterian minister, played the accordion each week at the Kiwanis Club and served on the local school board.[9] Life began to brighten all around. Wendy Munger does not remember the transition from one family structure to the next, but she soon became aware of the advantages.

"I always said I had the best of both worlds," said Wendy. "I immediately got two stepparents that I liked and lots and lots of new relatives. It was a smooth thing for me. Both my mom and my dad spoke highly of one another. I just loved it, being part of a big family."

AT AGE 76, CHARLIE MUNGER LOOKS back on those years and notes that time takes some of the pain out of losing a child. If it didn't, he says, he doesn't know how the human race could continue. Munger believes that by coping as best he could with the tragedy of Teddy's death, he was doing the only rational thing. "You should never, when facing some unbelievable tragedy, let one tragedy increase to two or three through your failure of will." As for the end of his marriage, the years have given Munger a mature perspective on that as well:

> I don't spend much time regretting the past, once I've taken my lesson from it. I don't dwell on it. Certainly I had more sense when I was 32 than I did when I was 22. But I don't have any feeling of terrible regret. We ended up with nice children. I think my ex-wife has been reasonably happy in a different situation.

Years later, Munger compared the marriage process to the investment process, though perhaps he wasn't speaking specifically of his own experience. "Life is a whole series of opportunity costs," said Charlie. "You've got to marry the best person who is convenient to find that will have you. An investment is much the same sort of process."

That pragmatic statement masks his devotion to his second wife, Nancy, and certainly throws up a shield around the trouble and sorrow Munger experienced before he finally settled into a happy situation. The second Nancy insists Charlie is very affectionate, but said he is a little "uptight" about showing his feelings. Charles Munger, Jr., Nancy and Charlie's first son, suggested that his father's strength, his ability to resolutely move on from the past, also is his Achilles heel.

"His son died, his marriage ended, he lost a lot of money," said Charles, Jr. "He just walks away from that (emotionally). Dad says to himself, that doesn't work. Don't revisit it. There are some things my dad could deal with better if he faced them more. My dad, if he had a bad experience in a town, in a restaurant, he would not go back. I'd try again."

And yet Munger did try marriage again, and in this second union, said Charles. "Both Mom and Dad found what they lacked in their first marriages."

CHARLIE'S DREAM OF A LARGE FAMILY was about to be realized, and Munger was determined that the children would be raised and educated well. He knew that if he was to earn sufficient income, he would have to apply all his talents to the task. He already was a hard-charging lawyer, and gradually his need for additional income drew him into the business world.

"He was always interested in money," recalled Molly. "He was always good at money. He invested in the stock market. He talked about business in a way that was animated and interesting though now I see he was almost broke. I knew he drove an awful car. But I never thought he was anything but a big success. Why did I think that? He just had this air—everything he did was going to be first class, going to be great. He was going to put in a patio on Edgewood Drive. He was going to get a boat for the island. He was going to build a house, build apartments. He had these enthusiasms for his projects and his future—his present. It was not as if you had to deny yourself in the present for the future. The focus was on how interesting things are today, how much fun to see them built. It was so much fun being in the moment. That's what he always communicated."

CHAPTER FIVE

PUTTING TOGETHER
A NEW LIFE

I liked the independence of a capitalist. And I always had sort of a gambling personality. I liked figuring things out and making bets. So I simply did what came naturally.[1]

Charlie Munger

"I MET CHARLIE IN 1955," said the second Nancy Munger. "We were married in January 1956. We've been married 43 years."

That simple statement covers a life that has been anything but simple. When Nancy Barry Borthwick and Charlie wed, it was as if he'd walked from a dark place into a bright field of new possibilities. The second Nancy had traits that either filled in gaps or compensated for Charlie's shortcomings.

"He's not a very good manager," conceded his daughter Molly. "He's the utter absent-minded professor. He buys on impulse. If he had expensive tastes, he'd be in real trouble. Along comes Nancy. She's calm, stable, hard-working, incredibly frugal, interested in the nuts and bolts of making it work. She manages it. She's the CFO, the Robert Duval character. She's putting it together. He has charismatic abilities. She adores him. She just thinks he's the cutest thing."

Nancy was youthful, healthy, and had energy. A skilled athlete, she played tennis and kept skiing well past the age of 60, and despite recent hip replacement surgery, still plays golf.

"She's a great self-investor," said Molly. "What you learn from Nancy is never give up on yourself. Just keep working on your stuff. She does very beautiful watercolor painting, which she began in her 50s. She cooks French food at a gourmet level."

Charlie and his second wife Nancy at their wedding reception.

NANCY HAD A CALIFORNIA-STYLE PEDIGREE not unlike the one Charlie brought with him from Omaha. Her father's family moved from Beaumont, Texas, to Los Angeles in 1902 and were real estate developers before the Great Depression diminished the family fortune. David Barry Jr., Nancy's father, was in the insurance business and was also involved in various real estate ventures. Among other things he was interested in botany and built greenhouses where he crossbred rare plants, particularly palms and bromeliads. Her mother, a native Californian, was a teacher.

Nancy's parents met at the most characteristically Californian of all colleges, Stanford University in Palo Alto. Stanford was founded in 1918 by Leland Stanford, a railroad baron who dedicated the college to his son who succumbed to typhoid fever while still a teenager. When their son died Stanford told his wife that the children of California now would be their children, and soon afterward the couple established the West's most distinguished university.

"I was born in Los Angeles at the hospital where Charlie is chairman of the board, Good Samaritan," said Nancy Munger. "I lived in

Los Angeles, and went to public school until the tenth grade, then I attended Marlborough School."

Nancy's mother was an only child but she benefitted from an extended family. The Wittenbrocks, her mother's grandparents, had settled in Sacramento around the time of the Gold Rush and prospered there.

Her grandmother had an uncle and six aunts, noted Barry Munger. "Each was given a house when they got married on a single block in Sacramento. When she visited as a child, Mother could run around from one house to another. The aunts' houses are still there on J Street, close to the state capitol. The original Wittenbrock home is listed as a historic landmark."

"The aunts," said Nancy, "were endlessly patient with checkers, tiddlywinks, and jackstraws. Each afternoon they chose someone's garden to gather in and gossip. They had fruit trees. They canned peaches and cherries."

Like her parents before her, Nancy also went off to Stanford. Five of the eight Munger children followed suit, and if Wendy's daughter Anna is accepted in 2000, she will make the fourth generation of her family to attend Stanford.

"I majored in economics," said Nancy. "I loved business law, but I didn't receive any encouragement to go to law school. Instead, I married and had a family shortly after graduating."

Following graduation Nancy's husband continued at Stanford Law School. Nancy took a job at a scientific laboratory at Moffett Field in nearby Mountain View. She worked in a section where wind tunnel and other research work was conducted for early supersonic aircraft.

"They asked me, 'would you rather be in the typing pool or use a calculator.' I said calculator. We used a Frieden machine, and I calculated the shapes of aircraft wings and fuselages," recalled Nancy.

It was Nancy's plan to earn a master's degree in American history, but before she could complete her studies the couple returned to Los Angeles.

NANCY BORTHWICK HAD BEEN DIVORCED for a short time and was living with her two young sons in a house in a canyon above old Bel Air. She and Charlie met on a blind date.

"Good friends lived up the street. They knew some friends of Charlie's, who said he'd like to meet someone, so they arranged for us to meet," said Nancy. The couple who did the introducing were Martha and Roy Tolles. Martha is a writer of children's stories and Roy was one of

Charlie's law partners at Wright & Garrett." Friends say that after Charlie and Nancy had their first evening out, Tolles asked how it went. Charlie assured him that everything went very well, but then scolded Tolles for not telling Charlie the most important thing about Nancy—that she had been a Phi Beta Kappa student.

"My mother and Charlie are both very bright, capable people and neither of them suffer fools particularly gladly or wants to waste time," explained Nancy's eldest son Hal Borthwick. "And I think that both having been married and both having relatively unfortunate divorces in terms of what was involved . . . in terms of emotional intensities and what not . . . I think they made a fairly quick decision as to whether the other person was worth a second look."

It is clear the prospects struck them both as promising.

"No one would write a novel this way. No one would ever name both wives Nancy," exclaimed Charles, Jr.

Hal Borthwick was about seven years old when his mother remarried and Charlie moved into her house on Roscomare Road not far from the north side of the University of California, Los Angeles campus. "It was just me and my younger brother, David. Teddy had died before they were married and the girls lived with their mother in Pasadena."

The Mungers were married and nine and a half to ten months later, Charles, Jr. was born. It became a his, hers, and ours establishment— Charlie's two girls from his previous marriage, Nancy's two boys and Charles, Jr. Roughly every three years after that a new baby arrived and together Charlie and Nancy had three sons and a daughter.

"Apparently I was a happy baby, fat little boy, always laughing," said Charles, Jr. His parents have told him, "We needed a son like you just then."

By the time Charles, Jr. came along, both families were settling into their new arrangements. The two older sisters had a fairly tame existence. Hal and David's father was no longer in the picture. He stuck around for a while after the divorce, but not long, said Hal. "He went back over to Honolulu where the family had a mortuary and other business interests and he was there for a while and then he moved to the Philippines and he was there for many years. He had various business interests, including some memorial parks and stuff like that."

It was many years before Hal and David Borthwick's natural father returned to the United States, and by that time the young men were well assimilated into the Munger clan. For Hal, the integration started quickly but did not go smoothly.

"I know that I had felt myself to be somewhat the man of the house, even as young as I was," said Hal. "Charlie would take Mother out for a date and I'd be up waiting for Mother when she came home, whether I was supposed to be in bed or not."

Hal's feelings intensified once there was another man in the house. "My personality is one of wanting to acquire whatever amount of territory I can expand into," admitted Borthwick. "And so I had acquired territory that I was going to be deposed from and it happened. It was as simple as that. Behavioral issues—I used to pound on my younger brother a lot and Charlie made short work of all that. It isn't easy to go through a divorce, to lose your dad. I was old enough so I remember the things that kids can remember about divorces. Fighting and stuff like that. My brother David was too young, so he doesn't have the same experience set that I do. But I still had damage from that."

Borthwick said his new stepfather was not afraid to spank, though Charlie had to be pushed before he would do so, and the spankings were not severe. Borthwick said he was the type of child who needed discipline and benefitted from it. "My brother David on the other hand was not that kind of child. I'm not aware of any of the other children that got paddled as much as I did. I'm sure Charlie didn't particularly enjoy it, but at the end of the day it got the job done."

The territorial issues took several years to resolve since Borthwick was a particularly pugnacious boy, and during that time, Hal felt angry.

"I gave those concessions up grudgingly, but ultimately I came to accept Charlie as my father in every sense of the word other than biological," said Borthwick. "Because what I am today, you know, he has contributed to materially. The way I approach life, my value structure, and what I will and won't do."

In the meantime, the brothers and sisters just kept arriving.

"There are 20 years between the oldest and youngest," explained Charles, Jr. "Molly and Hal are together, David and Wendy. Now the age differences matter less. But most of the time the family was a fuzzy muddle."

Carol Estabrook says that the commotion at home suited her brother perfectly. "I think he would have had 40 children. It was not from a lonely childhood. He was always gregarious, friendly. He had lots of friends."

Perhaps it was the example of the big, relaxed family gatherings at his great grandfather's house in Iowa; maybe he was inspired by the memory of the gang of children at Star Island in the summer.

"I didn't see life as a breeder's derby," said Charlie. However, he added, "I'm very glad to have had children. I don't want to crow that they are superstars—but we're pleased with them all."

Regardless of his motivation for having them, the upbringing of eight children was a daunting financial task. The family went to Star Island in the summer partly because it was an inexpensive vacation for such a big crowd. The pressure on Nancy was tremendous, but she recognized the need to build both family and financial stability.

"The early days were the scraping by days," noted Charles, Jr. "Trying to reestablish themselves after their lives had hit the rocks. She backs the plan, she was faced with a number of children for so long. Mother's mother or Mary Rhodes—Mom's childhood nurse—looked after us sometimes. My Grandfather Barry had built a house on Diamond Head Road in Honolulu, and our parents went there. At the end of a week's vacation, at the thought of going back, my mother burst into tears. The work at home was overwhelming."

Nancy's reaction was not surprising considering her many duties, but it seemed out of character.

"Mother is emotionally stable," said Barry Munger. "She does not suffer from much self-doubt, self-criticism. She's very loyal. Family is a sacrament."

Charlie wasn't the sort of man who came home and helped with the laundry in the evenings, and Nancy didn't expect that of him.

"I think my mother gave him an incredible amount of latitude to concentrate on his affairs and career," said Emilie Munger. "She did everything in the home. I *expect* my husband to help with the boys and go on family outings on the weekends."

The view a Munger child has of Charlie's presence in the home varies somewhat, depending on whether a younger or an older child is asked. To the older children, Charlie seemed always to be working. The younger children came along when he was more firmly established, and to them he seemed less busy.

"I'm not trying to paint an idea of a desert, devoid of all interaction between father and son," said Hal Borthwick, "there were family trips, we would fish back in Minnesota, and things like that, but, he was a very, very, busy man in those years."

Nevertheless, recalled one of the younger children, Barry, "He was always there. He was not the type of father who took off on ski trips or on business trips. He was always principally there, but he had an active business and social life, a lot of preoccupation."

To Emilie Munger, third from the youngest, "My father seemed like a traditional father. Everyone's dad was going to the office, coming back to dinner. We all sat down together for dinner. I didn't have the feeling that he was gone a lot. He played golf on Saturday, was around Sunday morning. He wasn't that involved in day-to-day discipline, but was a strong figure, so you knew if you ever broke a cardinal rule you would be in trouble."

Barry described his father as "high energy," out the door early in the morning and back in the door for dinner. He brought projects home and turned his attention to those after the evening meal. "He could go for a long time on nervous energy, on family flights, family trips. He would get on a 6:00 A.M. flight. My mother does not function early. She gets up early, but would rather not rush out the door."

Charlie habitually did several things at once. He would sit in a chair in the evening and read a book, at the same time following and interjecting comments into the family conversation.

"Both parents are stiff-upper-lip types. They are a team," said Barry. "You would never play one parent off another. You would never have had success. Their basic feelings about raising children, what they're allowed to do, not do, are similar. When we were young, a lot of attention was paid just to keep us from tearing up the car. He was strict, but not the Great Santini. You wouldn't lip off to him. They weren't the type of people you'd do that to. In the height of adolescence—I would mouth off, be sulky. I had the closest thing to a classic adolescence of the younger children. But I would say in terms of my peers, I was mild. I didn't run away from home. We weren't hell-raisers."

Despite the constant trips to school conferences, dental appointments, and loads of luggage when they went anywhere, those early years bonded three families into one.

"Mother treated Molly and Wendy as if they were her own," recalled Charles, Jr. "Father treated her boys as if they were his own. They forged a real family."

"He doesn't say children and stepchildren, he simply says we have eight children," said Wendy Munger. "He doesn't differentiate. That's just typical. In his treatment of the grandchildren, there is no distinguishing. He doesn't care at all. It is unimportant to him."

Even the soft-spoken David Borthwick, who bucked the family trend and became what Charlie calls "a coupon clipper," is deeply grounded in being a Munger. Molly lived fifteen or more miles away in the suburb of Pasadena with another set of parents, but she also felt part of her father's life.

"He bought me this car when I was in high school," said Molly. "Here he was struggling away. But I was driving the Mustang car with the white landau top. I had a clothes allowance. He was always there for me. I felt completely taken care of. It wasn't just financial. That was nice, but if he hadn't had that, he would have had something else."

Emilie Munger now has three small children of her own. She said motherhood has prompted her to wonder how her parents managed to raise eight successful children who share similar standards and who get along well together.

"As parents, part of their success was in transmitting values, human morality, and ethical codes to their children," said Emilie. "It wasn't through organized religion. We went to Sunday school at the Episcopalian church. We learned the golden rule, the basic rules. But it almost evolved through their example. I think he teaches through telling stories about people who are admirable in his eyes and those who are not. He was not hovering over us and telling us what was right or wrong with our own behavior. The siblings truly enjoy one another's company. There is not a lot of the weird things that can happen between brothers and sisters, parent and child, partly because we're all pretty moral and honest."

The Munger children often harken back to the lessons they've learned from growing up around a father with definite ideas of right and wrong. Hal Borthwick said Charlie drummed in the notion that a person should always "Do the best that you can do. Never tell a lie. If you say you're going to do it, get it done. Nobody gives a shit about an excuse. Leave for the meeting early. Don't be late, but if you are late, don't bother giving people excuses. Just apologize. They're due the apology, but they're not interested in an excuse. By the way, those are very useful rules, especially for people who have decided to go into service businesses. People are paying for your services with their own money. Return your calls quickly. The other thing is the five-second no. You've got to make your mind up. You don't leave people hanging."

"He asked us to do something," recalled Emilie. "If we came back and said we couldn't because (of this reason or that), he would send us back out to solve the problem and keep our word. Fine tune your judgment."

Nancy agreed that Charlie's limited involvement at home and her acceptance of that seems unusual, but it was typical of their generation. "He was not much of a helpmate around the house. I always say, he lives in a lovely hotel that others maintain. He's no putterer."

Nancy worked hard, but the whole family knew Charlie also worked hard to keep up his end of the domestic bargain. He was in his mid-thirties, starting his financial life over again, and managing several careers at once. Nancy used to tell their friends that Charlie "was a young man in a hurry," in a hurry to live a full life, in a hurry to get rich.

He often approached family life much like an executive would deal with a business situation, Nancy explained. "He was always ready to advise and assist the children, and the opportunity came along fairly often. When they grew older, however, we tried to limit advice to one or two important issues."

Though Charlie was reticent about expressing his feelings verbally, Molly said it was clear that he has always felt deeply about his family. It's just that a show of feelings might be dangerous.

"He probably feels that if he ever began, he would be overwhelmed by his emotions," said Molly. "But it's very much there. We all wish he would show it more up front. They both came from old-fashioned, repressive backgrounds. She's been very understanding and just worked along with what it is."

In addition to her domesticity, Nancy was Charlie's intellectual equal, someone with whom he could discuss ideas, though it is common for Nancy and Charlie to carry on a conversation with both talking simultaneously.

"On Nancy's seventieth birthday, there was a big party," said Warren Buffett. "I thought about it and decided to get her a Purple Heart." Buffett searched around in Omaha until he found an old soldier's medal in a pawn shop.

IN THE MUNGER'S HANCOCK PARK NEIGHBORHOOD, all the families seemed equally prosperous. Nobody made a big splash, said Charles, Jr., "Except Craig Hoffman's dad, who ran a candy company, which we toured." Charles, Jr. did not even know what his father did for a living.

"I never had a sense of his career. Dad woke up and left the house between 6:30 and 7:00 A.M., and would come home between 5:30 and 6:00 P.M. Dinner was at 6:30. That was our routine. What he did was mysterious to all of us. One of his offices was in a blue building. He had a big desk. I didn't understand what was on it. I never showed a great deal of interest in what my parents did. I had no idea."

ONE REASON THE MUNGER CHILDREN were unaware of the nature of their father's work was that he seldom talked about it. And when he did, it tended to confuse the youngsters because so much was going on at once.

Early on, Charlie mostly just practiced law at Musick, Peeler & Garrett, using all the skills he could muster to get ahead. Chuck Huggins, president of See's Candy but no relation to the first Nancy's family, says he saw Charlie in action as an attorney, and found him to be a "go get 'em" type of lawyer.

During an early case on which Charlie was the junior law partner, he knew the clients would be coming in to discuss strategy on a certain day. Charlie thought about the case and decided that there were only three reasonable ways to resolve the issue. He thought through each approach. The next day the clients arrived, and after some discussion, instructed the lawyers to proceed along one of the paths that Munger had anticipated. The senior law partner asked Charlie to go off and draft a letter accordingly. Charlie told the group that if they brought in a stenographer, he could do the letter then and there and save the clients the trouble of returning the next day. When Munger rattled off the letter in a matter of minutes, the clients were wowed. When they did business with the firm after that, they asked that Munger help represent them.

Munger was especially fond of senior partner Joe Peeler, a native of Alabama who used colorful language and like Charlie's own father, was a great hunter and fisherman. From him Charlie learned a new word that he liked very much—"gumption."

"No wonder I liked him," said Munger. "Also, like me, he tended to delegate any task completely or do it all himself, and I liked his total delegation mode."

One of the firm's most interesting clients was Harvey Mudd, a wealthy engineer with worldwide mining interests who later financed one of the best science and engineering colleges in the country, Harvey Mudd College, part of a cluster of small colleges in Pomona, California. Though Munger did not have a lot of close contact with Mudd, he developed ties with Harvey's brother Seeley and one of Mudd's advisers, Luther Anderson.

Charlie recalls that Mudd would tell his lawyers, "I don't want to know merely what the law is and what I can accomplish without violating the law. I welcome your help in doing rightly, all factors considered."

Charlie made some mistakes as a young lawyer, including drafting legislation granting property tax exemption to university buildings under construction. The law passed as he wrote it, but Munger was embarrassed to realize that it covered the buildings, but failed to mention the land under the buildings. Another partner was able to get the situation corrected.

Nevertheless, Munger moved ahead nicely. But he also sometimes found himself punished for his outspoken brashness and tendency to show off his brains. His friend Chuck Rickershauser told Charlie that when he first started out in the law, the correct path was explained to him by a senior partner. "You must always remember that your duty is to conduct yourself so that everyone appraises you no higher than the third smartest person in the room. The client must be made to appear smartest, with me the next smartest, and only after this should any wisdom seem to reside in you."

The leading partner at Musick, Peeler was Roy Garrett, and though Munger admired Garrett's legal skills and his ability to attract important business to the firm, he and Garrett never became as close as Munger was to Peeler. Despite the fact that Garrett gave some of his personal legal work to Munger for handling, Charlie said that deep down, he knew Garrett didn't like him very well.

"Roy Garrett was a dominant personality, and he and I naturally clashed," said Munger. "One day, fairly early in our relationship, he called me in and chewed me out for running up $20,000 of billable time, with no collection, on some small-looking account he had assigned to me. I replied, 'Roy, you have no right to talk to me this way until the first time I fail you in billing and collection' and we left it at that. A couple of weeks later I collected $50,000. This sort of being right got mixed reactions from Roy."

Charlie lived by principles he'd learned at his grandfather's knee—first, the surest way of building a business is by concentrating on the work already on his desk, and second, by underspending his income and amassing a pile of cash that could be invested to build future wealth.

"Munger learned a lot about business as an attorney," said Buffett. "He was involved in an International Harvester dealership, Twentieth-Century Fox. He was always seeing reality. He is unable to be around a problem without thinking about it."

Even things that were merely near at hand received close scrutiny, including an excellent mining property in California's Mojave Desert. "I would like to own that boron mine—boron is an element, the mine is in an open pit in a safe country. It has low costs and big reserves," said Munger. "It would be a really nice mine to own, but it is already owned by someone who knows it's a very nice mine."

Some of his clients, unfortunately, were not the types that Charlie would have liked them to be. He began to think more about his father's reaction when they discussed one of Al's clients, Omaha auto dealer Grant McFayden.

"I once complained that he [Al Munger] should have more clients like Grant McFayden and fewer like a certain other man," Charlie said. "I can remember my father's mock horror when he explained how McFayden treated his customers right, his suppliers right, and his employees right. A lawyer's family would starve, my father said, if all his clients behaved like

McFayden. It is a lesson I have never forgotten and it has helped my business career, even though I find, like other businessmen, that it is harder to starve the lawyers now than it used to be. The lesson helped me prefer McFayden types as clients and McFayden behavior as the right example for myself."[2]

The problem with law, Munger felt, is that the people he most enjoyed working with didn't get in much legal trouble, and the people who needed him most sometimes were defective characters. On top of that, in the 1950s and 1960s, practicing law wasn't necessarily a road to wealth.

Munger gradually accumulated money from his legal practice and began investing in securities and joining friends and clients in business endeavors, some of which proved to be graduate-level courses in the school of hard knocks. He'd done some legal work for a small transformer manufacturing company in Pasadena and got along well with the clients. Charlie hoped they would come back to him for more business. One morning, while driving past the company offices on his way in to work, Charlie decided that he was being too shy. He shouldn't wait for the clients to call him. He should make a personal visit to them. He did a U-turn in the middle of the street and went back. After chatting with the business owners for a while, he did get more work. Eventually, he took an ownership position in the business, borrowing some of the necessary funds. Munger's first formal partner was Ed Hoskins, who now is in his mid-90s and lives in a golfing community near a small mid-California city.

"Ed Hoskins is a great guy. He had created Transformer Engineers. He reached a disagreement with his venture capitalists who wanted to replace him. We worked out a deal for him to buy them out, using large amounts of credit. It was an early leveraged buyout. It was a nonlegal solution to what looked like a legal problem."

The company was a job shop, making highly specialized transformers that Hoskins designed for military rockets and the like. Because the Korean War was in progress, an enormous amount of military work was underway in Southern California. Despite the opportunities presented by the war, the business was plagued with problems. One of the key officers, a young man, died slowly of cancer and as he did so, was carried financially by his partners.

It was obvious that the company would have to expand rapidly to pay off the debt from the buyout. At the same time, however, competing companies spotted the wartime opportunities and also expanded rapidly. Soon there were too many producers. The business aspects of their lives became miserable, accounting for much of the financial pressure on

Munger around the time of his divorce. The upside of the story was that Hoskins and Munger became good friends.

"Ed worked 90 hours a week" recalled Charlie. "He designed every transformer in the early days. I can't tell you how close we were and what a wonderful man he proved to be. We had troubles that made his hair fall out. Terrible struggles. The worst trouble came from buying William Miller Instruments, Inc. That was not a good idea. It produced a complicated cathode ray recording oscillograph. That business took forever to get off the ground."

Finally the product started to move, and Hoskins and Munger sold the company. It was none too soon. The cathode ray recording oscillograph rapidly was made obsolete by more sophisticated magnetic tape technology.

"In the end all we had was the transformer business," said Charlie. "That was a bad business when the war was over. We were stretched financially. With the help of Harry Bottle, the controller, we finally righted it by firing all the customers who wouldn't let it make money and downsizing to a much smaller company. It was a lot of struggle, a lot of nerve pain. We damn near lost everything. We finally made it work out, but not fabulously. But we got a very respectable return on investment eventually."

Munger went into the partnership with Hoskins in the 1950s and got out of it in 1960 and 1961. Munger got a good start on a business education during those years with Hoskins. For one thing, "I never went back to the high-tech mode. I tried it once and found it to have many problems. I was like Mark Twain's cat that, after a bad experience, never again sat on a hot stove or on a cold stove either."

This, despite Munger's love and respect for science. Additionally, Charlie began to realize that buying high quality businesses has certain advantages: "It's not that much fun to buy a company that you hope liquidates at a profit just before it is destined to go broke."

He also learned how to define a good business: "The difference between a good business and a bad business is that good businesses throw up one easy decision after another. The bad businesses throw up painful decisions time after time."

CHAPTER SIX

MUNGER MAKES
HIS FIRST MILLION

The rabbit runs faster than the fox, because the rabbit is running for his life while the fox is only running for his dinner.[1]

Richard Dawkins, *The Selfish Gene*

IT WAS A BALMY NOVEMBER DAY in Southern California, cool enough to be comfortable, warm enough to go jacketless, Charlie Munger eased his sleek black Lexus LS400 between a row of garages, revisiting the Pasadena condominium projects where he made his first real money.

Maneuvering the car wasn't as easy as it looked. At 75, Munger is blind in his left eye and has little peripheral vision in the other. He has adapted, developing tricks to figure out where traffic is, and when he has a clear shot to enter or exit the flow. A powerful automobile engine allows him to act on his decisions quickly.

After searching for a while along the streets of a working-class Los Angeles suburb that has changed little over the past 30 years, Munger next located Alhambra Village Green, his largest real estate development project. On this day three decades later, Charlie is visibly pleased to see that the lawns are clipped, the spa and pool area swept, and several elderly ladies are gliding back and forth in the blue water, doing their daily exercise laps.

"Those olive trees?" he said, pointing across the grass. "We paid less than $100 each for them. Got them from an olive grove that was being torn out." Like the women swimming their laps, the olive trees had retired long ago, but they were still going strong.

Leaving Alhambra Village Green, Charlie looked around for somewhere to have lunch. "Usually a shopping center has some place," he said, gunning the Lexus across the street to a strip mall that has obviously had several facelifts over the years. It was still no Houston Galleria, but it swarmed with shoppers. He found a Baker's Square coffee shop and told the hostess, "Oh, seat us anywhere," then changed his mind and asked for a booth. A cheerful young Hispanic waiter introduced himself and enthusiastically described the chicken stir-fry salad, the stir-fry pita sandwich with french fries, and the plain old stir fry. "Those are my favorites," said Gabriel. Charlie ordered a club sandwich with french fries and iced tea. "Save some room for pie," advised the zealous waiter. At the end of the meal, Gabriel explained that although Charlie hadn't requested it, he'd given him the senior citizen's discount.

"I'm not old enough for that," Munger chortled.

Charlie picked up the check and stopped at the cash register. Gabriel dashed forward, "I'll take care of that for you, sir."

The young waiter had no idea that the gentleman in the chino pants and tweed jacket built the entire city block of condominiums opposite the coffee shop. He did not know that he'd just served a sandwich to a billionaire, and it was obvious that it wouldn't have mattered if Gabriel did know. He would give the same service to anyone.

"Are you our waiter?" blurted Munger.

"Yes, sir."

"Well, keep the change then," said Charlie, shoving two $10 bills across the counter for a bill that couldn't have been more than $15. Munger then charged for the door.

"I don't look at waiter's faces, so I never recognize them later," grumbled Charlie. "It's a terrible habit to live with. Very embarrassing."

Why doesn't he look at people?

"I'm always thinking about other things. I forget to look around."

"Charlie has enormous powers of concentration," said Otis Booth, Munger's partner on his first two real estate projects. "When he concentrates, everything else goes away."

AT THE 1998 BERKSHIRE HATHAWAY ANNUAL MEETING, a shareholder asked why Warren and Charlie shied away from real estate investments:

"Here's an area in which we have a virtually perfect record extending over many decades," said Munger. "We've been demonstrably foolish in almost every operation having to do with real estate that we've ever touched. Every time that we had a surplus plant and didn't want to accept the bid of some developer that planned a development, we'd have been better off later if we'd accepted the bid and done something with the sales proceeds in a field where we had expertise."

It is true that Berkshire seldom puts money into real estate ventures as a passive investment, although after Munger made this statement Buffett invested an undisclosed sum in motels operated by the Red Roof Inns chain. While it is quite possible that Berkshire has a poor record in managing the real estate properties that become surplus to normal operations of its companies, it is misplaced modesty to say that Munger personally has a certified record of failure in real estate.

In fact, the story is quite different. While Charlie was at first fascinated with industrial companies, he found that making money in manufacturing was fraught with danger. On the other hand, people were moving to Los Angeles at the rate of 1,000 per week in the 1960s. With Southern California's explosive growth and plentiful land, Munger could see that people were becoming wealthy as land developers.

"HOW IT HAPPENED IS AN INTERESTING STORY," recalled Munger. "I had a client—two, a father and son. The father's father had owned the end of a city block across from Caltech. The father had no use for the property—we were supposed to sell it off in probate."

Those clients were Otis Booth and his father. Otis Booth is a great-grandson of Harrison Gray Otis, who in 1894 founded the *Los Angeles Times*. Booth calls himself a "shirt tail" cousin to the Chandler family, who recently sold the newspaper to the Tribune Co., owners of the *Chicago Tribune*. Booth's father was an oil wildcatter and rancher and once worked for a talc-mining company. Like Munger, Booth went to the California Institute of Technology, where he earned an engineering degree. He and Munger attended college at the same time though they were in different programs and didn't know one another. Later Booth went to Stanford business school, where he may have met the second Nancy, but didn't get to know her well.

Booth first met Munger in the late 1950s when he went to consult with his father's attorney, Roy Garrett, because he hoped to buy a printing plant. "Roy said, 'I've got a young guy here about your age, why don't I turn you over to him.'" Munger and Booth were both in their mid-thirties.

"Charlie was the same then as he is now," said Booth. "Hungrier, more aggressive. We did run around, the two of us together, and made this deal, which was buying a rotogravure printing plant. The printing plant's major customer was the *Los Angeles Times* Sunday magazine, then called the *Home* magazine."

Because Booth worked at the newspaper and the *Times* was the plant's largest customer, he, of course, had to advise his employer of his intentions. Booth planned to quit the *Times* and run the printing plant. Because the *Times* had no labor unions and the plant was unionized, Booth thought that the newspaper's management would not want to buy it and would be pleased to have him own it as a reliable supplier of services to his former newspaper.

"But at that juncture in the *Times'* history they were just beginning to diversify their holdings. They brought in McKinsey & Co. to advise them. The partner in charge was Jack Vance. Jack looked at the terms of the deal and said, 'Hell, you didn't buy it, you stole it.' He said, 'we'll take it. You'd better cooperate.' The *LA Times* was crazy to take it on, but they did buy it. I had the pleasure of bailing it out for them later," said Booth.

"In the course of the deal, I got to know Charlie very well. It took us several visits to negotiate with the owner. We developed a considerable liking for each other. And I, at least, found we thought along parallel lines. If he started to say something, I knew what he was going to say."

The Mungers introduced Booth to his wife Dody. "A couple of years after, I called him for lunch at the California Club. I said, 'I want you to be the first to know—Dody's pregnant.' I wanted to have another child in this second marriage. I was 44. Charlie grinned and said, 'I think there's something you should know. Nancy's pregnant.'"

Booth's wife gave birth to a daughter, Stephanie, and the Mungers had a son Philip and the couples became godparents to one another's children. Since those early days Booth and Munger have fished together in New Zealand, Australia, and other distant waters. Munger goes every year to a trout fishing club Booth discovered in northwest Colorado, Rio Blanco Ranch, which is on the headwaters of the White River above Meeker. They celebrated the year 2000 fishing in Tierra del Fuego at the tip of South America, where Munger caught an 18-pound brown trout.

"He's my best friend in the world," said Booth. "Very much so."

It was around 1961 when Booth came to Munger to handle the probate settlement, and Charlie instantly advised Booth to keep the property and develop it.

"I said to Otis, build your own apartments." said Munger. "You should not allow those two houses forming the whole end of the block to go into other hands. You buy them. Tear them down, re-zone, build, and sell own-your-own apartment units. Otis said, 'Charlie, if this is such a good idea, and you're so sure it will work, why don't you put up some of the money and join me. I won't do it without you.'"

"He shamed me into demonstrating the wisdom of my own advice," chuckled Munger.[2]

This happened not long after the own-your-own concept of apartment occupancy started to become popular in California.

"Charlie and I went in together," said Booth. "We each owned half. We bought the other half, adjacent to Caltech. It's still there."

When Munger and Booth joined forces in real estate development and construction, it was a totally new experience for them, but Munger fell back on principles and skills he'd learned in other businesses.

The units across from Caltech are more than 35 years old, and have become so integrated into the neighboring landscape that they fade into the background. Yet, in a part of the country where housing sometimes seems disposable, the projects have endured and still hold their own in a respectable neighborhood.

"We gave our occupants more land and a better size and it turned out people really liked it. Moreover we had a good location," said Munger. "It worked out very well."

"It was slow, there was a recession we had to wait out," agreed Booth. But in the end there was a "very substantive profit – 400 percent. We put in $100,000, got back $500,000."

When the Caltech units, completed in 1967, were sold, Charlie and Otis then went to work on a site in Pasadena on Orange Grove Avenue, a broad street where apartments now encroached on 1900-era mansions. With this project, they applied the lessons they learned on the Caltech units and made more money faster.

Charlie and Otis noticed that the ground-floor apartments in the first project sold out quickly, but the upstairs units seemed to sell molasses slow. They decided to make the next project one-story, with a price that reflected a lower density of land use. Even with a higher price tag, the single-level condos sold quickly. Munger stuck with the single-level floor plan on a third, fourth, and fifth project, and again, despite boom-and-bust real estate markets, the units were profitable.

Munger continued to practice law and was involved in other activities while he worked on the real estate ventures. For years he took no money out, rather he invested in one project after another. Munger said that throughout the process he was learning from Booth, and Booth said he too learned much, especially about Munger. He came to understand Charlie's somewhat taciturn nature.

"Charlie isn't secretive," said Booth, "but simply very compartmentalized in his communication. He follows the 'need-to-know' rule."

Charlie's stepson Hal Borthwick pointed out that today lawyers seldom get involved in deals with their clients because their firms fear losses from malpractice claims, but in the 1950s and 1960s, it was a common occurrence.

"Relationships were more genteel," he said. "It was a different era."

With so many projects underway, Munger's free time was limited. "The kids would spend the day with dad at the construction site. We liked to pick up the metal plugs from the electrical boxes, like little coins," recalled Charles, Jr.

After Booth and Munger had completed their two projects, Charlie became involved in a third deal in which Booth did not participate because he thought the conditions of the land ownership might cause problems. Charlie saw the risks, but decided he could make it work.

"I had a client who came to me after I used to beat him at the poker table. He had shopping centers in Alhambra. Across the street, he had ground leases on surplus property owned by the city of Pasadena," explained Munger. "He wanted to protect his shopping center from more retail influx. He hired me to work on his legal problems, but I didn't like the way he was doing it. I said 'I quit' as his attorney. He turned the tables and said 'put on paper what *you* would do.' I said, 'if you put up the ground lease, I'll do all the development work, financing, etc. and give you half the profit.' "

Rather than share in the profits, the shopping center owner preferred to have cash up front, which turned out to be a mistake. Half the profits would have been a much better deal.

In Alhambra, Charlie and his partners built 442 one-story own-your-own apartments on two 11-acre sites. This was the lowest priced, lowest-end of all the Munger projects. Each unit sold for around $20,000. Again, the apartments went fast. By then, Munger felt he knew what buyers were looking for. He and the builders did not cut corners on design or construction details. Then when the project was finished, they made sure the units were attractively landscaped.

"Lush landscaping," declared Charlie. "That's what sells. You spend money on trees, and you get it back triple. Stinting on landscaping is building malpractice."

Munger took on a new partner when he started Alhambra Village Green, hiring Al Marshall as an unlikely sales manager. Charlie met Marshall because Nancy and Martha Marshall played golf together at the Los Angeles Country Club. Charlie and Al joined them for a husband and wife tournament. California was still a relatively small state at the time, and families who had been around for a while often found they were connected in some way. As it turned out, Marshall, a petroleum engineer, had been a classmate of Nancy's first husband at Stanford.

Charlie and Al were introduced at the first tee. On the second hole, Charlie asked, "What do you do?" Marshall had worked for Shell Oil and some small independent oil companies. The oil business was in a rocky period, and Marshall didn't want to make too much of the fact that he was unemployed. Instead he told Charlie about some oil rights he was bidding for. On the third hole, Charlie asked how Marshall was going about the bidding. When Marshall told him, Charlie replied, "You're doing it all wrong."

"I said okay, if you're so smart, why don't you do the legal and financing work and I'll do the rest," said Marshall. Munger structured the deal in an ABC trust, which was a type of tax shelter that was legally correct at the time, but was so much abused that it has since been outlawed. But Marshall said that their ABC trust was properly done and has held together.

"I'm still getting two to three thousand dollars a month from that. We only put up $1,000 each and we've each probably made a half a million out of it."

The Marshalls still own their shares, but Munger gave his to his children.

When the Alhambra project came along, Munger asked Marshall if he was interested in putting up $15,000 and going into the project with him. Marshall was still casting around for employment, and although the money was a stretch for him, he agreed.

"The business he was in was going to hell under him, and he had five children," said Munger. "I knew he was a great guy and he needed something else to do. I brought him in to do sales. I told him, 'Build your own department.' He'd never done it before, but he was naturally talented. He liked what he did. It was screamingly successful."

Marshall often teased Munger that he would advertise the Alhambra units as "Rancho Sewage," because the land had previously served as the city of Pasadena's sewage treatment plant.

Booth had opted out because the property was not owned, but rather came with a 49-year-lease from the city. Ordinarily lenders wouldn't issue loans for developments with less than a 50-year-lease, but that did not deter Munger. He knew that a local savings and loan, State Mutual, had recently raked in $60 million by increasing its passbook rate by one-half of 1 percent. The lender was racing to get the money out and earning interest in the form of loans. When Charlie and Al met with the loan officer to look at the property, Al said the lender all but asked if they wanted an even bigger loan than they had applied for.

The way Munger handled the situation convinced Marshall that Charlie had the ability to think through a future event and come to a conclusion different from what others assumed it would be, "and I've hardly ever seen him wrong."

Charlie saw things this way: ". . . just out of our respective graduate schools, my friend Warren Buffett and I entered the business world to find huge, predictable patterns of extreme irrationality. These irrationalities were obviously important to what we wanted to do, but our professors had never mentioned them. [Understanding the problem of irrationalities] was not easy . . . I came to [study] the psychology of human misjudgment almost against my will: I rejected it until I realized that my attitude was costing me a lot of money and reduced my ability to help everything I loved."[3]

Munger's originality in dealing with business problems was comforting to Marshall.

"One of the good things about working with Charlie," said Marshall, "was that there was no doubt about who should be boss."

When Marshall agreed to run the sales and marketing operation of Alhambra Village Green, he warned Charlie that he didn't know much about sales. Marshall said he didn't ever want to tell prospective buyers something that wasn't true. When customers inquired about the ground lease, and what might happen after the 49-year-expiration date, Marshall told them that he didn't know what would happen. It would be up to the homeowners and the city to work something out. About two-thirds of the potential customers backed away at that point, but the units sold out quickly, despite the fact that Los Angeles was going through one of the worst real estate recessions that it had ever experienced.

Part of the attraction was the one-story units, but another advantage was a location just 20 minutes from downtown. In time, the city changed its policy and sold the underlying land to the homeowners' association.

Although Munger's venture into real estate came with its own set of problems, they were relatively mild. There were never any lawsuits or follow-on problems from the own-your-own apartments. Once they were sold, and later when the financing was repaid, the projects were done and behind them.

Furthermore, in the process of development, Charlie discovered that he had the soul of an architect. He had vision and a passion that translated itself into durable and liveable spaces. Munger enjoyed development and construction, but it worried him that a successful builder was dependent on debt financing on an ever-increasing scale. Charlie and Al Marshall developed one more project, but decided it would be their last.

On the final project, the Huntington Granada, Munger put up a comparatively small number of units on Huntington Drive. The land actually was in Alhambra, but it was so close to upscale San Marino that it seemed to be part of the more desirable address. Again, the project sold off in a flash. The hard work at last paid off. Munger walked away from the real estate phase of his career with enough money to finance his foray into the world of independent investing.

"When it was over, I had $1.4 million as the result of my real estate involvement," said Munger. "That was a lot of money at that time. Some was in seconds (trust deeds), and so forth, from people who bought apartments. Later the seconds were paid. It was a substantial backlog of economic security. I did a total of five projects, then stopped. I didn't like constantly borrowing more money. Also, it was an activity with many details, each crucial, difficult to handle as a full-time activity and extremely difficult as a part-time activity."

CHARLIE WASN'T TOTALLY NEW TO CONSTRUCTION when he took on the projects. He had built his own home on Edgewood Drive shortly after he arrived in Los Angeles, then in 1960 he acquired a mansion on two large lots in Hancock Park. He demolished the large house and sold one lot at a substantial profit. On the remaining lot he built a house for his new family. The Mungers still live in the home, albeit after several extensive remodeling projects.

Emilie Munger, the youngest of the daughters, was born when the Mungers lived on Roscomare Road in the house Nancy brought to the marriage. The family moved to June Street in Hancock Park on her first birthday. The new home made life much easier for the Mungers, since Charlie would no longer have to drive across Los Angeles in rush hour traffic to and from his law office.

"We rode our bikes to school and rode around the neighborhood," said Emilie. "Now it's in the middle of the city. Then it was like a little town. I had eight girlfriends in the houses around us. I was lucky. There were always kids my age. We had a happy, stable family, good friends."

Emilie attended the Third Street school near her home until the sixth grade. She then went to the private Marlborough School for grades seven through twelve. "Where my mom went. I loved that school. I still have a group of girlfriends who get together all the time. Though occasionally a movie star's child would attend, Marlborough wasn't really a Hollywood school. It is more traditional. I had a great biology teacher. I loved that class."

Charlie and Nancy Munger still consider the June Street house their primary residence.

"It's pretty amazing to be 40 and to go back and have the same house. My friends are still there—most of my friends. Many families would have fallen apart, or at least moved. It is a gift to kids to be in the same neighborhood," said Emilie Munger.

Coincidentally, Buffett too has stayed in the relatively modest house in Omaha where his children were raised, and the Buffett children express similar feelings to those articulated by Emilie.

To see some tangible result from his work pleases Munger, and he still likes to be involved in construction projects. Munger often tells people, "I don't believe in doing everything with lily white hands, nor would I care to be like [early financier] Russell Sage, remembered only for skill in buying and selling little pieces of paper."

Remodeling, a room addition or a new dock, is almost always underway at Star Island. When David Borthwick and his wife, who like her stepsister-in-law is named Molly, bought a country home in England, they consulted extensively with Charlie before making an offer on the property. Munger financed the remodeling of Molly Munger's home in Pasadena from a trust fund set up for her, and he grumbles that Wendy won't agree to do the same with her big old house in South Pasadena. She likes her home the way it is and thinks it is suitable for the neighborhood.

The Munger Science Center at Harvard Westlake School had substantial design input from Charlie. He met with the architects, went through several iterations until they worked out the proper design for the site. Munger seems to be able to get his wishes fulfilled without alienating the architects and builders.

"No, he doesn't offend people," said Otis Booth, who also serves on the Harvard Westlake School Board. "He has a great ability to turn a phrase and make things amusing."

Munger employed this technique in planning the Munger Science Center, when he saw boys and girls bathrooms of the same size. "You're going to do this in a building where you teach biology?" he asked.

There was another building on campus, said Booth, a combined gymnasium and arts complex. It was difficult and time-consuming to continuously convert back and forth from a gym into a theater, and there was discussion about whether to spend the money to make it one or the other. Charlie told the board, "Look, man has only one instrument that serves two functions and it always gets him into trouble."

Munger agrees that humor helps—as does being plainly right—when reversing expert's ideas in their own territory, but he thinks that he sometimes causes resentment. It requires constant vigilance to keep from going too far.

Not long ago he did another commercial development, this one in Santa Barbara on property owned by Wesco Financial. Wesco's former thrift association, Mutual Savings, got the 22-acres of pristine oceanfront property in a 1966 foreclosure.

The development's official name is Sea Meadow, but Buffett calls it "Mungerville" after "Pottersville" in the movie, *It's a Wonderful Life.* "He's constantly trying to sell me things in Mungerville," groused Buffett.

Mungerville is in a pricey waterfront neighborhood on the south edge of Santa Barbara—tucked between the Pacific Ocean and the coastal range of mountains. The area is studded with citrus groves, eucalyptus and olive trees, oleanders, acacia, fuchsia, all gracing the gated walls of early California-style estates.

It took years of haggling with local building authorities and the California Coastal Commission to reach an agreement on the plans for the Sea Meadow project. Only about half of the houses have a significant ocean view. Munger said that due to the high cost of private streets, sewage, utilities, and various other charges, including heavy archaeological obligations, the houses would be costly and the profit from the development would be limited. "We have 'given' a very large fraction of the value of our land to the County of Santa Barbara in exchange for permission to use it at all," he said.[4]

"I developed it because I didn't want to let the zoning authorities rob me the way they wanted to. And now I know that if I had let them rob me, we would have had better financial results."

In 1989 Munger reported to shareholders, "Reasonable, community-sensitive development of this property has been delayed over 14 years in the course of administration of land-use laws. But, miraculous to report, eight houses, plus recreation facilities, are in various stages of completion on the property as part of an authorized development into 32 houses interspersed with large open areas. Mutual Savings plans to make the development first-rate in every respect, and unique in the quality of its landscaping."[5]

By today's standards, the land, which was carried on the books for $2 million, was bargain priced. In fact, Charlie and Nancy paid $2.1 million for just two lots on which they built a house where they now spend many of their weekends.

Otis Booth believes that Munger responded to governmental requirements creatively. "Sea Meadow in Santa Barbara is beautifully done. The piece of land was so constrained by rules, he really had to be imaginative. He made a beautiful enclave."

Despite the attractiveness of Mungerville, the units sold poorly, and many of the buyers are Munger's own friends and colleagues. The residence list looks like the directory of Munger's former law firm. Roy Tolles, Chuck Rickershauser, and Ron Olson each own homes there.

Booth also bought a home in Mungerville, but under some duress. "I bought it because Charlie gave me a hard time. I didn't need another house."

WHILE MUNGER WAS BEGINNING TO EARN his first million in the risky business of real estate development, back in Omaha Warren Buffett, whom he had yet to meet, was laboring in his own trenches, building assets in the Buffett Partnership. During this time, Dr. Carol Angle took Buffett's evening class on investing, and she and her husband Dr. William Angle invested in the Buffett partnership. Both Bill Angle and his brother John, by now an executive at Guardian Life Insurance in Lincoln, had been Charlie's chums and fraternity brothers at the University of Michigan. The number of mutual friends they shared was growing, but still Munger and Buffett had not crossed paths.

CHAPTER SEVEN

A COMBINATION
OF BIG IDEAS

I can see, he can hear. We make a great combination.

Warren Buffett, speaking of his partner
and friend, Charles Munger.

Omaha, Nebraska, businessman Lee Seemann often went duck hunting with Charlie Munger's father Al along the marshes, lakes, and rivers surrounding Omaha. Lee also hunted with another member of the family, Bob Munger. Bob was a big wine-colored mixed-breed, along the lines of a Chesapeake or a setter. Al Munger had many friends, but Bob was his very best. Al called Bob a college-educated dog, said Seemann, and along with his other talents, Bob held an advanced degree in retrieving ducks. If the dog missed a bird, Al would say, "Bob, there's another duck out there." Bob would look around, then scurry back out, and when he returned with the duck, Munger would scold him gently. "To think a college-educated dog like you would miss a duck."

Bob had lots of tricks. When guests were visiting the Mungers, Al would say, "Bob, what would you do if I told you to go to the basement?" Bob would zip off to the basement. After a while, Bob would amble back and lie down beside his master's chair. Then Al would repeat the statement, making it shorter. "Bob, what would you do if I told you . . ." and Bob would jump up and head for the basement. Finally, Al would simply say "Bob, what . . ." and off the dog would trot.

One day Lee, Al, and several friends went to a lake near Omaha to hunt. "It was bitterly cold in the valley," said Lee. "Bob picked up a lot of ducks, although he was extremely old for a dog. The water was deep, and we had to hold the decoys with ropes. It was too windy for weights. Bob got the final duck, then he became stuck in the ropes. Al went crazy. He climbed in the boat to go get him—by then Al was no longer young. He'd already had one heart attack. He started rowing out to get Bob, but he was not very strong or agile, so when he leaned over to pull Bob into the boat, it tipped over. There were ice sheets on him in a matter of seconds. I went out, worried more about Al than Bob. They were hanging on to the boat. I flipped the boat up and Bob climbed in. He was working with us, just looking around like it was fun. We pulled Al in. He said, 'Don't you ever tell this to Toody.' "

Other members of the hunting party rushed up the embankment to the railroad tracks where the car was parked and got the motor running and the heater going, and none of them told Munger's wife what happened. Al Munger survived the accident with no ill effects.

"Grampa Al died in 1959—he was like a Norman Rockwell grandfather," recalled Wendy Munger. "Rimless glasses. He had a little treasure chest where each child could pick out a candy."

HIS FATHER'S DEATH LEFT AN ACHING VOID, yet the end of Al's life launched a new phase of Charlie's. When Munger went home to take care of his father's estate, he was introduced to young Warren Buffett, a meeting that would change the lives of many people. It also is a perfect example of the sort of success matrix Munger often talks about, the converging of several great ideas to produce outstanding results. In this case, it was the coming together of two people with superior intellects and shared objectives.

"Warren and I got along from the start and have been friends and business associates ever since, although with various investments on both sides which do not overlap," said Munger. "With my background, how could I fail to take to a man who preferred reading and thinking to delivering groceries and who had learned something from everything he ever read, including the manuscript his grandfather left behind entitled, "How to Run a Grocery Store and a Few Things I Have Learned About Fishing."[1]

Following their initial conversations in Omaha, Buffett and Munger continued their discussions by telephone, often talking for hours at a time. Though Munger and several friends were poised to launch a new firm, Buffett urged him to give up law and become a professional investor. In Buffett's famous speech "The Superinvestors of Graham and Doddsville," he said that when he met Munger, he told him, "law was fine as a hobby, but he could do better."[2] Munger's experiences with the industrial companies and in real estate development had whetted his appetite for business and the notion attracted him, though he wasn't quite ready to let go of his legal practice.

Because Buffett's friend and former colleague Ben Graham had retired and moved to Beverly Hills, Warren and Susie had become acquainted with California and were captivated by the climate and people
they met. They visited whenever possible.

"Not long after [meeting Munger], I went out to California to see Ben
and Estey Graham, and we went to see the Mungers. They still lived on
Roscomare Road. Nancy was appalled by my eating habits."

She was indeed.

"I remember that Charlie came home and said he'd met this brilliant
man," said Nancy Munger. "He was excited about meeting Warren. About
a month later, he came to dinner. I planned a steak dinner. We had three
vegetables. I noted that Warren didn't eat a single vegetable. We had ice
cream for dessert, and he was happy about that."

Emilie Munger was an infant when Buffett first visited the Munger
home, and she was still quite young when she noticed that Warren Buffett
was an important visitor. "I remember his coming and thinking how
similar Dad and Warren were," said Emilie. "Their voices, their laughter.
He was a picky eater. He loved Pepsi—for us kids, it was funny to have an
adult who loved soft drinks so much."

Molly, the oldest of Munger's daughters, says she can't recall exactly
when Buffett entered their lives. "I do remember the symptoms. Daddy
was on the phone now all the time to Warren."

During the time the relationship between her father and Warren was
blossoming, Molly was becoming increasingly involved in her own affairs. First, over her father's objection, she decided to enroll in a high
school where none of her friends went, a school attended mostly by low-
income and minority students. As Charlie gave in to his willful daughter,
he said, "Molly, you are insisting on raising yourself. Make sure you do a
good job."

After high school graduation, she faced the stress and uncertainty of
going east to attend an Ivy League school. She graduated from Radcliffe,
then stayed in New England to go to Harvard Law School. When Molly
returned to California, several important events had occurred. Her father
had turned 50, he possessed several million dollars, and his business life
had become entwined with Buffett's. It was an arrangement that seemed
to fit the long-term plans of both men.

"Daddy had always been buying small companies," said Molly. "With
Warren, they had so much more capital."

Though Munger had worked with several partners already, Buffett had
been working mostly on his own. "We saw that we had odd personalties
that happened to fit fairly well, and we've been partners in one way or

another ever since," said Buffett. "We weren't formally business partners, but intellectually we've been partners ever since." Buffett sometimes calls Munger his "junior partner in good years and senior partner in bad years."

Although they agreed to collaborate shortly after meeting, the partnership evolved gradually and naturally, based on trust and a solid respect for one another's intelligence.

"We were certainly business partners at Blue Chip Stamps," recalls Munger. "We certainly were business partners when we formed Diversified Retailing to buy department stores, buying at less than the liquidating value of the company, a Ben Graham type of play."

From the 1960s and through the turn of the century, the two analyzed business opportunities often on the telephone, talking many times a week. When the time came to close a deal, they got together in the same place. When one couldn't be reached, the other had the authority to act. "We know so much about how each other thinks that we may move pretty far along even if the other isn't available," Buffett said.

Buffett was only 29 when he met Munger, but he already had strong investment credentials. He grew up listening to his stockbroker father talk and hanging out at the brokerage offices in Howard Buffett's building. Money fascinated Warren and investing was his obsession from boyhood on. As a student at the University of Nebraska, Buffett read a recently published book, *The Intelligent Investor* by Ben Graham, and his course was set. The year was 1949, and Graham, known as a sort of intellectual Dean of Wall Street, was one of the most successful and best known money managers in the country. Buffett enrolled in the graduate business school at Columbia University, where Graham taught, and later he briefly worked at Graham's New York investment firm. When Ben retired and closed the business, Buffett returned to Omaha to set up his own investment operation. His first clients were relatives, who already knew how bright he was, and some former Graham investors who were looking for the next Ben Graham and had reason to believe Buffett could pull the sword from the stone.

Munger brought a business law perspective to this rich mix, but from his independent forays into the commercial world, he also understood how businesses work. "Charlie can analyze and evaluate any kind of deal faster and more accurately than any man alive. He sees any valid weakness in 60 seconds. He's a perfect partner."

As they studied and acquired retail stores and companies such as Blue Chip Stamps and See's Candy, both Munger and Buffett were pushing themselves and venturing into higher realms. They also were learning how to be effective partners.

"A partner ideally is capable of working alone," explained Munger. "You can be a dominant partner, subordinate partner, or an always collaborative equal partner. I've done all three. People couldn't believe that I suddenly made myself a subordinate partner to Warren. But there are some people that it's okay to be subordinate partner to. I didn't have the kind of ego that prevented it. There always are people who will be better at something than you are. You have to learn to be a follower before you become a leader. People should learn to play all roles. You can divide up in different ways with different people."

When he worked with Rick Guerin, Munger's relationship was different from the one he had with Buffett, even though what they did was similar. In fact, Guerin was sometimes a partner in the deals Munger and Buffett put together.

"Charlie is older than I and had legal experience," said Guerin. "He was the senior partner, you might say. He's always willing to listen. Always had an open mind. If you said 'Charlie, stop talking and listen to me, to what I'm trying to say,' he would listen."

A friend once noted that "Charlie is about as much like Warren as you can get. One of Warren's strengths is that he's very good at saying no, but Charlie is better. Warren uses Charlie as one last litmus test. If Charlie can't think of a reason for not doing something, they'll do it."[3]

Buffett has called Munger "the abominable no man," but Lou Simpson said that's more of a joke than anything. There is more to Charlie than negativity. "Charlie thinks outside of the box. He thinks quite differently and this leads him to some interesting conclusions. He has the ability to zero in on things that are really crucial to making good decisions. Charlie will give lots of negatives, but [he and Buffett] finally come up with a similar conclusion."

The tendency for him and Buffett to think alike hasn't always been an advantage. "If a mistake goes through one filter, it is likely to go through both," said Charlie.[4]

The relationship between Munger and Buffett, however, is more than a business arrangement. Though Munger can be self-willed, preoccupied, and abrupt, says Buffett, "He's just the best pal a guy could have."

A LESS OBVIOUS ELEMENT OF THIS MENTAL MATRIX, one that was woven deeply into the background, was the old master of the investment game, Ben Graham. Because Graham was now living in the same town with Munger, the two became acquainted. In certain ways, the similarities between Buffet's two closest associates were eerie. Both men admired and purposely emulated Benjamin Franklin. All three, Franklin, Graham, and Munger, lost their beloved first sons to diseases that, had they occurred even a few years later, most likely would have been cured or prevented.

Both Graham (who died in 1976) and Munger shared a wry and occasionally silly sense of humor and a deep interest in literature, science, and the teachings of the great thinkers. Both liked to quote the classics. One of Munger's favorite ideas is from Aristotle, "The best way to avoid envy is to deserve the success you get."

Like Munger, Graham was known for his integrity and dedication to objectivity and realism. Graham often told his students that there were two requirements for success on Wall Street: the first is to think correctly and the second is to think independently.

Munger also urges independent thought: "If, in your thinking, you rely entirely on others, often through purchase of professional advice, whenever outside a small territory of your own, you will suffer much calamity." Charlie recognizes the need to hire a doctor when he needs medical advice, an accountant or other professional help when necessary. But he doesn't take the experts entirely at their word. He considers what they say, continues his research, seeks other opinions, and in the end, reaches his own conclusion.

As Lou Simpson pointed out, Munger probably does not realize how much his mind works like Graham's. That said, there were major differences between Munger and Graham. Graham was an unrepentant ladies man until the end of his life but Munger has no such reputation. The important women in Charlie's life are his wife and three daughters. Differences in investment philosophy became increasingly apparent as Munger's career progressed.

Munger was among those who attended a now famous conference that Buffett organized in Coronado, California, in 1968. A group of Buffett's investing buddies met with Graham to discuss the best way to react to the flagging stock market. At that meeting, Buffett introduced Munger and his law partner Roy Tolles to friends he'd made when studying and working in New York. The Graham acolytes included Bill Ruane, founder of the Sequoia Fund, Tom Knapp of Tweedy Brown, Walter Schloss, Henry Brandt, David "Sandy" Gottesman, Marshall Weinberg, Ed Anderson, Buddy Fox, and Jack Alexander. These were investors of the high caliber that would impress Munger.

However, Charlie did not share the special affection and admiration that Buffett felt for Graham. Some of Graham's precepts, did not impress him at all. "I thought a lot of them were just madness," he said. "They ignored relevant facts."

Specifically, said Munger, "Ben Graham had blind spots. He had too low an appreciation of the fact that some businesses were worth paying big premiums for."[5]

Yet Charlie agreed with Graham's most fundamental teachings and they have been part of the Buffett-Munger success formula from the start. "The basic concept of value to a private owner and being motivated when you're buying and selling securities by reference to intrinsic value instead of price momentum—I don't think that will ever be outdated," said Munger.

Though Munger isn't interested in Graham's old-fashioned "cigar butt" stocks that have one puff left in them, Charlie is still too conservative to overpay for an asset. "I never want to pay above intrinsic value for stock—with very rare exceptions where someone like Warren Buffett is in charge," said Munger. "There are people—very few—worth paying up a bit to get in with for a long-term advantage. The investment game always involves considering both quality and price, and the trick is to get more quality than you pay for in price. It's just that simple."

Buffett has had a lifelong connection with most of the people who were in Coronado with him that summer, and he gives Graham a lot of credit for what happened to them afterward. "They were all moderately well-to-do then. They're all rich now. They haven't invented Federal Express or anything like that. They just set one foot in front of the other. Ben put it all down. It's just so simple."[6]

It may not have been obvious in Coronado that Munger was replacing the ailing Graham as Buffett's confidant and advisor, but the transition had begun. Carol Loomis, an editor and writer at *Fortune,* explained that while Buffett maintained his respect for Graham's ideas, Munger helped him expand his approach, to take the next big step forward:

> When he met Buffett, Munger had already formed strong opinions about the chasms between good businesses and bad. He served as a director of an International Harvester dealership in Bakersfield and saw how difficult it was to fix up an intrinsically mediocre business; as an Angeleno, he observed the splendid prosperity of the *Los Angeles Times;* in his head he did not carry a creed about "bargains" that had to be unlearned. So in conversations with Buffett over the years he preached the virtues of good businesses. By 1972, Blue Chip Stamps, a Berkshire affiliate that has since been merged into the parent, was paying three times book value to buy See's Candies, and the good-business era was launched.[7]

Buffett agrees with Loomis' explanation. "Charlie shoved me in the direction of not just buying bargains, as Ben Graham had taught me. This was the real impact he had on me. It took a powerful force to move me on from Graham's limiting view. It was the power of Charlie's mind. He expanded my horizons."[8]

Buffett says he slowly came around to Munger's point of view on many points. "I evolved," Buffett said. "I didn't go from ape to human or human to ape in a nice, even manner."[9]

To that Buffett has added a simple observation: "Boy, if I had listened only to Ben, would I ever be a lot poorer."[10]

In spite of what he says, it didn't take long for Buffett to put together what he had learned from Graham and what he was learning from Munger. "I became very interested in buying a wonderful business at a moderate price," he said.[11]

The 1968 meeting that Buffett organized in Coronado developed into a combination study group/party held every other year. The original Buffett Group was comprised of 13 investors. Now more than 60 top corporate executives and personal friends of Buffett attend. Buffett and Munger exchange ideas with old friends like Al Marshall, Walter Schloss, and Bill Ruane, and newer friends such as Katharine Graham and Bill Gates.

"Our group," as Buffett calls it, has met at Lyford Cay in the Bahamas; Dublin, Ireland; Williamsburg, Virginia; Santa Fe, New Mexico; Victoria, British Columbia; and more than once in Monterey, California. One year they booked the Queen Elizabeth II for a cruise to England and it rained the entire trip. Members take turns playing host, and whoever hosts the event gets to pick the location.

The group holds seminars on public policy, investments, charitable giving, and life's toughest and silliest moments. Once Munger gave a lecture on Einstein's Theory of Relativity. Few people were interested, but most felt obligated to go. One member recalls, "If Buffett was there, he probably understood it. I don't think anyone else did."[12]

CHAPTER EIGHT

POUND-FOR-POUND, THE BEST LAW FIRM

You know, someone once told me New York had more lawyers than people.[1]

Warren Buffett

"CERTAINLY WE WERE NEVER GROOMED FOR THE LAW," said Wendy Munger, an attorney who teaches arbitration and negotiation part-time at the University of California at Los Angeles Law School. But, she added, "We do tend to be a pretty verbal bunch."

Emilie Munger was definitely influenced by family tradition when she decided to enroll in law school. Law was "a way to understand the family," explained Emilie. "I think we're all analytical that way. Philip didn't chose law, but could have. He likes to read and think and analyze. He twice won the California state championship as a high school debater."

There was no grand plan, but the Munger children have tended to follow family tradition when it comes to careers. Four of Nancy and Charlie's eight children are attorneys, and five of their children are married to lawyers.

Molly Munger was the first of her siblings to take the step, though she probably chose law more by instinct than by reason. "My family had no particular consciousness—girls grew up and got married and you should have something to do—in case your husband died or something. That thinking had an influence on me. My last year at Radcliffe, in the spring the other girls all had the diamond rings. I didn't think 'I'm going to Harvard Law like my dad,' but when I realized I didn't have a job, I thought I should go to grad school. I wasn't good enough in math for economics. Then I filled out this Harvard Law questionnaire, which asked, did any member of my family attend Harvard. . . ."

For Molly, a light went on. She knew it was the right thing to do. Charlie Munger, usually reticent about expressing his emotions, let his first daughter know how he felt about her decision in an indirect way.

"Only extremely rarely had he done anything at Christmas or birthdays other than a check or cash," said Molly. "The idea of him out shopping is extremely funny. He bought us all Brooks Brothers gift certificates, He loves Brooks Brothers. Or once he was enamored with a certain type of briefcase, so he bought all of us one. He's the kind of man that when I graduated from college, I said 'I've graduated.' Then I said, 'I think it would be nice if you bought me a watch.' He looked up from his paper and said 'Oh yes, that's very appropriate. Go out and pick yourself out a watch and send me the bill.' And as I left he looked up again and said, '. . . and have it engraved, from your loving father.' So imagine my amazement my freshman year at law school, living in a seedy Cambridge student duplex with such poor heating that one person spent the whole winter standing in front of the oven. I was unwrapping this package from my father. It's this thing. This nicely framed set of head shots of four people. My great grandfather, my grandfather, my father, and my high school graduation picture. Some little note from him. Well '—love from Daddy.' I *clung* to that object."

Despite her original ambivalence, Molly took to the profession deeply and happily. She worked in the U.S. Attorney's office in Los Angeles as a prosecutor, then built a private-practice career bringing suits against perpetrators of complicated financial scams. In time, she followed her heart and went into public interest law. Molly was among the leaders of a coalition in the late 1990s who made a futile attempt to defeat a proposition that eliminated affirmative action in California schools and government. In the late 1990s, she, some colleagues, and her husband Steve English, founded a public-interest law organization called the Advancement Project. There, Molly continues the sort of work she formerly did for the National Association for the Advancement of Colored People and other civil rights organizations.

IN 1962—THE SAME YEAR Buffett started buying shares in the beleaguered New England textile manufacturing company, Berkshire Hathaway—Charlie Munger helped established two new ventures in Los Angeles. The first was a law firm and the second was a securities firm called Wheeler, Munger and Company.

A breakaway group of Musick, Peeler & Garrett colleagues prevailed upon Charlie to join them in creating a practice that quickly became known as a group of "superlawyers," a premier small firm with clients not only in Los Angeles, but across the nation. Charlie had been with Musick, Peeler & Garrett for 13 years when he and six other attorneys, including Roderick Hills (later chairman of the Securities and Exchange Commission) and his wife, Carla Anderson Hills (who in time became the U.S. Trade Representative), struck out on their own. Their idea was to be a democratic organization, meet the highest standards of conduct, recruit only the best, and build the finest law firm anywhere.

Roy Garrett by this time had developed heart trouble and in order to ease the load on himself, brought into the firm a high-level man who Charlie described as a "control freak." Munger was among the seasoned attorneys who finally got fed up.

"The formation of the new law firm was not at the time perceived as a pure sad loss for Musick, Peeler & Garrett," said Charlie. "Everyone hated to see Fred Warder and Dick Ebenshade leave, but many welcomed the departure of others, particularly Rod Hills and Charlie Munger. The new managing partner especially hated Rod Hills' constantly maneuvering himself into responsibilities that, at other firms, were not handled by lawyers so young."

Nancy Munger recalls this period of rebellion as one of the most exciting phases of her life: The real estate ventures were underway and "Most of the discussion about forming the new firm went on at our house. Charlie also established his first investment company. He cut loose from our past. I didn't have sense enough to be scared. I had faith. I didn't worry a lot. I had more children and just lived."

Her confidence in the new projects was bolstered by her knowledge of her husband: "He judges people pretty well—which ones to join with and which ones not to join," said Nancy. "He has avoided attaching himself to people who are problems—that's helpful."

Rod Hills, rather than Charlie, was actually the driving force behind the new firm. A street-smart lawyer, Hills talks fast, and covers a lot of ground. He was born in Seattle, but when he was still very small, his father lost his job and the family headed for California. Their car broke down in Oregon and they hitchhiked the rest of the way to Los Angeles. Hills grew up in East LA, played football well enough and earned good enough grades to get a scholarship to Stanford. He found his calling when he enrolled in law school and ended up clerking at the U.S. Supreme Court. It was Munger who recruited Hills for Musick, Peeler, & Garrett.

"It was not the hardest firm to get a job with," said Hills, "but they had a couple of people like Charlie who were quite unusual. After three years, the firm offered me a partnership. I decided I didn't want to accept, for a lot of reasons. We had a baby, my wife was Assistant District Attorney, there was a senior partner I didn't think much of. I decided to quit. Charlie said he'd quit, too. We'd share office space. He said he didn't really want to practice law anymore. I said okay, as long as I can use your name on the firm. Charlie is the most unique person I've ever met. In many respects, he reminded me of Justice Frankfurter. He has the same kind of mind. He wouldn't accept anything on face value. His interest in almost everything can be so intense, he will have a perspective that others will not have. He's a fair person, he can understand the prejudices and weaknesses of other people and make allowances for them. He is not as judgmental as others. He wasn't a lawyer like other lawyers. He would take on clients that he cared about. He worked for people that I would not have worked for. He used to say, 'Why do you insist upon being a traditional lawyer? You guys were first in your class at Harvard, Yale, and Michigan; many of you clerked in federal court. Do things that other people aren't doing.' "

When they branched out on their own, Hills was 31 years old and Carla Anderson Hills was 28. To them Munger, who was only 38 but had the demeanor of a much older person, represented grey hair and maturity.

Carla Hills was a native Angeleno who attended Stanford, where she made a name for herself playing tennis. She then went on to Yale Law School, and after graduating in 1958, worked for two years as Assistant U.S. Attorney in Los Angeles.

"My father had a great working relationship with Carla Hills," said Molly. "He thought she was a great working lawyer." Though Molly wasn't consciously aware of it at the time, her father's respect for Carla Hills may have been a signal that it was acceptable for Molly to study law as well.

Some of the lawyers brought clients with them into the new firm and Charlie was no exception. Rod Hills estimates that in the early years, Charlie's clients provided at least 10 percent of the work. In addition, Hills said Munger was instrumental in helping them hold on to existing clients and attract new ones.

"We started out with Aerojet General and Federal Mogul," recalled Hills. "They all came with us because it looked like we had some substance with Charlie there. Charles Rickershauser had been with Gibson, Dunn and Crutcher, but was California's corporations commissioner. He wouldn't have joined our firm if Charlie hadn't been there. Because he did, we got the Pacific Coast Stock Exchange as a client."

Hills said the practice started off with a healthy burst and quickly got even better. "The first year we made any real money in the firm, all of a sudden I was rich, I'd made money. Somebody had made a suggestion about a tax shelter investment. I said, 'Charlie, I've got this terrific invest-ment opportunity.' I thought it was great, but Charlie said, 'I have a much better idea for a tax shelter.' He said 'Give me the money.' I said, 'As a mat-ter of interest, what are you going to do with it?' He said, 'I'm going to keep it. You're going to lose it either way. I'll pay the taxes on it and will be eternally grateful for the contribution.' I took that as my lesson not to invest in this tax shelter."

Rod and Carla Hills were partners in the firm from 1962 to 1974. Carla gained experience in anti-trust and security cases and also taught at the University of California at Los Angeles as an adjunct professor. The Hills switched to careers in politics when in 1973 Carla was offered the post of Assistant U.S. Attorney General in the administration of Richard M. Nixon. The offer became void after Attorney General Elliot L. Richardson resigned in the "Saturday night massacre" of the Watergate affair in Febru-ary 1974. However, William B. Saxbe, the next attorney general, renewed the offer. Hills became Assistant Attorney General in charge of the Justice Department's civil division. In 1975, she was nominated Secretary of Housing and Urban Development by President Gerald R. Ford. She served as U.S. Trade Representative from 1989 to 1993 in the cabinet of President George Bush. She now has a consulting firm, Hills & Co., that works with corporations on trade issues.

Rod Hills also clambered up the White House political ropes. He left Munger, Tolles in 1974 to become White House General Counsel to Presi-dent Gerald Ford and then ended up as chairman of the Securities and Ex-change Commission. He now has a consulting firm, Hills Enterprises, and spends most of his time on corporate workouts, reorganizing or closing down troubled companies. His most publicized assignment was with the now defunct Drexel, Burnham Lambert following its junk bond scandal. Most recently Hills has worked with Federal Mogul Corp. and Waste Man-agement Inc.

Once ensconced in Washington, the Hills stayed but they remain connected to Munger, Tolles. Of the Hills' four children, three became lawyers. Their daughter Allison married Kelly Klaus, an attorney in the Munger, Tolles' San Francisco office.

During those early years, Charlie kept cementing relationships that he felt were valuable to the firm, including attracting Chuck Rickershauser, another former clerk at the U.S. Supreme Court, as a partner. Munger and Rickershauser met in 1965 when Munger was moonlighting as a real estate developer. A new statute had been enacted in California dealing with condominium-like projects. It was a change in the concept in real es-tate law, and Munger thought the legislation hadn't been written properly.

Rickershauser was about 36 years old at the time and was serving as corporations commissioner under Governor Pat Brown.

"Charlie wanted a slightly different version of the law than what was written. I refined it to change it," said Rickershauser. Several years later they met at a party, and Charlie helped recruit Rickershauser for Munger, Tolles. Of the young lawyers brought aboard in the early years, Ronald Olson and Robert Denham have become the best known.

Ron Olson graduated from the University of Michigan School of Law in 1966, spent a year at Oxford, then in 1968 clerked with U.S. Court of Appeals Judge David Bazelon in Washington, DC. He had decided to stay in Washington when his appointment was over until a law school classmate suggested that he come to LA and join him at Munger, Tolles.

"Two weeks before our son was born I told my wife I was going out to California to take a look," said Olson. "I came back and told my wife I thought we ought to go. Why? I never met a more interesting group of people. Charlie was not with the law firm. But his values were very much part of it. I heard stories about him when I was recruited, and to this day, recruits who come through this firm hear Charlie Munger stories."

When Olson eventually met Munger, his first impression was typical of what others saw. "Gee, he's an old man," thought Olson. "He was in his 40s. For years his mother probably told him, 'Charlie, you should act your age, meaning you should be more mature.' Charlie, from the first day I met him, was the most wise, most mature, most sensible man I ever met. Now his chronological age is just catching up with the wisdom he accumulated very early in his life."

To be sure, said Olson, "He can be maddening. He can talk over the best conversationalist I know. His opinions are never hidden. Our political opinions are quite different. He's a conservative Republican and I'm a Democrat and we differ on how to solve a social problem, but in the end, we come out the same."

California Law Business once described Olson, who grew up in a small town in Iowa, as one of the country's top "rainmakers"—a partner who lures new business to a firm. Olson won recognition for arranging a $400 million settlement between his client Merrill Lynch and Orange County in a famous case involving junk bonds. Not bad, considering that the county was seeking $2 billion in damages. Olson advises clients such as Atlantic Richfield Company, Universal Studios, and Michael Ovitz, the former Walt Disney president.[2] In 1998, when California lawyers ranked themselves, Olson took the top spot in the list of most influential lawyers.

Katharine Graham, a regular member of Buffett's inner circle, was impressed with Olson when they met and had lunch in Washington. "He is dynamic. A really fabulous guy. He was Warren's securities guy for a long time. The most prominent deal maker in Los Angeles. Wasn't that $90 million Ovitz settlement amazing?"

Graham was referring to the settlement package of Michael Ovitz, former number two executive at Disney Inc., who left after a falling out with top executive Michael Eisner. The Ovitz's package is sometimes valued as high as $140 million or much lower, depending on the price at which Disney's stock is trading.

Robert Denham, who served as Munger, Tolles managing partner from 1985 to 1991, gained national prominence when Buffett and Munger called him and Olson to New York to help sort out the bond-trading scandal at Salomon Brothers, Inc. Denham was in New York for seven years and before he left, he became Salomon's chairman.

Denham grew up in West Texas and learned about Munger, Tolles when he was a student at Harvard Law, where like Munger, he won a Sears Prize. "In 1969 to 1970, Rod [Hills] taught at Harvard. Carla was writing an anti-trust book. Very interesting people. The Hills had my wife and me to dinner. Molly [Munger] was there. Molly was a senior at Radcliffe."

After talking to Hills, Denham decided to give Munger, Tolles a once-over by working there in the summer of 1970. He was impressed with what he found. "The firm stands for value oriented toward business. It stands for integrity. The same thing Charlie stands for, this firm stands for."

Denham first encountered Munger the summer he worked as an intern. "My earliest impression was of someone who was very smart, very focused, had a lot of really close human relationships, who cared a lot about his friends. As I began doing legal work for him—in 1971 or 1972—that gave me a much better perspective on him. He is an unusually smart client. He understood legal work quite well and the business issues. Working for him was hard, demanding, but it's the best work you can do, because you learn a lot from it. Any good law firm is fundamentally in the business of selling judgment. That's a critical part of the way Charlie practiced law. Solid legal skills and understanding of business issues."

Thanks in part to Munger's name and his connections, explained Denham, "We've been able to recruit very, very well. Part of that recruiting success is that we can recruit into elite declination. Lots of very able people get turned down. This is an intellectually elite institution." One applicant went so far as to describe it as "elitist, snobby, and competitive."[3]

The hiring rules are strictly followed, no matter who the applicant. Not long after she graduated from Harvard, Molly Munger applied at Munger, Tolles for an associate's position. She interviewed with Carla

Hills, but Hills did not offer her a job, allegedly because Molly had not made the *Harvard Law Review*. Apparently in Hills estimation, that meant Molly's credentials weren't quite up to Munger, Tolles's standards.[4]

When new graduates are interviewed at Munger, Tolles, they are told that grades are the main criteria by which they will be evaluated. "Even your undergrad record is picked over," said one applicant. "God help you if you only graduated cum laud [sic], rather than magna or summa."[5]

Of its 130 lawyers, 17 are former U.S. Supreme Court clerks. MTO (as its members call Munger, Tolles) added seven new partners in the year 2000, graduates of Georgetown University Law Center, the University of California at Los Angeles (UCLA), the University of Southern California (USC), the University of Michigan Law School, Stanford Law School, and Yale Law School. While most law firms have two associates per partner, with the associates carrying the heaviest work burden, Munger, Tolles partners have to do more of their own work, since only about half the lawyers on the staff are associates.

Perhaps one of the most nurturing things Charlie Munger did for MTO was to bring in a small group of companies as clients, a group that later became Berkshire Hathaway Inc. As Berkshire grew in size, influence, and prestige, so did Munger, Tolles.

"Berkshire-Hathaway has had a huge impact on the firm . . . the ability to work for Warren Buffett and the opportunity to be the lawyer for Berkshire-Hathaway?" noted Hal Borthwick. "And I'm not saying, by the way, that Berkshire's business produced massive amounts of gold. It's consistent work, but by and large Warren and Charlie run that business so as to stay out of trouble. At the same time, in the early days they bought businesses that had troubles they thought they could fix. Blue Chip Stamps was a case in point where they took over control of a company that had, I don't know, 10 cases against it? Their calculated judgment was that they would win or cheaply settle all the cases. They did. It cost some money, took a long time, but they got a good deal, right? But it's a tremendous amount of help to have something like Berkshire built into the client base. It's a stamp of approval. Some general counsels will say, 'You know, if they're good enough for Warren Buffet, I think they're okay for us, too. Give 'em a call.' "

Because Berkshire's business grew at a steady but manageable rate, Munger, Tolles was able to keep pace, adding staff and expertise as required. Today, the offices of Munger, Tolles & Olson occupy several floors in a russet marble wedge, one of a pair of skyscrapers on Bunker Hill. The offices are across the street from the Los Angeles Museum of Contemporary Art, in a part of town that has magnificent edifices, but is only blocks from areas that look like the back streets of Mexico City. A short distance from the cappuccino shops and elevators filled with people dressed in exquisitely tailored suits, the streets are redolent with the aroma of taco stands, the sounds of sidewalk vending stalls and Latin music.

Munger, Tolles & Olson now specializes in corporation, securities, and business litigation, labor relations, anti-trust law, taxation, real property, trust, probate, and environmental law. The firm has a particularly large business litigation practice.

In addition to being Berkshire's chief counsel since the 1970s, Munger, Tolles has represented the Philippine government in its efforts to recover funds from Imelda and Ferdinand Marcos. They represented the Alyeska Pipeline Service Co. in disputes arising from the Exxon Valdez Alaska oil spill. They were legal counsel in the restructuring of Vons Cos., a western-states grocery store chain. They have done substantial work for the Northrop Corp., Litton Industries, Southern California Edison, Bank of America, Unocal Corp., and MCA Inc. MTO performs pro bono work for numerous groups, including the Western Center for Law and Poverty and for the homeless of Los Angeles.

Munger, Tolles is known for creating a democratic and fairly unique compensation system designed to make the firm a meritocracy. As a result, when conditions are right the highest-paid partner can earn at least five times more than the lowest paid.

Every January the partners—there are now 62—get a ballot listing the names of all the partners with a blank after each name. The firm's net income for the previous year is printed at the bottom of the ballot. Each partner fills in the amount of money he or she thinks every participant should make, with no rules other than that the numbers must add up to the net income for that year. There are no points, no shares, no extra credit for seniority. When the partners vote, they can take seniority into consideration, but they also consider a person's ability to find business and represent clients successfully.[6]

"We vote on disbursement, then everybody gets to see how everyone else voted," explained Olson. "There isn't a compensation committee—a lawyer-by-lawyer pitch on how valuable he or she was to the law firm. It's a whole different dynamic. Rod, Roy [Tolles], and Charlie together were the ones who came up with the process. It's a yearly check on how you are perceived."

After the ballots are in, the firm then plots the numbers and names on a grid, allowing each attorney to see how he or she ranks in the eyes of every other, by name. The compensation committee reviews the numbers, talks privately with each partner, and then settles on a final compensation figure. The system, claim the partners, encourages good manners. People think twice before riling anyone who will influence their salaries.

"People have said this must be very brutal," says John Frank, a Munger, Tolles partner. "It is open, but it's not brutal. You can't give a whole lot of money to one person without taking it away from others, which imposes a certain civility on things."[7]

"They think of themselves as a more intellectual bunch than most law firms," said Anne Larin, a former associate who later joined the legal staff at General Motors Corp. "And I liked that."[8]

Although he has not worked there for years and his name is no longer on the brass plate, Rod Hills claims, "Pound for pound, it is the best firm in the country."

CHARLIE WAS STILL PRACTICING LAW, though not full time, when he, Jack Wheeler, and later Al Marshall were running Wheeler, Munger. The Wheeler, Munger offices at the Pacific Stock Exchange were so cramped that if Charlie got a sensitive call from a client, he asked Al and Vivian, their secretary, to step outside so that he could maintain confidentiality. Al and Vivian would stand around in the hall, on one foot and then the other, and wait.

Within three years of founding Munger, Tolles, Charlie dropped out. He finally left the firm in 1965 because he believed that he would never again need to rely on legal fees. He transferred his remaining balance at the firm into the estate of a partner who died young. Clearly, Munger had been plotting his escape from law for quite a while.

Al Marshall said Charlie once summed up practicing law this way: "Too often, if you absolutely kill yourself over an impossible client and get a ten strike, your reward is you get to do it all over again for an equally impossible client." Despite his love of his father and grandfather and respect for their work, it was a relief to Munger to quit the law.

"I hire lawyers, oversee lawyers, it's not that I don't use law or lawyers. But I was entirely willing to give up working for other people as a lawyer," said Munger. "I had a huge family. Nancy and I supported eight children. . . . And I didn't realize that the law was going to get as prosperous as it suddenly did. The big money came into law shortly after I left it. Also, I preferred making decisions and gambling my own money. I usually thought I knew better than the client anyway, so why should I have to do it his way? So partly, it was having an opinionated personality. And partly, it was a desire to get resources permitting independence."

Munger hoped to use his wealth, when he felt secure with it, to emulate his childhood idol, Benjamin Franklin. "Franklin was able to make the contribution he did because he had (financial) freedom." Munger came to understand that in order to be truly wealthy, a person needed to build ownership in a business.

"It was a classic thing my mother-in-law talks about," explained Hal Borthwick. "She says, it's always the lawyer who has the wonderful lifestyle, with the kids in the schools and the nice home in the nice neighborhood. She says, of course, you are living at a level your clients are living at, right? What you forget is your clients are building capital where, as an attorney, you're not. There is no capital value to your practice, so when you do retire one day, your income disappears. You have nothing other than maybe your house and so you sell the house and move to the desert or whatever."

Charlie changed, the profession of law was changing, but even if he had stayed in the practice, he probably would have been dissatisfied. There is now more money to be made from law, but less time to enjoy it.

"I think many lawyers now have love-hate relationships with themselves and their profession and it is definitely the case now that you really have to work very hard to have traditional relationships with your clients," said Borthwick. "Because things have really changed a lot in law practice. It is now a business where you have to be a good lawyer and a good businessperson to survive. Before, you could just be a nice person with a good sense of values."

Borthwick, a member of Charlie's hang out, the California Club, says that 20 to 25 years earlier, after lunch the club lounges were full of men playing cards or dominoes. Today there is practically nobody there in the early afternoon. The lawyers and brokers and other professional people often take lunch at their desks, or if they do go out it is for a business lunch and they rush back to their offices as soon as possible. "It's a different deal now," said Borthwick. "The gentility has gone out of these things and you have to make the best with a limited amount of time."

Although Munger is disassociated from the profession of law, his connection with his former firm remains solid.

"You know, even though he hasn't drawn any income out of that firm for probably 35 years, he's always had his name on the door, he's always had an office there or near," Borthwick continued. "He's used that firm heavily. He's just changed his relationship to the firm. He's a client instead of a lawyer."

Ron Olson says that the lawyers at MTO consider Munger a resource as well as a client. The lawyers gather for lunch in the office's cafeteria three times a week, and on Mondays they bring in an outside speaker. The speakers have included the mayor of Los Angeles, a writer for the television show *Frasier,* Robert Kenney, Jr., and of course, Munger. "He will periodically be asked to talk to the assembled lawyers. He does this about once a year. We have yearly retreats to discuss longer term issues, and he has participated in those as a panelist. He's part of our social life. He comes to the annual holiday party."

And because Berkshire Hathaway leases office space there for Charlie to use, "He's physically here, very accessible, his door is always open. He likes it, is stimulated by it. He loves to think about problems."

As for Munger's name still being on the door, Bob Denham said, "From the firm's standpoint, it would be crazy to change it. From Charlie's point of view, it gives him a certain satisfaction."

AS HIS LAW CAREER WAS PHASING OUT, Munger discarded the elements from his life that no longer worked for him, and built upon those he found valuable. Relationships with his colleagues continued to be central to his success.

When Molly Munger returned to Los Angeles to begin her own legal career, she said, "The law firm was up and running. It was prestigious. I quickly learned it was a very hot firm. I've benefitted my whole career from being Molly Munger. Nobody in my business life realized my father wasn't over at Munger, Tolles practicing law."

Molly once thanked the managing partner at Munger, Tolles for building such a respected firm, one that even though she didn't work there, allowed her to walk proudly in its reflected light.

"It's okay," said the lawyer. "In the early days, Charlie put me in his business deals. I think we're square."

CHAPTER NINE

OPERATING WHEELER, MUNGER OUT OF A UTILITY ROOM

The opulence at the head office is often inversely related to the financial substance of the firm.

Charlie Munger, paraphrasing Parkinson

"WE USED TO PLAY GOLF in a pick-up foursome. You know how personable and charming Charlie can be," said one of his earliest business partners, Al Marshall. He and Charlie would meet someone new and the four of them would have a great game of golf. "The next day we'd be in the elevator at the office, and one of those golfers would get on the elevator and say hello to us. Charlie would just stare straight ahead.

"Why didn't you say hello to that guy?" asked Marshall.

"What guy?"

"The guy we played golf with yesterday," Marshall explained.

"Oh. I didn't see him," Charlie replied.

"This was even before he had his eye operation," said Marshall. People sometimes became angry at Charlie when he seemed to ignore them, especially members of the California Club or the Los Angeles Country Club, places where members don't expect to be snubbed. Marshall, usually without success, would explain to the offended party that Munger did not act with malice, but simply was lost in a world of his own thoughts. But, conceded Marshall, Charlie also occasionally needled people consciously, subtly, and with a purpose in mind.

"We used to play golf with this Army officer, a West Point guy," recalled Marshall. A few moments before the officer was to address the ball, out of the clear blue sky, Charlie commented, "I don't know, but I think a little communism is good for the military." The West Pointer's face reddened and he missed his putt.

WHEN THE 1960s dAWNED, the young John F. Kennedy was the newly elected president of the United States and the Viet Nam War was still a whisper in the back halls of the Pentagon. Charlie Munger was 36 years old, practicing law and was in the midst of promising real estate development projects. The connection he had made with money manager Warren Buffett proved deep and abiding, and Buffett assured Munger that he, too, could earn a living as an independent investor. Charlie realized, however, that he would be taking a big risk.

When he'd ventured into real estate, said Munger, The situation seemed less risky. "I never thought I'd lose everything. Real estate took leverage, but the development process always had risk limits in place. The big loans had clauses that we'd guarantee completion, but we didn't have to pay the money back if the completed project couldn't be sold above cost." In case the condominiums didn't sell, the bank might take ownership of the property and Munger would be dented but he would not be ruined. However, Munger was not satisfied with his dual career as a member of a new law firm and a real estate developer. In 1962, Munger made the commitment to spend at least part of his time acting as a professional investor using other people's funds. He took the step that Buffett had repeatedly suggested to him. Charlie, along with his poker pal and legal client, Jack Wheeler, established Wheeler, Munger & Company, an investment partnership similar in format to Buffett's partnership. Wheeler, a Yale graduate, was by profession a stock exchange floor trader and a co-owner of two specialist posts at the Pacific Coast Stock Exchange.

Wheeler, Munger acquired the specialists posts, locations on the exchange floor where buy and sell orders are called out and trades are made. The posts help smooth out the market, making certain that there are ready buyers and sellers for listed securities. Often, one post is the exclusive market-maker for a particular stock, and in that case, owning a post can be highly profitable. The posts generated a generous amount of excess income and when that was combined with the capital Charlie raised from family, friends, and former clients, there were funds well above those needed for trading. It was Charlie's job, with help from his law partner Roy Tolles, to invest the excess capital.

Wheeler, Munger, and many of the people at the Pacific Coast Stock Exchange were small operators who purchased memberships so that they could maximize their trading profits.

"In the 1960s there was a fixed commission system," said Rick Guerin. "The only way to beat that was to be a member of the stock exchange. You could then trade without commission. Those little costs are significant."

It was a low-budget, make-do arrangement. Wheeler and Munger worked out of a tiny mezzanine office at the stock exchange, which was on Spring Street amid the headquarters of major financial institutions, but also very near the Skid Row section of Los Angeles. Munger and his partner shared a pipe-riddled, but larger front office while their secretary worked in a tiny private room in the back, adjacent to the toilet. The entire office suite had only two windows, each looking out over a grubby alley. It suited Munger because the rent was cheap, $150 per month with all utilities included.

The penny-pinching wasn't entirely necessary. When Wheeler, Munger was formed, Munger had accumulated a net worth of about $300,000, which was more than 10 times his annual rate of personal expenditure. A fair amount of the money had come from investments in securities.

By the time Charlie started Wheeler, Munger, he and Buffett were talking often, discussing approaches and spinning investment ideas by one another. Nevertheless, Jack Wheeler was Munger's first formal partner in the securities game. Before and after this, Munger also invested informally with others, among them, Rick Guerin and Roy Tolles. He met Guerin while he and Wheeler were setting up their business.

"In 1961 a friend called and said he was going to buy into a downtown (LA) trading firm because someone was selling out," said Guerin. Rick decided that he too would join in the investment and would help run the company.

The seller was Jack Wheeler who was disposing of his portion of Wheeler, Cruttenden & Company because he planned to go into a new arrangement managing money with Charlie Munger. When Guerin arrived to settle the deal, Munger was present. They started to talk. "I was just going to this meeting for the closing. I was going to deliver a check and take a stock certificate. We were joking with Munger, when this light went on in my brain. 'I'm on the wrong side of this transaction.' "

Guerin realized he wanted to be where Wheeler was going, not where he had been. Guerin's intuition was correct. In part, Wheeler was selling his interest because he was not seeing eye-to-eye with his partner. Arrangements between investment partners are tricky and rely on a combination of brains, judgment, and trustworthiness. If partners are incompatible in any of these areas, even a small issue grates like sand in a shoe.

Munger had advised Wheeler to simply get out of his former arrangement and concentrate full-time on Wheeler, Munger. Using the only $40,000 he then had, Guerin bought into the less promising half of a splitting partnership and later lost the entire investment.

"But by then," said Munger, "he'd learned a lot and was doing very well."

WITH THE ADVENT OF WHEELER, MUNGER, Charlie's business life took on a new direction, as did his social life.

"Charlie started to go down to the stock exchange very early every day," said Buffett. "First he would check the board, then he and his friends would roll dice to see who would pay for breakfast. They had a ritual of eating breakfast at the Stock Exchange Club on the top floor of the Stock Exchange Building. Rick had some fairly modest job there but was always listening in. In a sense, he was attending class."

Guerin was learning, and he, like Munger, was making new buddies. Guerin would become another of Munger's many "best friends," but the one least like Charlie. "My mother was a seamstress, a Rosie the riveter," explained Guerin. She died from alcoholism when Rick was a teenager. Guerin trained to be an Air Force pilot but dropped out, although for years afterward he flew his own plane. He spent three years at IBM, then five to six years as a stockbroker.

"It took me three years to extricate from that (early) partnership," said Guerin. "Charlie—and Jack Wheeler to some extent—became my mentors. I then founded my own partnership, modeling it after the Buffett and Munger partnerships."

J.P. Guerin & Co. imitated Wheeler, Munger in every way including the operation of a specialist post. In his famous essay, "The Superinvestors of Graham and Doddsville," Buffett described Rick Guerin's investment record. "Table 6 is the record of a fellow, a pal of Charlie Munger's—another nonbusiness school type—who was a math major at USC. He went to work for IBM after graduation and was an IBM salesman for a while. After I got to Charlie, Charlie got to him," Buffett wrote. "This happens to be the record of Rick Guerin. Rick from 1965 to 1988, against a compounded gain of 316 percent for the S&P, came off with 22,200 percent, which probably because he lacks a business school education, he regards as statistically significant."[1]

Guerin did deals with Munger and Buffett, but also invested independently. He became a major shareholder and director of Pacific Southwest Airline, which in 1988 was merged into USAir. Guerin says that he learned from Munger how to make deals, but he also began to think deeply about the importance of personal values.

"I think I've been affected by Charlie," said Guerin. "It was in me to see these values and to respond to them immediately, but he shaped me. Being around Charlie and Warren has made me a better man." Guerin saw how clearly logical it is to be ethical, rational, and honest. "It is easier to tell the truth."

Guerin is Buffett's age and is married to a woman 26 years younger than himself. They have a five-year-old son. Rick also has a 42-year-old daughter. Between them, he and his wife Fabienne have seven children—five girls and two boys. Munger, Guerin, and Otis Booth still play bridge at the Los Angeles Country Club with a circle of friends that sometimes includes Mayor Richard Riordan. In addition, Munger and Buffett once played bridge at nearby Hillcrest Country Club with the late comedian George Burns, then in his late 90s. To accommodate Burns' cigars, the Hillcrest posted its rule: "No smoking by persons under 95."

Charlie admires a long-standing practice of the Hillcrest Country Club of demanding a generous charitable giving history as a condition of membership. "I have heard that, long ago, a big-time theater owner tried to join, delivering a yellowing newspaper clipping reporting on a World War II savings bond rally held in one of his theaters. Back came the reply of the membership committee: 'This is a very useful piece of paper. For instance, you could wipe your ass with it. But it won't get you into this Club.'"

THE REAL ESTATE DEALS WERE WRAPPING UP, the law firm doing well, and about that time, Charlie approached Al Marshall and asked him if he would like to come into Wheeler, Munger as business manager. Munger had discovered that his style differed from Jack Wheeler's, and he needed someone around who was more compatible.

Wheeler "was not from Omaha but he was a very smart man," said Marshall. "He once told me that he'd taken a course in [late 1920s style] pools and the management of pools, which of course are totally illegal today. He was a big spender, lived big. He was very good at what he did, but he also would suffer big reverses once in a while, which did not appeal to Charlie."

Finally Charlie persuaded Wheeler to turn the operation of Wheeler, Munger over to himself and Marshall, and they would pay Wheeler a cut of the profits. "There was no acrimony between them," insisted Marshall. "Wheeler just sort of retired."

Marshall, who ultimately became a general partner, wasn't surprised that Charlie approached him a second time to join in a business venture. "If he trusts you, he trusts you completely," said Al. It still amazes Marshall that for years Charlie listed him as a signatory on a personal checking account. Charlie knew Al's character and didn't think for a minute that Marshall would run off with the money, and of course he didn't.

Munger, ever the absent-minded professor, had Nancy to keep things straight at home. At the office he needed a lieutenant like Marshall. "We had a secretary named Vivian," said Marshall. "When she left, we had two or three secretaries after her, but Charlie just kept calling all of them Vivian. I've always said it's a good thing his second wife was named Nancy, too. Otherwise he'd never have remembered her name."

Marshall liked his new position, but it also had drawbacks.

"One of my more obnoxious jobs was to watch the specialist posts," said Marshall. Floor traders tend to be action-oriented individuals who have a lot of adrenaline in their systems. Once one of Marshall's traders objected to something that had been said and jumped up and slugged another trader. It took Marshall several days to negotiate a peaceful settlement with the battered trader and the exchange's governors. But the traders also were clever and creative. One of Wheeler, Munger's men set up a complex four-way arbitrage in the securities of the pharmaceutical company, Alza, which at the time was just a start-up. Marshall established a $2 million line of bank credit to finance the arbitrage, but at one point, the credit line was drawn out to $3 million. A banker came over to the stock exchange to investigate and to ask Marshall, again, what the credit line was being used for. Even after Marshall explained, the banker went away confused. The trader unwound the arbitrage after three weeks with a profit of $600,000.

Marshall recalled that one evening he needed to talk to Charlie about a business situation, so he went over to the Mungers' June Street home. Marshall had five children of his own so he knew what a busy household was like, but even he was surprised that Charlie could concentrate under the circumstances. Charlie was sitting in a big chair, and "One kid was climbing on his shoulder, another was pulling his arm. Another was yelling. It was bedlam, but he didn't send them out or correct them. It didn't bother him a bit."

WHILE WHEELER KEPT AN EYE on the specialist posts, Charlie concentrated on investing the surplus capital. Sometimes he, Buffett, or Guerin—or all three together—invested in the same companies. They scoured the exchanges, the newspapers, and talked to friends, searching for deals. Buffett described both—Buffett Partnership and Wheeler, Munger—as classic hedge funds, similar to those that again became popular in the late 1990s.

"We bought some operating businesses," said Munger, "including a company that made automotive chemicals. At one time, as part of a bargain-priced package, we bought a manufacturer of car wash machines and a group of loans to car wash operators. Every time it rained, people called Marshall to explain why they weren't paying. That was not one of my happier moments. So we had a lot of experiences, good and bad."

Because the companies they bought were small and sometimes closely held, the investors became involved in peculiar situations. This was the case with the tiny automotive chemicals company, K&W Products.

"I spotted it in the newspaper, an estate sale," said Rick Guerin. "It turned out it was a company that made a substance that, when poured into an automobile radiator, would seal up a leak in the car's engine block. The inventor of the product had launched it into the market by, time after time, driving his car into an auto repair shop, calling together the mechanics, and then drilling a disastrous hole in his car's engine block, which he fixed by pouring his product into the car's radiator. This proved quite effective as a sales aid, and the company made a fair amount of money."

"The company came up for sale because the controlling shareholder [not the original inventor] had died. It was rumored that this owner, a doctor, had died because he over-prescribed addictive drugs to himself. He had borrowed money from his wife's aunts to invest in the company, and the estate owed the aunts $80,000 each. The only asset in the estate was the stock. For some reason the doctor left his estate to his wife, but made his mistress the executor. Needless to say this caused some rancor between the executor and family members. The aunts had not been receiving interest payments and for several years were not able to get any money. Charlie proposed that he and Guerin buy the two $80,000 notes held by the elderly aunts.

"Under the circumstances, it would be typical to bid less than face value," said Guerin, but Charlie insisted on paying the full $80,000 for each note. "Charlie was not willing to benefit from their distress. He could have taken advantage of them, but did not. I did the leg work. I found the old ladies. Charlie and I became the creditors, then later traded the notes for ownership."

Next, Munger, who was at best a little awkward when dealing with women, telephoned the mistress/executor and invited her to lunch at the California Club so that they could discuss the matter. Munger was taken aback when the woman showed up at the office. She had flaming red hair, eyes enhanced by bright green contact lenses, and was wearing a snug nurse's uniform that showed off her ample bosom. Charlie was flustered, but there was no way of getting out of accompanying the woman to lunch at his conservative businessmen's club, with its dark paneled walls, leather furniture, and valuable collection of old California art.

Eventually, Charlie and Rick became fifty-fifty owners of a controlling block of stock in the company, with its management owning the rest. After some time passed, a situation arose where Guerin needed to cash out of the investment. "I still was very poor. We had an informal understanding that one would take the other out if either needed to get out. I went to Charlie and said I need to use that money elsewhere. He said fine, figure out what you want."

Guerin looked over the accounting statements and thought about it. "I told him it was worth $200,000. Charlie said 'No, you're wrong about that.' I said to myself, 'Oh darn,' because I needed $200,000. He said, 'It's worth $300,000.' And he pulled out a check and wrote it. I would have been delighted with $200,000. I would have been the happiest man on earth. It was an opportunity for him to show me how stupid I was," Guerin said with a chuckle. "Charlie has a saying, 'Think about it a little more and you will agree with me because you're smart and I'm right.'"

The automotive chemicals business was fully acquired in the mid-1970s and ultimately became part of Berkshire Hathaway. Berkshire sold it in 1996 to a group of investors that included a former president of the company.

THOUGH OTIS BOOTH WAS TOO CONCERNED about the risk to participate in Munger's final real estate ventures, he quite willingly put money into the new Wheeler, Munger partnership. "I became the largest participant, and I remained so."

When he initially went into Wheeler, Munger, Booth had some concerns about what he was doing. "I worried about partnership interests being just pieces of paper. I was taking them on trust. This guy was straight, but there was not a great deal of documentation. But I didn't think it was going to go south. I knew Charlie well enough."

Charlie's partners say he has a flair for structuring a company in the most effective form and for postponing the tax consequences as long as possible. When it came to Wheeler, Munger, Charlie borrowed a format from Warren that Warren had borrowed from Ben Graham.

"The structure of the Buffett and Munger partnerships was very important." explained Otis Booth. "At the end of each year profits were distributed, and ownership was reallocated. The reallocation was not a taxable event. Profits were given according to partnership interests at the previous year end. First 6 percent to capital, limited and general partners alike. After that, a huge majority share to capital and a much lower share to general partners. When there were taxes to pay, all partners bore their share according to their interests."

Buffett explained that Munger followed the fundamentals of value investing, though his portfolio was far less diversified than those established by the managers of traditional value funds, such as Buffett's friend and former co-worker at Graham-Newman, Walter Schloss.

"Charlie's portfolio was concentrated in very few securities and therefore his record was much more volatile but it was based on the same discount-from-value approach," said Buffett. "He was willing to accept greater peaks and valleys of performance, and he happens to be a fellow whose whole psyche goes toward concentration, with results shown."[2]

Some analysts might claim that Charlie was willing to assume more risk than Graham, Buffett, or Schloss would tolerate. "Yes," agreed Otis Booth, "but Charlie feels he has better insight and assessment of risk and he says 'Yes, I'll do that.' But Warren also bought stocks that were out of favor, such as American Express. The real risk was less than the perceived risk at the time."

As he became more and more experienced in business, Munger found small but reliable ways to make risk more tolerable.

"In no way was there a desire to run foolish risks as many gamblers do," explained Booth. "None of that. And particularly when we were younger and hungrier. He would look for each little edge you could get. The seat on the stock exchange. Ability to get an option on land where the zoning could be changed, whatever."

Charlie does not consider himself more daring than Buffett where investments are concerned. "Warren is very adventurous when it relates to his lifelong interest. When it has to do with Berkshire, he'll try new things. But when it comes to trying the leg of lamb versus the prime rib, he's not at all interested."

Molly Munger said during the time he was building his business, her father became acutely aware of the impact of taxes when capital gains were compared to ordinary income. "He made a lot of money in this or that deal and didn't have to pay as much in taxes. He said, 'If I'm a lawyer

I have to pay more. The capital gains tax is less, and in my case it doesn't seem fair.' "

DURING THOSE YEARS AT WHEELER, Munger, Charlie and Warren kept up the telephone conversations. Although they didn't always buy the exact same securities in the same quantities, their portfolios overlapped in part. They shared investment in two chains of retail stores owned through a company named Diversified Retailing. Together with Rick Guerin, they bought working control of Blue Chip Stamps. Buffett was the largest shareholder and Munger the next largest in the California retail trading stamp company.

"We were of a 'raiders' generation," observed Guerin. "That of Sol Steinberg, Harold Simmons, and so forth. But we are not like them." The group never made a tender offer without management's consent and never engaged in a proxy fight.

By the time he quit practicing law in 1965, "I had more confidence that Wheeler, Munger would work out, and I had much greater wealth," said Munger.

"I was not particularly surprised when he gave up law," said Munger's sister Carol. "That's what happens . . . when someone finds something that is his real love."

Munger was getting close to his dream of financial independence observed his stepson David Borthwick. "He needed to work for himself. Even with friendly partners in a law firm, you're still in service of clients who call on your time to fit their schedules."

In his book *The Big Test,* Nicholas Lemann said that Daniel DeFoe, not Benjamin Franklin, was behind Munger's lust to be his own man. When Charlie's grandparents read and reread *Robinson Crusoe* to him, they planted a notion in his head. "He wanted to be rich so he could be completely independent, like Crusoe on his island, and not have to do what anybody else said."[3]

IN AN ESSENTIAL WAY, HOWEVER, Charlie Munger remained in the service of clients—those clients being the other investors in Wheeler, Munger. The fact that many of the investors were family members, former colleagues, or friends did not ease the pressure. As fate would have it, during Wheeler, Munger's existence, while the stock market had ups and downs, the overall direction was sideways. By the late 1960s, Buffett was talking about getting out and eventually, at the end of 1969, did liquidate his partnership. Munger and Guerin stayed in longer, especially with a large investment that was made late in 1972, a registered investment company named Fund of Letters.

Bob Denham had arrived at Munger, Tolles, and part of his early work for Munger was the acquisition of the Fund of Letters. The stock market in the late part of the 1960s—the go-go years—had been torrid. A popular investment at the time was "letter stock," a security sold without SEC registration and therefore not saleable for an extended period of time in ordinary stock market transactions. Under the securities laws, it was necessary to put a rider on the stock saying that the investor was not allowed to sell until an SEC registration or some other key event had occurred.

The Fund of Letters was a venture capital fund that its founders had formed in a highly touted initial public offering allowing liberal sales' commissions to stockbrokers. When it was first organized, the fund raised $60 million, but when underwriting fees and other costs were subtracted, only $54 million remained for investment purposes.

"It was as if," said Charlie "the customers had asked their brokers 'What shall I do with my money?' and the brokers had responded: 'First, give 10 percent of it to me.'"

Because the Fund was a closed-end registered investment company, no new shares were sold once it was established. The Fund grew only if its money was invested wisely and its asset value increased. As typically is the case with a closed-end fund, the Fund of Letters soon traded well below its net asset value. Moreover, when the market went into a prolonged decline, the Fund tanked with it.

After Guerin and Munger bought control of the troubled Fund of Letters, they changed almost everything about it. They renamed it the New America Fund, reorganized the board, and redirected the investment style to a value approach. They quickly liquidated assets chosen by former managers. Guerin was the chairman, but Munger's investment philosophy was written all over the New America Fund and, as might be expected, the philosophy ran against the pack. In 1979, *Business Week* published an article entitled "Shareholder Heaven at New America Fund."

"New America eschews the common industry practice of paying fat fees to outside investment advisors," wrote *Business Week*. "Instead, the work is done internally under Guerin's supervision. What's more, the latest fiscal year, director's fees were only $25,000, and remuneration for all officers and directors came only to $54,950."[4]

New America Fund exhibited "a propensity for publishing and broadcasting investments," continued the article. "In recent years its record has been outstanding: The net asset value per share increased from $9.28 in October 1974, to $29.28 on September 30, 1979. Like most closed-end funds, New America sells at a discount to net asset value. On November 16, shares closed at $18.25, a 25.9 percent discount from net asset value of $24.64."[5]

Among New America Fund's holdings were Capital Cities Communications and 100 percent of the Daily Journal Corporation, publisher of a Los Angeles legal newspaper. Regardless of how wonderful New America Fund looked to *Business Week* in 1979, its purchase by Wheeler, Munger caused many sleepless nights.

In its first eight years, Wheeler, Munger had a stunning performance, although, said Munger, "We never did get a large amount of money under management. I never did manage a lot of other people's money on a compensated basis."

When the years 1962 to 1969 are measured together, Wheeler, Munger's average annual return, before the general partners' override, was 37.1 percent per annum which beat performance of the Dow Jones Average by a large margin. Then, in the three-year period ending with 1972, Wheeler, Munger's return dropped to only 13.9 percent, barely topping the Dow's 12.2 percent.

Discouraged by market conditions, Buffett liquidated his partnership at the end of 1969. Within a few years, Munger probably wished he'd followed suit. But Munger did not follow Buffett's example, and 1973 and 1974 were a nightmare. Wheeler, Munger was off 31.9 percent in 1973 (versus a negative 13.1 percent for the Dow Jones Industrial Average) and down 31.5 percent in 1974 (compared to a minus 23.1 percent for the Dow).

"We got drubbed by the 1973 to 1974 crash, not in terms of true underlying value, but by quoted market value, as our publicly traded securities had to be marked down to below half of what they were really worth," said Munger. "It was a tough stretch—1973 to 1974 was a very unpleasant stretch."

Others were also finding 1973 to 1974 unpleasant. For example, Berkshire Hathaway, still mostly a textile operation, saw its share price fall from $80 in December 1972 to $40 in December 1974. Gloom and doom permeated the news of Wall Street. Headlines proclaimed "The Death of Equities."[6]

The main cause of Wheeler, Munger's poor relative performance was its ownership of big blocks of common stock in New America Fund and Blue Chip Stamps. They had purchased New America's predecessor, the Fund of Letters, during a time of stock market exuberance at the end of 1972, paying $9.22 per share, substantially under liquidation value, for their controlling block. And even after the great stock market decline, as *Business Week* noted in October 1974, Fund shares had an asset value of $9.28, a little higher than Munger and Guerin had paid in 1972. So why Munger's agony? After all, Munger and Guerin had made a big investment at an unpropitious time but had dodged the natural consequences, mostly because of the "margin of safety" of the purchase as required by the principles of Benjamin Graham. Moreover, the Fund possessed a tax loss carryforward that would enable it to make large gains for many future years with no income taxes due.

Munger's distress was caused by the limited partnership structure, the fact that some borrowed money had been used in buying Fund stock, increasing declines in partnership net worth, and the fact that by 1974, Fund shares had a market price very much lower, indeed over 50 percent lower, than the asset value per share that could have been paid out in a Fund liquidation. Like it or not, Munger had to report results to his limited partners at the end of 1974 valuing the partnership's large block of Fund stock at only $3.75 per share.

In addition, Wheeler, Munger was in a similar position with respect to its substantial block of Blue Chip Stamps. This stock had been purchased at an average price of $7.50 per share, had a market price of $15.37 per share at the end of 1972, yet a market price of only $5.25 per share at the end of 1974. Munger believed that Blue Chip Stamps stock was virtually certain, "not too far ahead and regardless of what the stock market did, or whether any more trading stamps were sold," to reach a value much higher than $15.37 per share. Yet at the end of 1974, Munger faced a stubborn fact: the market price of Blue Chip Stamps stock was then only $5.25, intrinsic value be damned.

As Wheeler, Munger's investment numbers went to hell, Charlie realized that some partners would suffer hard-to-bear distress. After all, an investment of $1,000 on January 1, 1973, would have shrunk to $467 by January 1, 1975, if the partner had never taken any money out during the period. In contrast, a similar $1,000 investment that performed in line with the Dow Jones Industrial Average over the same period would have shrunk much less, leaving $668. Moreover, following precedents in the Graham and Buffett partnerships, all Wheeler, Munger partners drew cash from their partnership accounts at one half a percent per month on start-of-the-year value. Therefore, after regular monthly distributions were deducted, limited partners' accounts in 1973 to 1974 went down in value even more than 53 percent.

At the end of 1974, after the big stock market crunch, the net asset value of the entire Wheeler, Munger partnership was only $7 million. Of this, $4.3 million or 61 percent, was in 505,060 shares of Blue Chip Stamps, selling at $5.25 per share, plus 427,630 shares of New America Fund selling at $3.75 per share. Measured from this nadir, what was the subsequent price history of these two positions?

New America Fund stock did fine. By the late 1980s, each share that had traded at a $3.75 market value at the low point had turned into about $100 in cash and securities. The Blue Chip Stamps stock did much better, measured from the same low point. Each share of Blue Chip Stamps, then valued at $5.25 became 7.7 percent of one common share of Berkshire Hathaway. With Berkshire common stock selling in March 2000 at about $48,000 per share, this means a former Blue Chip Stamps share was then worth 7.7 percent of $48,000 or about $3,700 per share. Each dollar of 1974 market value thus became about $700 in year 2000 market value. This represents an increase of about 28.5 percent per annum, compounded, for 26 years, with no income taxes due for any shareholder who held on to the stock. Furthermore, because Blue Chip was held within a corporate structure, there was no fee from Munger and Buffett for management services.

"Over the course of Wheeler, Munger's first 13 years of life, ending with 1974, an investment mimicking performance of the Dow Jones Industrial Average, after counting all dividends received, would have produced a nominal return just above zero," explained Munger. After the ravages of taxes, inflation, and withdrawals of funds for use, the real return would have been embarrassingly negative. Wheeler, Munger, during its entire lifetime, did much better. Limited partners who stayed the course after 1973 to 1974 fared exceptionally well and 95 percent of the partners did stay the course. For instance, Otis Booth stood pat after 1973 to 1974, and stood pat again with securities distributed in Wheeler, Munger's liquidation at the end of 1975."

There was one major, galling exception. A new limited partner had put in $350,000 just before the 1973 to 1974 crash and panicked out at the bottom. For this partner more than half the funds vanished. Charlie could not talk the partner out of the decision to withdraw. "A lawyer is supposed to be an expert in persuasion, and I flunked a persuasion test that I think I should have passed," said Munger. "There was something in the mix of personalities, including a low pain threshold and a strong will in the limited partner, that somehow made me fail."

When dealing only with his own money, investment losses never bothered Munger much. To him it was like a losing night in a regular poker game where you knew you were one of the best players—you'd make up the difference later. But he now found that reported, temporary quotational losses in the Wheeler, Munger limited partnership accounts gave him tremendous pain. And so, by the end of 1974, he had resolved, like Buffett, to stop managing money for others in a limited partnership format. He would liquidate Wheeler, Munger after its asset value made a substantial recovery. And he would liquidate soon enough so that he would not take any general partner's override when the main investment positions were distributed.

In 1975, Wheeler, Munger did make an impressive recovery with a gain of 73.2 percent, and Munger and Marshall liquidated the partnership early in 1976. Even counting the dreadful times, during the 14 years Wheeler, Munger operated, the partnership turned in an average annual return of 24.3 percent before the general partners' override. (For a chart of the fund's performance, see page 251.)

"When the dust settled, my family had about $3 million from Wheeler, Munger and about $2 million more from real estate, and so on," said Munger. "It was a lot of money at that time, and it was a good time to have that much money. I owned wonderful securities, and other wonderful, bargain-priced securities were then available in the market."

When Wheeler, Munger was liquidated, the investors got securities in Blue Chip Stamps and Diversified Retailing, companies that later were folded into Berkshire Hathaway in stock swaps. Diversified Retailing, a company that was formed to buy one of the department store chains competing in the Baltimore metropolitan area, from the beginning had been mostly owned by the Buffett partnership, and by now was mostly owned by former members of the Buffett partnership. Wheeler, Munger owned 10 percent. The original purchase price was below the liquidating value of the business acquired, making it a classic Ben Graham type of play.

Diversified Retailing had borrowed about half the purchase price for the Baltimore acquisition, using a bank loan quickly replaced by long-term debentures that had almost no covenants limiting the borrower. Very soon thereafter, Buffett and Munger realized how intense Baltimore retailing competition was, and that they had made a mistake. They reversed course and sold the Baltimore department store chain for cash at almost no loss. The debentures were left in place offset by cash. Meanwhile Diversified Retailing had purchased for nearly nothing another chain of stores that threw off a profusion of cash. And so, during the great 1973 to 1974 stock market crash, Diversified Retailing had large amounts of investable assets, considerably more then twice what Buffett and Munger had paid for their original stockholdings. With stock prices at such a low level, it was a shopping spree in a bargain basement for

Buffett and Munger. "It has been a source of satisfaction to me for decades that such a poor start was turned into a large success," said Munger. And again, shareholders who stuck with them were rewarded.

"We didn't know Diversified Retailing would become Berkshire," said Otis Booth. "I gave some shares [of Diversified] to the Los Angeles Natural History Museum. Over the years I had to beat on them hard to keep them. They kept two-thirds of the Berkshire that came out of it. They once had 1800 shares of Berkshire; they're now down to 1200." Though he doesn't always prevail in his recommendations, Booth still serves on the board of the museum.

Booth ended up with a 1.4 percent stake in Berkshire Hathaway, a little less than Munger's 1.5 percent holding—making him one of the largest investors in the company.[7] Other members of Munger's inner circle also prospered. Ed Hoskins, Munger's original partner in the electronics manufacturing business invested in Wheeler, Munger, and as a result, eventually ended up with some Berkshire Hathaway stock, as did Guerin, Marshall, Tolles, and, of course, Munger himself.

"The money in Berkshire Hathaway stock outperformed the rest," said Munger. "Little else could compound that way. As late as 1974, it was trading for $40 per share on shares now [in June of 2000] trading for $60,000." At times, Berkshire's price has reached more the $90,000. Munger's own cost basis for his Berkshire shares is less than $40, because he acquired them by swapping for stock that was purchased at a much lower price.

AT THE TIME OF WHEELER, MUNGER'S liquidation, limited partners among other things, got stock in New America Fund, which Munger and Guerin continued to operate until 1986 when the fund also was liquidated completely. As a small part of the New America Fund final liquidation, shareholders received stock in the Daily Journal Corporation.

BY THE TIME THIS PHASE of their careers was over, Charlie and Al Marshall had worked side by side in the same office for about two decades. The real estate projects amounted to a major deal for a young lawyer with a big family, and Munger says having good partners like Marshall was crucial to their success. "They were big things to take on," recalled Munger. "Buying Blue Chip Stamps with Guerin and Buffett was a big thing. All my life, I had high grade partners, some of the very best that could ever be. Even now that he is so famous, people underrate how fine a partner Buffett is. Jack Wheeler was great, even though he drank too much. Al Marshall was wonderful—worked hard on projects, made a big partnership contribution in pushing so hard for the purchase of See's Candy. I never had any flannel-mouthed baloney in the operation. I dealt with quality people."

During the 20 or so years they worked together, Al Marshall found himself having to pull Charlie out of all kinds of social messes. Every once in a while, said Marshall, Munger would go on a talking spree, and gab so long and rapidly that nobody was able to interrupt or change the subject. One evening at a dinner party, the host cornered Al and begged him to go in the other room and get Charlie, who had consumed several glasses of wine, to shut up. "Nobody can get a word in edgewise. He's lecturing them on difficulties religions have in describing heaven, something he called a thousand-year orgasm."

On top of that, Munger didn't mind turning up the heat when Marshall got into a little hot water. When the Mungers and the Marshalls were vacationing together at Nancy's parent's home on Oahu, the two couples were shopping in a grocery store. Al and his wife Martha were standing side-by-side at the meat counter picking out steaks for dinner when Martha Marshall stepped away to look at something else. Al didn't realize she was gone, and reached out and grabbed the rear end of some other woman. Al was startled to learn the buttocks were not those of his wife, and the victim was furious. Munger, who was at the other end of the meat counter shouted out, "You know, he does that to all the women." Charlie's comment only made the woman angrier.

Despite the jokes, Marshall said he learned a lot during the decades he worked with Munger. "I learned to make money," Marshall said. But additionally he came to believe that "Hard work, honesty, if you keep at it, will get you almost anything."

WHILE MUNGER WAS GOING THROUGH this period of enormous change, expansion, and development, his family sometimes were in a quandary when they tried to describe what Charlie did for a living. Molly Munger had trouble explaining her father to her friend Alice Ballard, a Philadelphia blue-blood and debutante. Alice had scored 800 on the verbal portion of the SAT and like Molly, attended Harvard Law School. To a California girl, Alice seemed worth impressing, but Charlie was of no help.

"My college roommate's father was a partner in an old-line Philadelphia firm. She was descended from William Penn. Charlie called on Fred

Ballard (Alice's father), who later said, 'I have no idea who [Munger] is from what he said of himself. He could be working for the CIA.' Daddy made no coherent explanation of himself. He had this ratty little office in the stock exchange. What did he do—working in a ratty little office? And a fledgling law firm—he bought odd companies like K&W—the automotive chemicals company." Nevertheless, Molly's faith in her father was unshaken. "It didn't matter to me. It seemed like, 'You just don't know him. If you don't know it now, you'll know it later. He's fabulous.' "

CHAPTER TEN

BLUE CHIP STAMPS

I've accused Father of being negative. He has a buoyant, cheerful upside, but also a negative side. He said, "No, no, I'm not negative. I jump like a little trout if it's a good idea." His hand went up in the air.

Molly Munger

C HARLES MUNGER, JR. KNEW SOMETHING was afoot in Munger's financial life when his father came to him to discuss a math problem. Charles, Jr. was studying to be a physicist and his math skills were advanced. The exercise involved a California company called Blue Chip Stamps, which had a pool of reserve funds to meet the obligation of redeeming stamps in the years ahead. It had a float account, similar to those used by insurance companies, to hold premiums for covering probable future losses—an account that is invested with investment returns accruing to the company. Each year a predictable number of Blue Chip Stamps were redeemed, causing a decline in funds, which in turn was offset by the proceeds of issuing stamps. What Munger really wanted to know was how fast Blue Chip's investable funds would decline under various scenarios.

Blue Chip Stamps had been in the news because of a dispute it had with a group mom and pop retailers who wanted to participate as owners of the company alongside big retailers who had founded it. At the time Rick Guerin was just recovering from his losses in the company sold to him by Jack Wheeler.

"Three years later, I got my capital back together, which was next to nothing, and Charlie and I talked a lot about investment ideas," said Guerin. "I'd read about Blue Chip Stamps in the newspaper, and I had an idea," Charlie said, 'I'll take you to my friend who knows more about float than anyone.' "

When Guerin was introduced to Warren Buffett, Rick realized, as he had when he first met Munger, that he was talking to someone exceptional. Rick was pleased when Buffett immediately saw the same potential value of Blue Chip's float that he had seen. Just by investing the float alone, the company could amount to something. Buffett, Munger, and Guerin slowly began accumulating shares, with Buffett buying the stock both for his personal account and for the Buffett Partnership.

Tracing the story of Blue Chip Stamps from its inception to the present is confusing, but it is central to understanding how Munger, Buffett, and Guerin became so rich, and how Berkshire Hathaway evolved into the company it is today. Blue Chip became the vehicle through which See's Candy, the *Buffalo News,* and Wesco Financial were acquired, and these three companies later became essential to the cultural and financial foundation of Berkshire.

First, the history: An early precursor to frequent flyer miles in the 1950s and 1960s, trading stamps, such as Green Stamps, Blue and Gold, and Blue Chip, were handed out as a customer incentive by merchants. Retailers deposited money at Blue Chip in return for their stamps, then the money was used to operate the stamp company and to purchase the merchandise handed out when stamps were redeemed. Shoppers were given a certain number of stamps for each dollar spent in a store, which they pasted into books, then redeemed for prizes such as toddler toys, toasters, mixing bowls, watches, and other items. Because it took time to accumulate enough stamps to redeem merchandise—and because some customers tossed the stamps in the back of a drawer, forgot them, and never did redeem them—the float built up. By the early 1970s, Blue Chip's sales amounted to approximately $120 million per year (around $400 million, in today's dollars). Its float at the time was nearly $100 million.

Stamps were popular with housewives and with merchants, who liked the increased sales and profits. One of the first trading stamp companies was S&H Green Stamps, but according to S&H's rules, only one type of retailer—a single grocery store, gasoline station, or drugstore—in each area could offer S&H stamps. A group of nine retailers, including Chevron Oil, Thrifty Drugs, and important California grocery chains, wanted the same competitive advantage, so they got together in 1956 and created Blue Chip Stamp Company. The Company was controlled by the nine retailers who organized it. Other store owners were allowed to offer the stamps, but they had no say in how the business was run nor did they share in the profits. Blue Chip became by far the largest trading stamp company in California and was so successful that eventually it faced a law suit from the small retailers who thought they weren't getting a fair shake from the founders. They claimed that the founding owners had violated antitrust laws by not providing ownership rights to small merchants.

In December 1963, the Department of Justice filed an antitrust action against Blue Chip Stamp and the nine founding shareholders. After four years in court, a consent decree was entered in June 1967, calling for a complete reorganization of the company so that the founders could no longer exert complete control. Blue Chip Stamp Company then added an "s" to its name and became Blue Chip Stamps.

Under the court's decree, Blue Chip was required to offer approximately 621,600 shares of its common stock to the smaller, retail users of the stamps who previously were not shareholders. The shares were issued on a pro rata basis determined by the quantity of stamps given out by each of the nonstockholding retailers during a designated period. The offering consisted of three shares of common stock and a $100 debenture for a cash payment of $101. Any of the 621,600 shares not purchased by the nonstockholder users were to be sold on the open market. This new stock part of the offering amounted to 55 percent of the common stock of the company. To provide liquidity for old and new shareholders, the new Blue Chip shares were traded over-the-counter.

"Thousands of little retailers ended up with Blue Chip stock," said Buffett, and a market was born for the shares. "We saw this as a very cheap stock and bought aggressively. Charlie, Rick, and I ended up controlling Blue Chip."

They acquired their shares separately. "I started with $80,000," said Guerin, and built from there. Munger's investment matched Guerin's fairly closely.

"At Blue Chip Stamps, we finally took over the company. It was a friendly, gradual kind of takeover, but we took it over," said Munger.

By the early 1970s, Buffett's various entities had become Blue Chip's largest stockholder, Munger was the second largest and Guerin was somewhere behind. The three had accumulated enough shares to warrant positions on Blue Chip's board of directors.

"Blue Chip had an 'old boys' board, some of whom resisted new guys, especially these smart-alecky young guys," said Guerin. "Charlie went on the board first, then convinced them they should accept me, and finally Warren was accepted."

Soon, their shareholdings in Blue Chip became densely tangled. In 1971, Warren and Susan Buffett personally owned 13 percent; Berkshire Hathaway Inc., of which the Buffetts were 36 percent owners, held 17 percent, and Diversified Retailing Co. Inc., of which the Buffetts owned

42 percent, held 16 percent. In addition, Diversified Retailing owned shares in Berkshire, and Munger's partnership owned 10 percent of Diversified Retailing, plus 8 percent of Blue Chip. Guerin's partnership also owned 5 percent of Blue Chip. Eventually, after more purchases of Blue Chip stock, the liquidation of Wheeler, Munger, and the merger of Diversified Retailing into Berkshire, Berkshire's ownership reached 60 percent. Together Berkshire, Buffett, and Munger owned nearly 75 percent of the outstanding shares of Blue Chip.

For some years, trading stamps continued to be Blue Chip's main business. In 1970, Blue Chip sales peaked at more than $124 million, but soon the popularity of trading stamps waned, and by 1982 sales plummeted down to $9 million. Sales amounted to only $200,000 a year by the late 1990s when Blue Chip's trading stamps were primarily issued by a few bowling alleys.

Buffett and Munger gained control of the investment committee once they were board members, and so during the time that trading stamps were slipping from favor, the investment committee was at work building the value of Blue Chip's float.

Among the investments that Buffett and Munger acquired through Blue Chip was the largest block of troubled Source Capital, a closed-end investment company established in 1968 by the infamous "Go-Go" manager Fred Carr. Carr was a phenomenon for a while, but soon was discredited by the choppy stock market of the early 1970s. When Carr quit Source Capital, the fund had $18 per share in asset value, but was trading for $9. It was a situation much like that at the Fund of Letters, except that after Carr left, portfolio managers at Source Capital had considerable talent and a mind-set similar to that of Munger and Buffett. Blue Chip acquired 20 percent of the fund and Munger went on the board where he got along well with the main portfolio managers. Source Capital remained an independent company and is stilled listed on the New York Stock Exchange. Munger and Buffett referred a lot of management clients to Source Capital in subsequent years.

Most of Buffett's and Munger's acquisition attempts went smoothly, but they did not get all the properties they sought to acquire. In 1971, Blue Chip was outbid in an attempt to buy the *Cincinnati Enquirer.* The *Enquirer* at the time had a daily circulation of 190,000 and a Sunday circulation of 300,000. E.W. Scripps Co. was being forced to sell the newspaper to settle a U.S. Justice Department case charging it with having an illegal monopoly in the Cincinnati market. Blue Chip offered Scripps and its affiliate, Scripps-Howard, $29.2 million for the newspaper but was turned down. The *Enquirer* is now owned by the Gannett Company.

By 1980, Blue Chip had five areas of business: the remainder of its trading stamp business, See's Candy Shops, Wesco Financial, the *Buffalo Evening News,* and Precision Steel.

Along the way an uncomfortable incident involving Blue Chip's acquisition of Wesco Financial. The reaction of the Securities Exchange Commission caused Buffett and Munger to re-evaluate the way they were conducting their business.

The story began in the summer of 1972 when a broker offered Buffett and Munger a block of Wesco Financial, the parent company of Pasadena-based Mutual Savings and Loan Association. Wesco's stock was trading in the low teens, less than half its book value. Buffett and Munger agreed that it was a bargain, and through Blue Chip, acquired 8 percent of Wesco's shares. Even that early in its history, a $2 million stake was a relatively minor investment for Blue Chip.

Then in January 1973, Wesco's management announced plans to merge with another savings and loan, Financial Corp. of Santa Barbara. Buffett and Munger felt that Wesco was selling itself at a fire sale price. The deal called for Wesco shareholders to swap their undervalued shares for those of overvalued Financial Corp. Munger and Buffett didn't think the deal was a good one for shareholders on the Wesco side.

Said Buffett: "I read these terms, and I didn't believe them. And I told Munger the terms and he couldn't believe it either. But it was there in black and white on the Dow Jones tape."

Munger wanted to buy more Wesco stock to fight off the merger, but Buffett did not. Charlie prevailed, and for six weeks, Blue Chip bought every Wesco share it could find, accumulating about 17 percent of the company. They couldn't buy more than 20 percent without regulatory approval and that would take a long time to obtain.

Munger called on Louis R. Vincenti, Wesco's president, to inquire about his reaction to the existence of a large unhappy shareholder. Without being acrimonious, Vincenti said that Blue Chip was free to vote against the merger if it wished and to solicit other shareholders to do the same, but the outcome would be determined by shareholders, not Vincenti. This was the kind of straight talk Munger liked. He immediately developed an admiration for Vincenti, and Buffett soon did the same.

For shareholders to vote the merger down, Munger and Buffett would have to persuade Elizabeth Peters, a San Francisco heiress who owned a Napa Valley vineyard, and her brothers, to go along with them. Peters' father had founded the S&L and took it public in the 1950s and the Peters still owned a large block of shares. Elizabeth Peters hoped that the Financial Corp. merger would inflate Wesco's flagging share price. Donald Koeppel, Blue Chip's president, tried to persuade Betty Peters to change her mind, and when he failed, Buffett gave it a try.

"I flew out and talked to her—out and back in one day—we talked in the American Airlines lounge at the San Francisco airport," said Buffett.

Peters insisted that something had to be done to improve the S&L's performance, and Buffett said he'd like to try it himself. She was impressed with his self-confidence, but asked a question that would be posed again and again as Berkshire grew.

"Mr. Buffett, if I buy you, what happens if you get hit by a truck at the intersection? Who would save Wesco then?" Buffett assured her that Charlie Munger was waiting in the wings.[1]

Warren persuaded Peters to vote against the merger and to ride along with her family's Wesco shares, remaining as a Wesco director on a board that Munger would join. This turned out well for Peters, since Financial Corp. went bust and Wesco prospered mightily with the help of Buffett and Munger aboard.

After squelching the merger, Munger and Buffett could legally buy only another 3 percent of Wesco's outstanding stock and they set out to do so. They had been paying about $17 per share right up to the time the merger was cancelled. They knew that Wesco stock was sure to decline in the short term. Nonetheless, they offered $17 per share, thinking it only fair since it was they who had interrupted the merger. "We decided in some quixotic moment that it was the right way to behave," said Munger.[2]

After some period of time passed and the regulatory hurdles were leaped, Blue Chip made several subsequent tender offers, and eventually raised its Wesco stake to 24.9 percent. By mid-1974, Blue Chip owned the majority of Wesco shares. Munger and Buffett would have acquired more Wesco shares, but stopped at 80 percent at the request of Peters, who remains a large minority shareholder.[3] Buffett lets Peters set Wesco's divided policy and she increases the payout slightly every year.

All through this, however, the SEC for some reason had been tracking the activities of Buffett and Munger and had some questions about the Wesco deal.

"I've always suspected that someone who wanted the Financial Corp. merger to go through complained to the SEC," said Munger. And yet, he admitted, the convoluted ownership at Blue Chip did appear suspicious.

"When the SEC started looking, there were all these criss-crossed ownerships. That happened by accident. But it was complicated and because so many people create complications to hide fraud, the SEC delved and delved and finally fixed its attention on something—how we got Wesco. People assume if what you're doing is enormously complicated, you're probably doing something wrong."

Indeed, Buffett, Munger, and to some extent Guerin, owned stakes in an incredibly intertwined bundle of companies. The three men's investments had grown this way and that, taking whatever structure seemed logical and fair at the time. The organization was a little too disorganized for the tastes of the SEC. But there also was a legal question.

The SEC's concern was whether Blue Chip had unlawfully manipulated the stock of Wesco in some way. The SEC rightly concluded that Munger and Buffett bought shares at an obviously higher-than-necessary price, and suspected some sort of preemptive motive, rather than a benevolent one. Buffett responded to the inquiries by shipping three cartons of documents, memos, stock transfer documents, and so on to Washington. Buffett reacted calmly; Munger, on the other hand, was impatient.

The SEC investigation became an impediment to Blue Chip's everyday business, and in the fall of 1974, Munger wrote to his attorney, Chuck Rickershauser, "I hope the foregoing will satisfy everyone at the SEC and that, if not, you can arrange that I receive the promptest possible response, preferably by direct telephone calls to me, so that we can clear up any problems and get our merger consummated."[4]

Instead, the SEC opened a full-scale investigation of Buffett's investment practices: *In the Matter of Blue Chip Stamps, Berkshire Hathaway Inc., Warren Buffet* [sic], HQ-784.

"Blue Chip, Berkshire, Buffet [sic], singly or in concert with others . . . may have engaged in acts which may have directly or indirectly operated as a device, scheme, or artifice to defraud; or included in an untrue state of material of fact or omitted . . ."[5]

In the meantime, the Washington DC rumor mill churned with the news that Munger's former law partner, Rod Hills, had been offered the job of SEC chairman. Rickershauser, who also was acting as Buffett's lawyer, called Hills and asked him to reject the job offer, claiming that if he took the post, the SEC might feel compelled treat the Blue Chip case more harshly just to make sure there was no suggestion of favoritism. According to some reports, Munger called Hills several times and berated him for not standing by his friends, but Hills said that Munger never called him about the matter. They never discussed it at the time or later. At any rate, Hills dismissed Rickershauser's request as inappropriate and accepted the job anyway.

The SEC did not stop its probe with Wesco. It extended the investigation to Source Capital, and when Buffett and Munger realized that their financial relationship had become so complex that it was difficult to explain it to the SEC, they decided to restructure their holdings and simplify matters. Charlie already had closed down Wheeler, Munger and assumed the chairmanship of Blue Chip at a salary of $50,000 per year.

Buffett had closed his partnership and had turned his attention to Berkshire Hathaway.

In 1975, Munger testified before the SEC about the Blue Chip case, doing his best to convince regulators that he and Buffett only intended to play fair when they offered the higher-than-necessary share price after the Financial Corp. merger blew up. The SEC countered that it was a corporate investor's job to make a profit for its shareholders, not favor anonymous sellers on a stock exchange. Munger explained, with little effect, that he and Buffett hoped that conduct demonstrating fairness would enhance Blue Chip's reputation and this ultimately would benefit all shareholders. Munger and Buffett particularly hoped to make a good impression on Lou Vincenti, whom they wanted to stay on at his old job as CEO, which he did for many years. Such considerations got no favorable reaction from the SEC.

Following a standard practice, the SEC filed and concurrently settled a lawsuit against Blue Chip, charging that the company had purchased Wesco not just as an investment, but to defeat the merger. It also asserted that Blue Chip artificially propped up Wesco's share price for several weeks after the merger collapsed. Without admitting or denying guilt, Buffett and Munger agreed not to make the same mistake again. Blue Chip was required to give more than $115,000 to Wesco shareholders whom the SEC decided had been damaged by the business practices.

It was a stressful time, but as a result, Berkshire Hathaway became a larger, simpler company. In the reorganization that followed, Blue Chip Stamps sold its interest in Source Capital, which by then had doubled in value. Wesco, for tax purposes, was consolidated with Blue Chip Stamps as its ownership proportion reached 80 percent. Both Diversified Retailing and Blue Chip were merged into Berkshire, finally giving Munger a formal position at Berkshire. Munger got 2 percent of the stock of Berkshire and was named vice chairman, keeping his old salary of $50,000.

Bob Denham, who worked on some of these legal maneuvers, said the organization of the company under a single corporation eliminated almost all appearance of conflict of interest. Before they were merged, Blue Chip and Berkshire had different shareholders, and when a true bargain investment came along, the possibility might exist that Buffett would allocate the bargain to one group of shareholders at the expense of the other. That could no longer happen.

Until the merger, Blue Chip shareholders were sent their own annual report with a message written by Munger. When the merger took place, Buffett and Munger together wrote a letter to shareholders: "It will be somewhat simpler for us to run a combined enterprise, reducing some costs. Also, simplicity has a way of improving performance through enabling us better to understand what we are doing."[6]

By the time Berkshire and Blue Chip merged, Berkshire held 60 percent of Blue Chip stock. On July 28, 1983, Berkshire acquired the 40 percent interest that it did not already own. Each outstanding Blue Chip Stamps share was exchanged for .077 of a share of Berkshire.[7]

The combined assets of the merged companies amounted to $1.6 billion. Shareholders met at Omaha's former Red Lion Inn to approve the new corporate structure. Warren and Susan Buffett held enough shares to enact the merger on their own, but told other shareholders they would vote for the merger only if it were approved by a majority of the remaining shareholders.[8]

Years later, Munger said the merger was the right thing to do. "It is so much less complicated now. Since then we have one of the simplest structures there is. At a high level, it's one big company, Berkshire Hathaway. But way down in the organization, there is still some complexity. Some of our companies are owned 100 percent, some 80 percent, and some positions merely involve big blocks of stock."

What Charlie finds interesting when thinking back about all this progress is how few big business decisions were involved in creating billions of dollars out of less than $40 million, fewer than one every three years. "I think the record shows the advantage of a peculiar mind-set—not seeking action for its own sake, but instead combining extreme patience with extreme decisiveness."

Munger's stepson Hal Borthwick gives Charlie enormous credit for helping to work out Blue Chips' various problems. "Charlie made really tough calls in the early days. Those guys were still cigar butt investors. They were, you know, looking for assets on the cheap. And Charlie helped solve those problems."

"WE BEGAN THE 1970s WITH a single business, trading stamps, which was destined to decline to a small fraction of its former size, and a portfolio of securities, offsetting stamp redemption liabilities, which had been selected by previous owners and would have led to a disastrous result if held through to the present time," Munger wrote to shareholders in 1981.

As for the original business of Blue Chip Stamps: "I presided over a reduction in trading stamp sales from over $120 million down to less than $100,000. So I presided over a failure of 99.99 percent," said Munger. "Even so, the company did wonderfully with the capital we invested elsewhere. But in terms of the trading stamp company, I laid an egg. So did everyone else. There is no big trading stamp company left in the United States."[9]

"But we had no expectation that the trading stamp business was a big winner—as it turned out it went bloo-ey. Meantime, we bought See's, *Buffalo News,* and Wesco and made successful investments in marketable securities with the float and other capital. The money compounded like crazy," said Munger.

In 1972, Blue Chip's balance sheet net worth was about $46 million; By the end of 1981, net worth had increased to about $169 million, up 267 percent in 10 years. Return on shareholders investment in the company for the 10 years was 15 percent per year.

Later, the gains were larger, according to Munger. If Blue Chip had remained a separate company, it would be a powerhouse today. Its former operating subsidiaries now earn over $150 million pretax. Moreover, Wesco has more than $2 billion in marketable securities, and by now Blue Chip, on its own, would have owned much more.

Though it is buried deep in the filing cabinets of Berkshire Hathaway, Blue Chip remains an intact company. When people dig into the back of their kitchen drawers or open their deceased mother's trunk and find books of Blue Chip Stamps, they can be redeemed.

"Most trading stamp companies just disappeared. Blue Chip still exists, a minuscule stamp business—redeeming stamps issued in 1961 and 1962," explained Buffett. "The numbers say they were issued 30-odd years ago. We keep this little redemption company. We've got a good looking catalog. We offer the same value we did 25 years ago."

He and Munger are determined that the Blue Chip office will remain open as long as they believe that some significant number of unredeemed stamps are going to turn up. It also tickles them that Berkshire Hathaway became a great investment for the small retailers who fought for a piece of the company.

"Years ago, before Warren and I bought our stock, Blue Chip Stamps mailed minor amounts of Blue Chip stock out to filling station operators as a litigation settlement in the antitrust case brought against the founders by small merchants," said Munger. "My wife told the guy who owns the automobile repair shop where she takes her car to hold onto it. Well, the other day when she stepped out of her car he hugged and kissed her. So maybe we should buy into another dying business."[10]

THE SECURITIES AND EXCHANGE COMMISSION was finally placated, but Berkshire's problems with Blue Chip were not yet fully resolved. The remaining

issue involved some of those filling station and other small business owners who were issued shares in the 1970s. Some 20 years later, a tiny group
of shareholders who had forgotten about or lost track of their stock realized they'd missed out on an important event.

The shareholders claimed that their stocks were lost in transfer agent
records and that they were unaware that they were now holders of Berkshire shares. Under state laws, after a certain amount of time such shares
are escheated, or turned over to the state for care taking, which Berkshire's transfer agent did. In some cases, the states were still holding the
shares, which in the meantime had increased in value almost a hundred-
fold. In other cases, the states sold the Berkshire shares and held the
money in the name of the original Blue Chip shareholder.

In 1993, legislation was passed in California permitting the state to
save escheating costs by selling the stock it held as unclaimed property.
The state then placed the funds in numbered accounts to hold in trust for
future claimants. In November 1995, the State of California sold all Berkshire stock it held at $31,177.77 per share. By the time the misplaced Blue
Chip shareholders learned what happened (with the help of a bounty
hunter) and filed suit, Berkshire was selling at $37,950 per share.[11]

The New York and San Diego law firm of Milberg, Weiss, Bershad,
Hynes & Lerach, which is well known for handling shareholder class action lawsuits, sued Berkshire for failing to make enough effort to find 400
early Blue Chip Stamps shareholders to let them know that they now
owned Berkshire shares. They wanted shareholders to be compensated
for the growth they'd missed out on after the state sold their shares.

"The issue is, they should've dropped me a note and let me know,"
said plaintiff John E. DeWitt, 61, who owned gasoline stations and delivered petroleum products in South El Monte, California. "We've been located in the same spot since 1972."[12]

Although they were not listed as defendants, Munger, along with
Warren Buffett and his wife Susan, were named in the complaint.

"There is no truth to the stories that little retailers were taken advantage of," said Buffett, claiming that in some cases the shareholders simply
ignored their mail. In the end, "People got their money. They are just mad
because the state sold the Berkshire shares. We've found Berkshire holders from the 1930s. They are millionaires now."

The court threw out the shareholders suit, saying that the statute of
limitations had expired on their action. If the suit had run its full course,
Berkshire may have had no liability anyway. Some stocks were "lost" long
before Berkshire bought Blue Chip, and at any rate, due process had been
followed for unclaimed shares.[13]

"Some shareholders are always going to get 'lost,' meaning out of contact with the corporate transfer agent. The inevitability of that outcome is why all advanced commercial nations have escheat laws," says Munger. "And Berkshire works harder than most corporations in pushing transfer agents to find lost shareholders."

As IMPLIED EARLIER, THE RELATIONSHIP between Buffett, Munger, and Vincenti, chief executive officer of Wesco, worked out just as Buffett and Munger had hoped. Vincenti, one of Pasadena's best business lawyers, had become CEO of his best client. "He was brilliant, principled, decisive, and parsimonious," said Munger. "And he stayed on as CEO for many years, loving the business. Finally he got Alzheimer's disease. By that time we liked him so much that we kept him coming in as CEO until he could no longer function. Betty Peters cheerfully joined in this unusual decision."

AMONG THE SHAREHOLDERS BERKSHIRE inherited from Blue Chip was legendary investor Philip L. Carret. Carret had owned Blue Chip shares since 1968 and converted to Berkshire at about $400 per share. Carret had been involved in portfolio management for 78 years. He founded one of the first and most successful mutual funds, the Pioneer Fund, which operated through all sorts of economic conditions from 1928 until 1983. The annual total return for the Pioneer Fund in that period averaged 13 percent, compared with 9 percent for the S&P 500.

Born in 1896, Phil Carret died May 28, 1998, at age 101. Just a year earlier he'd attended the Berkshire Hathaway annual meeting in Omaha and although he was confined to a wheelchair, Carret spent much of the day chatting with other shareholders. Carret worked until two weeks before his death and was sharp of mind until the end.

FROM THE TIME THEY STARTED buying Blue Chip until the time it was merged into Berkshire, Buffett and Munger slowly but surely cemented their partnership. There never had been a written contract covering the terms of their work together. Rather, Munger and Buffett simply went forward on trust.

"To those of us who became lawyers," said Wendy Munger, "the lesson of his business life is that you don't want to do business with people you can't trust. The economics are irrelevant if you don't have trust. Most people are just thinking about the economics, thinking that the contract will save you when entering into a transaction with someone you can't trust. You *must* do business with high-grade people—that's all he will deal with."

Charlie also puts it this way: "Never wrestle with a pig because if you do you'll both get dirty, but the pig will enjoy it."

CHAPTER ELEVEN

SEE'S CANDY TEACHES A LESSON

Generally, I'm not in favor of a social system that throws huge rewards to people who don't improve the factories, don't invent better systems, and so forth. Of course, you can argue that I'm condemning myself. All I can say is it's almost intentional.

Charlie Munger

THE MUNGER FAMILY MEMBERS WERE having their first dinner together in the new "great hall" at their Star Island retreat. A cooperative design effort among the adult children, the communal gathering room had been generously funded by their father. As the Munger clan had grown, collecting spouses and grandchildren, it was increasingly troublesome to find one space where everyone could get together for dinner, or to play games, or to simply sprawl around a fireplace and gab. This lodge room will do the job. An open-beamed ceiling rises above a massive, fieldstone fireplace. A full-sized pool table at one side of the room already is surrounded by teenagers. There are two long banqueting tables for grown-ups, and a small dinner table for the younger children. As happens most evenings, the teenaged Mungers have decided to dine together—elsewhere—and have set up their own party on a picnic table near the end of one of the Munger boat docks. It's cool out over the lake and there are fewer bugs and no parents.

Back in the lodge room, there are toasts to the new addition, all-around thank yous to the people who collaborated by fax, e-mail, and ordinary telephone to plan this expansive, woodsy room, the small kitchen, and a second small dining/workroom. A meal of mixed grill, fresh creamed corn, risotto, and salad is served from a buffet. Ice cream is the dessert. Most people hold their hands over the top of their wine glasses to keep the insects out, but those who don't are treated to a mouthful of gnats. No matter. Everyone's chattering and having fun.

Molly Munger, who is seated next to her father, turns to him and quietly thanks him for providing the wherewithal for the family gathering, and especially for this wonderful great hall. Charlie stares straight ahead, not responding to her comment, not blinking.

"Did you hear me, Daddy?" Molly asks persistently, quietly. "Yes," he murmurs, continuing to stare straight ahead.

Suddenly one of the Munger children appears with a box of See's Candy, taken from a case that had been shipped from the factory in advance of the family's arrival. The guests begin poking around, looking for their favorite cream center or caramel, stopping just short of sticking a finger in to see what the filling might be. The Mungers and their guests are too polite for that, but some are tempted. Nancy Munger speaks to her husband from the opposite end of the table, "Charlie," she calls. "Charlie! He never listens to me," Nancy complains to her dinner partner. "Charlie, Charlie," she calls louder. "Tell the story about the pipes." She gets his attention. "The pipes at the See's factory."

Now he's online and proceeds to recount an episode when See's hired a new employee experienced in candy-making and took him to review the kitchen where the candy is cooked. "The employee spent some time looking around, then puzzled, asked a manager where the water pipes were. The guy could only find two pipes, one marked 'cream' and the other marked 'whipping cream.' He was *amazed* to learn that they don't use any water when making See's, so there were no water pipes."

When See's Candy celebrated its seventy-fifth anniversary at a luncheon in Los Angeles, the crowd had surprise visitors. A man in a white jumpsuit, wearing goggles and an antique leather helmet, drove onto the stage astride See's 1920's trademark black-and-white, restored Harley Davidson motorcycle with its matching delivery sidecar. The driver hopped off the motorcycle, flung off his hat, and ripped off the jumpsuit. At the same time, a figure rolled out of the back door of the sidecar. There, before a laughing audience stood the driver, Warren Buffett, and his passenger, Charlie Munger.

"I particularly enjoyed coming here today," Munger told the assembled employees, suppliers, and customers. "It gave me the chance to look a lot spryer than I really am. If you coil a guy up like a spring and put him in a narrow receptacle, he will pop out like a kid. While I was in that receptacle, I thought of my favorite business analogy—the mouse who says 'let me out of the trap, I've decided I don't want the cheese.' There are a million business traps. You can get sloppy, you can get alcoholic, you can get megalomania, you can not understand your own limitations. There are a million ways to gum it up. To survive and prosper as long as this company has—started by a woman who was 71 [years old], that I really like. And it's an amazing example. See's has stayed out of a lot of traps."

"The ordinary candy company puts in too many stores," Charlie continued. "You have this huge overhead you're carrying through July and August, and you just can't get well at Christmas. But See's has always had the discipline of knowing their own business. That's harder on the employees, by the way. They have this huge crunch in the stores at Christmas, but it's part of the secret of See's.

"And of course the fanaticism about the quality of the product and service is the heart and soul of the business. I love the fact that this room is full of long time customers and long time suppliers. You get suppliers who are good and who are trusted because they deserve trust, and you behave the same way toward your own customer, then you are a little part of a civilization that is a seamless web of deserved trust. This is the way the world ought to work. It is a better example for everyone else. It is the right way to build up a state or a civilization. It was just marvelous for us to become associated relatively early in our business careers with a culture that was so fundamentally sound. It is Ben Franklin (or his business philosophy) all over again, alive and well at See's after all these years."[1]

Summer is the slowest season for candy-makers, since there are no candy-centric holidays. At the La Cienega Boulevard factory in Los Angeles, the summer staff shrinks to around 110. During the Christmas to Easter season, the staff swells to 275 or more.

The summer candy-makers are the long-termers, the lifers, and many are Hispanic. See's prides itself on a sense of family that allows mother, daughter and granddaughter, husbands and wives, brothers and sisters, to work side by side. The southern plant makes about 40 percent of the candy, concentrating most on those with hard centers. The remaining sweets are made in the South San Francisco plant. Factory workers are paid hourly wages and receive full health benefits as negotiated by their union, the Bakery and Confectionary Workers Union. Hundreds of See's workers have been with the company 15 years or more. At the Los Angeles factory's 1999 awards banquet, 21 workers were recognized for service ranging from 30 to 50 years.[2]

See's Candy—with its motto "quality without compromise"—represents more to Munger than an after-dinner delicacy. The acquisition of See's Candy was among the earliest deals that he and Warren Buffett did together and it was one of the first companies they purchased outright. But most important, the experience of See's taught Charlie and Warren a lesson that caused a major improvement to their investment style.

In 1972, using the float of Blue Chip Stamps, Buffett and Munger acquired the small Los Angeles-based See's Candy for $25 million. It was a major step for Charlie and Warren because it was their biggest purchase up to that time.

It was big news in California, where See's black-and-white candy shops are part of the local culture. A 16-year-old Cher was working at See's when she met Sonny Bono and left her job to move in with him as his housekeeper.

Mary See was 71 when she opened a small, Los Angeles neighborhood candy shop in 1921, although she had the help of her son Charles.[3]

Charles A. See had been a pharmacist in Canada, but changed careers after his two pharmacies were destroyed when a forest fire swept through the town where he did business. He took up work as a chocolate salesman and dreamed of starting his own candy company, using recipes developed by his mother. In 1921, he moved his family, including his widowed mother, Mary, from Canada to Pasadena, the beautiful and refined Los Angeles suburb that Charlie would later adopt as home. During the 1920s, Los Angeles was a booming city of 500,000 residents. It wasn't an easy go for the Sees, since there were hundreds of competitors. See and his partner, James W. Reed, decided to concentrate on building a reputation with a high-quality product.

When the stock market crashed in 1929 and the Great Depression hit, See was forced to cut the price of a pound of candy from 80 cents to 50 cents. He survived by persuading landlords to reduce his rents, arguing that lower rent was better than no rent. But he also saw an opportunity to expand his markets as other candy-makers went bankrupt. A second crisis came during World War II when sugar was severely rationed. Rather than compromise quality with inferior ingredients or altered recipes, See's decided to produce as much high quality candy as possible with the ingredients that were allocated to the company, and no more. Customers lined up around the block to buy the limited supply of chocolates, and once the supply was gone, the shop closed for the day. No matter what time the store closed, the sales staff was paid for a full day of work. This turned out to be a smart marketing ploy, since the waiting crowds added to the candy stores caché.

See's was already 30 years old when Charles Huggins joined the company in 1951. The head office was then in Los Angeles, but Huggins started in the San Francisco facility.

Huggins first saw San Francisco when he took furlough before going to Europe as a paratrooper in 1943. Huggins fell in love with the area. "I said, if I make it through the war, this is where I want to be." He made it, then enrolled in Kenyon College. After graduation, Huggins moved to San Francisco, where, after getting a referral from Stanford University's placement office, he went to work at See's.

He was sent around to work in all the departments and even to make candy. Huggins first big opportunity came when managing the packaging department, where employees thought they were doing things wrong, but couldn't get anyone to listen. Huggins went in, took the workers' advice, and made changes that improved the process. Little by little he was given more responsibility.

When Harry See, Mary's grandson, took over the company after his brother's death, Huggins was given responsibility for expanding the company's business. Harry See, Huggins said, "enjoyed life tremendously, was a world traveler, established vineyards in Napa Valley. After a while the family decided collectively to sell the company and cash in their chips. I was coordinator and liaison for that.

"We started in the spring of 1970. We had a couple of very serious suitors, such as a big-four sugar company from Hawaii that owned C&H and others. The family wanted a pretty heady ransom for the company and that dissuaded several buyers."

One company began an in-depth due diligence, examining the business, its many contracts, and so on, to the extent that even Huggins thought they were overly meticulous. "At the eleventh hour, literally at midnight the day before they were to sign the purchase agreement, they backed out. No harm was done, except the energy I expended. We've even kept in touch for years, they were such nice fellows," said Huggins.

About that time, Robert Flaherty, an investment adviser to Blue Chip, heard that the premier chocolate chain was for sale. He contacted William Ramsey, a Blue Chip executive, who was enthusiastic about buying See's. Ramsey call Buffett from Flaherty's office.

"Gee, Bob," Buffett said. "The *candy* business. I don't think we want to be in the candy business."[4]

For some reason, the phone line then went dead. Ramsey and Flaherty hurriedly tried to call Buffett back. Finally, after the secretary misdialed the number and several minutes elapsed, they reconnected. Before they could speak, Buffett burst out: "I was taking a look at the numbers. Yeah, I'd be willing to buy See's at a price."[5]

Warren immediately flew out to visit Harry See.

That was in November 1971, recalled Chuck Huggins. Harry See was fond of Hawaii, and "We were preparing to open our first shop there. I was commuting back and forth between Honolulu and the mainland. I got a call from Harry saying 'we've got some very serious potential buyers. I want you to come back and help me talk to them.' We were to meet them Saturday after Thanksgiving."

Huggins hurriedly caught a flight home for the meeting, which was held in a Los Angeles hotel. Harry See, See's chief executive officer Ed Peck, and a See's attorney were already there. Huggins saw Munger for the first time when he walked into the room with Buffett, Guerin, and Flaherty.

"So we sat and talked a couple of hours. Harry explained who they were, which didn't mean anything. Berkshire Hathaway—everyone thought that was a shirt company. Nobody knew who Charlie was and Rick was maybe involved in property development. He had some relationship with Blue Chip. Anyway, Warren made a lot of comments. Charlie would periodically interrupt and put in his comments. Rick didn't say anything. We got to a point where it was evident that they were serious about buying See's. There were two things to be resolved—how much to pay and how the business would be run. Warren said, 'Harry, we need to talk to you about the price privately.' Warren then said to Harry, 'If we go through with this, we don't run companies. I need to know who will run the company.'"

Peck was ready to retire, so the question presented a problem. "Harry looked around the room and saw me, and said, 'Chuck will.' That's how it happened. Warren said, 'That's fine.' Charlie and Rick and I would like to meet with Chuck tomorrow."

Huggins had some experience with such meetings already, thanks to the buyers who backed out at the last minute. He knew that Harry See had already told the potential owners all the good things about See's.

"I prepared myself by figuring what the company had been doing up to that point. I intended to tell them all the things I thought were problems, things we were working on, my view of the competition. The bad stuff. I gave them a list of my problems and solutions."

"Warren was very calm, down to earth," recalled Huggins. "Rick never did say much. Charlie would volunteer whether asked or not. There were Warren and Charlie talking at the same time—it gave me insight. But

I liked all three of them. There was no blowing of horns about what they'd done. I knew Charlie was a lawyer. That came out. Warren is like an old shoe. Charlie's a college professor or a chief justice of the Supreme Court, and my feeling about Rick was he was hip about everything. He is completely unrelated to those two, except that he was related. He never seemed serious, but he was."

Warren explained to Huggins that first the purchase had to be settled, but, "if that happens, here are a couple of things that are expected. First, we want you to run See's as president and CEO, and second, we don't want any Sees left with a relationship to the company. Some of the people have been around for a long time. Make a settlement and they can go their way."

Huggins said Warren and Charlie wanted him to have full control. "We want you to maintain company ethics and standards," said Buffett.

The See family was asking $30 million. But because of See's low book value, Buffett and Munger decided not to go above $25 million. The talks ended, but later See called back and accepted the $25 million.[6] Munger and Buffett purchased See's Candy on January 3, 1972, paying three times book value, something they'd never done before.

"I was thinking, Charlie lives in Hancock Park. Warren's going back to Omaha," said Huggins. He was worried about how he would communicate with his new employers.

Buffett told Huggins that he realized that the sale was coming at See's busiest time, since it makes more than half of its profits at Christmas. The group would get together after the holidays, said Buffett, and talk about how to proceed next.

"We shook hands. That was the last meeting I had until after Christmas," said Huggins. "I still didn't have a sense about Warren. I couldn't find out." Since that time, Huggins has learned a lot about both Charlie and Warren.

"The actual contract signing was January 31, 1972," said Huggins, and within a month Charlie and Warren were back in his office. "I would be sitting at my desk, the two of them in front of me. Warren would ask questions, Charlie would inject a lot of opinions."

Nevertheless, Huggins was feeling positive about See's new owners. "I got the strong feeling that we were the luckiest people in the world. Warren reminded me of someone I admired—Will Rogers. Homey, trustworthy, absolutely brilliant. It was as if he'd run a business just like ours. Charlie was similar—I was a little guarded with Charlie. He was very absolute. Warren left some room for your opinion. With Charlie, it was 'hep, two, three, four,' but I got used to that. It was just his style."

But, Huggins learned not to take Munger lightly. "If you've ever tried to get Charlie off a position, you're wasting your time. He sort of huffs and tosses his head, and you can forget anything from there on."

"While Blue Chip owned us, it was clear Warren, Charlie, and Rick were the owners," said Huggins. "I asked, 'you'll all disappear—exactly how do you want me to communicate with you?' Warren said 'Do what you've been doing. Let us know if there are danger signs, trouble, but you just keep us informed. Figure out some way to do that.' He said, 'If you can build on what the See family has done, make it more grand, that would be good.'"

Then Buffett added an observations about the candy itself, "You're priced well below the market."

Despite Huggins' positive feeling about the deal, there were problems. His immediate challenge was to convince loyal customers that See's would not change under the new owners.

First, in 1972 when the purchase was publicized in the newspaper, it became known that Blue Chip had bought it. "Well," said Huggins. "People didn't have a lot of respect for the company. They'd just been through an antitrust case—they looked bad. That left a bad taste in the mouths of our most faithful customers. In 1972 and 1973, I spent a lot of my time dealing with customers who were concerned, mad that the family had sold and now it was in the hands of a company that would ruin See's. Suddenly we got a lot of hate mail, people claiming the candy had changed."

See's long-term customers were used to a genteel experience when visiting the shops and were in a near panic. They filled their local stores to express their concerns, which in turn, upset the employees.

Huggins wrote in the company newsletter. "This must seem like a time of the most profound changes in the 51-year-history of our company. Yet there is even more that has not changed. We will not change our personal relationships with employees or customers. We want to go forward without losing any of the vital ingredients that have gone into the making of See's Candy." It took Huggins nearly two years to smooth over the uproar caused by the sale of See's.

Once the dust settled, See's started expanding into markets in Missouri, Texas, and Colorado and even as far away as Hong Kong. See's participated in the 1982 World's Fair in Knoxville, Tennessee, and the exhibit was such a success that See's opened a shop in Knoxville.

A recession hit in the 1980s, however, and many of the out-of-state shops were closed. Customers in distant locations were forced to order by catalog and telephone.

During this same period, the Retail Clerk's Union attempted to organize the salesforce in the stores. See's since has triumphed in four attempts to organize by the Retail Clerk's Union, mainly by paying higher than union-scale wages. See's later had problems with union truck drivers who delivered the product, but through a labor negotiator were able to cancel their contract and transfer the work to a private trucking company, which then rehired most of See's senior drivers.

At one time, See's came under attack by a major candy producer from the Midwest.

"In 1973, Russell Stover Candies [which traditionally was sold through other retailers] went heavily into their own stores. They decided to put on a campaign with See's and beat us out in our own marketplace," recalled Huggins. "They put in stores that looked exactly like See's, called Mrs. Stover's. They duplicated our identity and tried to grab our market. Of course, I informed Charlie and Warren about the fact."

Munger said, "If they are infringing on our trademarks in any way, we can go after them."

"Then, Charlie gave me a lot of direction of what to look for," said Huggins.

Huggins hired a photographer and told him to take pictures of things in the Stover stores that resembled See's trade dress, such as checkerboard floors, lattice in the windows, and old-fashioned photos on the walls.

"Charlie said 'I want this to be handled by a partner at Munger, Tolles. She was born in California, teaches at University of California at Los Angeles Law School. I will assign her to this action. I want you to come to the office and meet her.' It was Carla Anderson Hills. I met her and liked her. It took me about 30 minutes to realize that she was the same personality type as Charlie."

What kind of personality was that? "Go get 'em," said Huggins, snapping his fingers in the air. "It was fun. The upshot was, Charlie scared them to death with all these planned legal responses if they persisted. They backed off. They agreed they wouldn't put in any more copycat stores, and after a time would change the ones they had."

Part of See's competitive advantage is that it is a leader in its market. "In some businesses, the very nature of things is a sort of cascade toward the overwhelming dominance of one firm," said Munger. "It tends to cascade to a winner-take-all result. And these advantages of scale are so great, for example, that when Jack Welch came into General Electric, he just said, 'To hell with it. We're either going to be number one or number two in every field we're in or we're going to be out.' That was a very tough-minded thing to do, but I think it was a correct decision if you're thinking about maximizing shareholder wealth."[7]

During that period, Huggins came to the opinion that Munger was a very practical person. "The Ben Franklin thing is appropriate. Charlie's as corny as hell, but what more do you need?"

The problem with encroachment on its territory took several years to resolve, said Huggins, and there were other difficulties as well. During President Richard Nixon's wage and price controls, for example, the company had to operate differently.

Once the problems of the early days were under control and See's was running smoothly, Munger and Huggins spent less time together. "The personal and direct contact has diminished over the last 10 years." said Huggins. "I miss that. I now talk to Warren on a regular basis. We talk on the phone every 10 days or so. He and Charlie then talk. I don't need to call both."

IN THE 1990s, SEE'S STARTED a more cautious expansion, and rather than build more stores, they established counters at airports and in department and other stores.

At the end of the century, See's operates approximately 250 black-and-white shops across the United States, with two-thirds of them in California. The company sells 33 million pounds of candy a year. More than 75,000 pounds of candy was sold through See's Internet site, a competitor to its own toll-free order service. The company's 1999 sales were $306 million, and its pretax operating profit was $73 million.

Though it doesn't compare to the year-end holiday season, the Berkshire Hathaway annual meeting each May in Omaha is an important day for See's. "We did $40,000 [in sales] at the 1999 annual meeting," observed Huggins. "Warren's proud of that."

"SEE'S CANDY," REMINISCES MUNGER. "It was acquired at a premium over book [value] and it worked. Hochschild, Kohn, the department store chain, was bought at a discount from book and liquidating value. It didn't work. Those two things together helped shift our thinking to the idea of paying higher prices for better businesses."[8]

When they bought See's, Charlie and Warren still were bottom fishers. But as they learned and as the business grew, change was necessary. "You could once find value by just rooting around in the less traveled parts of the world—the pink sheets—you'd find a lot of opportunity," said Charlie.[9]

It was only luck that Blue Chip was able to buy See's at the price they paid. Munger credits Al Marshall for giving the final push toward the correct decision.

"If they had wanted just $100,000 more for See's, we wouldn't have bought it," said Munger. "We were that dumb back then."[10]

Even so, "When we bought the business, almost nobody was having much success selling boxed chocolates except See's, and we wanted to know why that was, and if the success was sustainable," said Buffett.

When See's turned out to be an excellent, ongoing business, Munger and Buffett realized how much easier and pleasanter it was to buy a good business and just let it roll along, than to buy a deeply discounted but struggling business and spend time, energy, and sometimes more money setting it straight.

"If we hadn't bought See's, we wouldn't have bought Coke," said Buffett. "So thank See's for the $12 billion. We had the luck to buy the whole business and that taught us a whole lot. We've had windmills, well, I've had windmills. Charlie was never in the windmill business. I've had second rate department stores, pumps, and textile mills . . ." which he decided were nearly as problematic as the windmills.

Munger says he and Buffett should have seen the advantages of paying for quality much earlier. "I don't think it's necessary to be as dumb as we were."[11]

See's is a slow grower, but its growth is steady and reliable—and best of all, it doesn't take additional infusions of capital.

"We've tried 50 different ways to put money into See's," explained Buffett. "If we knew a way to put additional money into See's and produce returns a quarter of what we're getting out of the existing business, we would do it in a second. We love it. We play around with different ideas, but we don't know how to do it."

Munger added, "By the way, we really shouldn't complain about this because we've carefully selected a bunch of businesses that just drown in money every year."[12]

Munger told Berkshire shareholders that there are a large number of businesses in America that throw off lots of cash, but which cannot be expanded very much. To try to expand would be throwing money down a rat hole, he said. Such businesses don't stir acquisition desires in most corporations, but they are welcome at Berkshire because he and Buffett can take the capital and invest it profitably elsewhere.[13]

Incidentally, that is the same reason Berkshire pays no dividends. Berkshire holds on to cash when Buffett believes retained earnings can produce more in market value for shareholders than would likely be possible if the earnings were not reinvested within the company.

From See's, said Munger, "We've learned that the ways you think and operate must involve time-tested values. Those lessons have made us buy more wisely elsewhere and make many decisions a lot better. So we've gained enormously from our relationship with See's."[14]

Despite See's place of honor in the Berkshire crown, it now represents only a tiny portion of Berkshire's value to its owners. Even if See's were now worth $1 billion, which is conceivable in light of its sales, that is less than 2 percent of Berkshire's market capitalization.

CHAPTER TWELVE

THE BELOUS CASE

Charlie has no enemies in the sense of fighting or confrontation. He has enemies in the larger sense—generated from envy. His personality is unique, but it does not appeal to everyone. I know women who don't want to sit next to him at dinner parties.

Otis Booth

ENGLAND'S KING GEORGE CALLED THE American colonist Benjamin Franklin the "most dangerous man in America," though Franklin was well received when he first arrived in England in 1757. Soon after establishing himself in London, Franklin realized that the British knew very little about the colonies. Often the wag, he took it upon himself to set the British straight. "To read the English papers," Franklin wrote, "one would think America didn't produce enough wool to make a pair of stockings a year; whereas the tails of American sheep were so heavy with wool, little wagons had to be tied under them for support."[1]

During his 16 years there, Franklin dazzled the British with his originality. He invented bifocal eyeglasses, a 24-hour clock for navigation, and urged the adoption of daylight-saving time. But he shocked Londoners by swimming in the Thames and working out with dumbbells totally in the nude. Finally, largely because of political differences but partly because some were jealous of his popularity, he was expelled from England.[2]

When Franklin sailed to France in 1776 to become the American ambassador, America's most famous citizen again was given a hearty welcome. According to the French Ambassador to the United States (in 1999) Francois Bujon de I'Estang, Franklin had qualities that "French people revere: He was cheerful, witty, and humorous. . . . The story goes that he had not been allowed to write the Declaration of Independence for fear he would hide a joke in it."[3]

Warren Buffett often teases Munger about how often he quotes *Poor Richard's Almanac* and preaches Franklin's moral messages:

> Buffett: "Charlie overdosed on Ben Franklin early in his life, and he believes that a penny saved is a penny lost."
>
> Charlie: "I can tell you a lot about Warren, he reminds me of Ben Franklin, I can tell you a lot about Ben Franklin."

"I am a biography nut myself," said Munger, "and I think when you're trying to teach the great concepts that work, it helps to tie them into the lives and personalities of the people who developed them. I think that you learn economics better if you make Adam Smith your friend. That sounds funny, making friends among the eminent dead, but if you go through life making friends with the eminent dead who had the right ideas, I think it will work better in life and work better in education. It's way better than just giving the basic concepts."[4]

Munger has studied the lives and scientific writings of Albert Einstein, Charles Darwin, and Isaac Newton, but his favorite eminent dead person has always been Franklin, a passion that he shared with Warren Buffett's first serious mentor, Benjamin Graham. Munger admires Franklin for being the best American author of his time, the best investor, scientist, diplomat, merchant, and greatest contributor to educational and civic causes. Though he admits that Franklin had a lusty side to his personality, and perhaps neglected his wife, Munger says that stories of how badly Franklin behaved reflect a shallow understanding of Franklin, his situation, and the times in which he lived.

It was from Franklin that Munger gleaned the concept of becoming wealthy so that he could be free to make a contribution to humankind. "I always cared more about being useful than dying rich," said Munger, "but sometimes I drift too far away from this idea."

Franklin was the son of a candle maker who had too many children, and at an early age Ben made his way from Boston to Philadelphia to escape an apprenticeship with a cruel brother. From an early age Franklin strove to be a better person and build a better life. After the phenomenally successful *Poor Richard's Almanac* made Franklin both famous and rich, he devoted his life mostly to public service.[5]

Like Franklin, Munger has learned that his ideas about a good and proper society do not always coincide with the beliefs of others. Though most of the French continued to find Franklin interesting and entertaining during his sojourn in Paris, the king became so jealous that he put Franklin's picture on the bottom of a chamber pot he gave to his mistress.

As SEVERAL HUNDRED FANS OF Warren Buffett and Charles Munger crowded the front entrance to Gorat's steak house in Omaha on the Sunday evening before the 1998 annual meeting, they confronted a disturbing sight. About a half dozen protestors trudged back and forth on the sidewalk, carrying lurid placards showing fetuses floating in bottles and proclaiming Buffett and Munger baby killers because they have been longtime supporters of human reproductive rights. One sign attacked Buffett's charitable foundation for its funding of tests for the RU-486 abortion pill.[6]

When asked at Berkshire's annual meeting about the company's contributions to pro-choice causes, Buffett explained that under the corporate contributions plan, shareholders are allowed to designate a charity of their choice and then gifts are given in proportion to the number of Berkshire shares owned. "The policy is designated by shareholders. There are a number of shareholders who designate Planned Parenthood. The Buffett Foundation contributes to Planned Parenthood. Charlie gives to Planned Parenthood. Put Charlie's name on the signs."

Charlie demurred: "I am perfectly willing to have that limelight passed."

Most of the protestors knew only that Buffett and Munger are longtime and generous contributors to Planned Parenthood and to other organizations committed to population issues. They were largely unaware that Charlie and Warren were pioneers in the abortion rights movement. Thanks to Munger, they were influential in getting the right to abortion legalized in California, a pivotal legal decision that preceded the Roe vs. Wade case in the U.S. Supreme Court.

"I would say 99 percent of Charlie's friends are Republican or very right wing. He's generally regarded that way. Most of Charlie's friends also were unaware of his pro-choice activities," observed Buffett.

Munger confounded other conservatives and irritated the religious right by his admiration and financial support of Garrett Hardin, author of the well-read 1993 book, *Living Within Limits*. Hardin was among the earlier scientific writers to warn of looming population problems. He and others point out that it took civilization until 1804 to reach one billion people, but only 12 years to jump from five billion to the current global population of six billion. In the next one hundred years, the population of the United States alone will double from 275 million to 571 million. Experts estimate that before world population growth stops or reverses, there could be 10 billion people on earth. Such a large population already is putting stress on the earth's resources, including production and distribution of food. At the end of the twentieth century, an estimated 800 million people were malnourished due to difficulties of growing or buying enough food.

A professor emeritus of human ecology at the University of California at Santa Barbara, Hardin has written extensively on biology, ecology, and ethics. During the 1960s, Hardin was known as "Mr. Abortionist" because he championed abortions in hundreds of speeches around the country.

Roderick Hills, who helped start the Munger, Tolles law firm, says the reproductive rights issue first came to Charlie's attention when he read an article in the newspaper about a criminal case that would be appealed to the California Supreme Court. He promptly persuaded his law firm members to help out on a pro bono basis. The case was that of Dr. Leon Belous, a doctor who had been convicted of referring a woman to an abortionist.

"You can go back to the Belous case, 1972 or so. We would talk about it all the time, Charlie was totally immersed in it," recalled Buffett.

As unusual as it may seem for a devoted family man with eight children, especially one with a conservative political bent, to support legal abortions, Munger made the decision to go forward.

"It was emotionally hard for me to become pro-choice because I do have reverence for human life," said Munger, "but when I thought through the consequences, I found it necessary to overrule that part of my nature."

Once Munger decided that it should be a woman's right to decide whether or not to become a mother, he went about seeking change with energy and resourcefulness. He convinced Buffett, who is fiscally conservative but socially liberal, to join him in helping to pay the legal defense of Dr. Belous. Munger and his law partners, particularly Rod Hills and Jim Adler, organized themselves and did the rest.

"Charlie took over the case, got one amicus brief from a blue ribbon group of legal luminaries and another brief from medical school professors," said Buffett. "Charlie made an enormous effort on that."

Hills was among the lawyers who helped assemble the two friends-of-the-court briefs. One was written by Munger himself and signed by 17 prominent lawyers. The other was signed by 178 medical school deans and professors.

During the time the Belous case was pending before the California Supreme Court, Munger and Buffett sponsored a "church" called the Ecumenical Fellowship that counseled women on family planning. The church, run by a legitimate minister who got in trouble with his own denomination for his pro-abortion activities, sometimes helped women get safe abortions outside the United States.

"Warren and I were revolutionaries," said Munger. "We created a church that was used as an underground railroad. We supported the Clergy Counseling Service. The minister running it was cashiered by his own church for helping women get abortions. First I tried to persuade the church to let him continue. That failed. I called Warren and asked him to help me establish our own church. That we did. For years this minister ran the thing. That was our contribution, trying to help so that society didn't force women to give birth—to be held in a system Garrett Hardin called 'mandatory motherhood.'"

When the Belous case was heard before the California Supreme Court, the outcome became uncertain when one of the Justices had to recuse himself because the abortionist was his family doctor. But in September 1969, Belous won a landmark victory in which, for the first time in U.S. history, an anti-abortion law was declared unconstitutional by a major court. The replacement Justice was the swing vote in a four-to-three decision. Not only has the decision been the legal precedent used in California ever since, "It was the first chink in the armor of abortion restrictions," said Munger.

The impact of the case widened even more when two years after the California decision, Belous was cited in the appellants' brief in Roe v. Wade, in which the U.S. Supreme Court established "the fundamental right of the woman to choose whether to bear children."[7]

"Charlie gives more than time," says Ron Olson. "He transforms the charities."

Indeed, the court ruling was not the end of Munger's work. Following Belous, he was for many years a trustee and the chief financial officer for Planned Parenthood of Los Angeles, which offered family planning services and, when necessary, referred patients to clinics where abortions were available.

"We were way ahead of the national office of Planned Parenthood in arranging abortions," said Munger. "The Planned Parenthood chapter in Los Angeles wanted to get into that business, but didn't know how. We merged our church, the Ecumenical Fellowship, headed by the same guy who headed the Clergy Counseling Service, into the Los Angeles chapter of Planned Parenthood."

When he joined the Planned Parenthood board, there was only one major benefactor, Anna Bing Arnold, the widow of the wealthy real estate developer Leo Bing. Despite her dedication, the organization was small and thinly financed.

"We were chronically short of money," said Otis Booth, who served on the board with Munger. The board expanded its contributor base, but as usual, with Charlie the organization took contrary positions. "There was a controversy over national dues. We told them [national] no. 'You're not contributing anything useful to us, we're not paying the dues.' We finally rejoined the national organization."

Despite the pressure from protestors and sometimes frightening actions of anti-abortion activists, Munger's fervor on the subject of abortion and population issues have not changed over the years.

Barry Munger recalled that at a party for Keith Russell, a well loved Los Angeles obstetrician who had been Charlie's stalwart ally in the abortion rights struggle, a patient toasted Dr. Russell for all the babies he'd delivered. Charlie raised his glass and declared, "I want to toast Dr. Russell for the thousands of babies he *didn't* deliver."[8]

In 1990, Munger fired off a stinging letter to *Fortune,* claiming that a review of Paul and Anne Ehrlich's book, *The Population Explosion,* had missed the point. The book reviewer, said Munger, "argues that human welfare will continue to improve as a result of desirable population growth accompanied by even faster technological development. Alas, it is not so simple. In a finite world system, subject to the laws of physics, two variables (population and per capita welfare) can't both be maximized forever."

Munger said it was nonsensical to expect, as the reviewer had suggested, that some technology, now unknown, will step forward to solve all the problems of pollution, erosion, and so forth: "No one contemplating the prospective environmental burden described by the Ehrlichs can be confident that such a 'benign demographic transition' will occur or that the population-growth-driven conditions won't be ghastly in 100 years or less. For one thing, the technological development that is necessary to permit a peacetime population increase will also make weapons both more effective and more generally available in a more crowded world."[9]

Buffett is just as solid in his view. In 1994, Buffett declared that the world would have far fewer problems, "if you could make every child born in this country and this world a wanted child . . . the closest thing we have to that is Planned Parenthood. Until women have that right to determine their reproductive destiny, we're in an unequal society," Buffett said.[10]

CHAPTER THIRTEEN

THE BUFFALO
EVENING NEWS

If thou faint in the day of adversity, thy strength is small.

The Bible, Proverbs

THE MUNGER CHILDREN HAVE NEVER forgotten the summer of 1977 after their father and his partner Warren Buffett bought the *Buffalo Evening News*. The youngsters scurried around their lakeside Minnesota cabin collecting coins, then went with Charlie to the telephone booth at the marina across the lake to help him feed money into the pay phone as he and Buffett plotted their strategy for the paper.

"The *Buffalo Evening News* was a big deal. In my mind a really big deal," said Molly Munger.

Molly said that with the acquisition of a well-known eastern newspaper, she felt that Buffett and Munger had stepped up to a higher plain. They were taking on a broader scope, moving away from small, regional companies and going for more visible properties. It was the beginning of a trend to buy companies with names that other people would recognize when you tried to explain what your father did for a living.

The *Buffalo Evening News* was among the most impressive acquisitions made with Blue Chip Stamps' float account, and for a long time, it was the most aggravating.

The *Buffalo Evening News* was established in 1880, and for years was operated by a single family, the Butlers. After Kate Robinson Butler died in 1974, the establishment-oriented Republican-leaning newspaper was put up for sale by her estate. It wasn't until the first Saturday after New Year's Day, 1977, that Buffett and Munger arrived in Weston, Connecticut, to talk to Vincent Manno, a newspaper broker who was handling the deal. Buffett first offered $30 million for the paper, but his price was refused. He then raised the bid to $32 million. The offer was high, considering that the *Evening News* had earned only $1.7 million pretax in 1976. However, the offer again was rejected. Buffett and Munger excused themselves to confer. They returned with a price written on a sheet of yellow legal paper. The amount, $32.5 million, was accepted. It was a daring move, since the acquisition price represented nearly 25 percent of the net worth of Berkshire Hathaway at that time.

Once the price was settled, Buffett and Munger flew to western New York to work out the details of the contract. They arrived there in the middle of the worst snowstorm in Buffalo's history. For someone who had become acclimated to California, Buffalo's severe winter climate may have been a shock to Munger. In a letter to Katharine Graham, Charlie referred to Buffalo as "a town where the statue of George Washington wears a Masonic apron, and the wind blows so hard that the mail in the chute goes up and not down."

When touring the newspaper's relatively new offices and printing plant Munger snapped, "Why does a newspaper need a *palace* to publish in?" Buffett jokingly dubbed it the Taj Mahal.[1]

Munger, with his passion for good architecture, was repelled by the design of the building's famous architect, who had impressed old Mrs. Butler by driving the same model of Rolls Royce that she did. He put in big balconies that were unusable in windy Buffalo and employed an "artsy-craftsy" construction method that caused unfixable leaks—all at great cost. This was not Charlie's concept of successful design.

But in the year 2000, the boxy cement-like building in the center of Buffalo's aging downtown seems reasonably spacious, though austere. It certainly is no more opulent than most other metropolitan daily newspaper facilities.

Like Graham's *Washington Post*, a newspaper in which Buffett had made a major investment in 1973, the *Buffalo Evening News* proved to be a difficult business proposition. In both situations, Munger and Buffett proved that though they prided themselves on fair dealing, they also could take tough positions and stick to them.

When Blue Chip bought the *Buffalo Evening News*, it had a solid readership base in western New York, although Buffalo was gradually becoming a classic rust-belt city. The newspaper had several other problems. Like the *Washington Post*, the *Evening News* had several extremely active unions. It also had a strong competitor in the *Buffalo Courier-Express*, a historic newspaper once edited by Mark Twain. Additionally, the *Evening News* published no Sunday paper. Though the *Evening News* outsold the *Courier-Express* four-to-one during the week, its lucrative Sunday edition kept the *Courier-Express* in business.

The new owners knew that long term, only one newspaper could survive in Buffalo, and that their new property would either perish or stand alone. The *Buffalo Evening News* plainly required a Sunday edition, hazards be damned. Immediately after Blue Chip bought the newspaper, Buffett and Munger dropped the "Evening" from the newspaper's name and started to publish on Sunday. At first the paper was given away to current subscribers and for racks and news stands, the price was only 30 cents a copy. The *Courier-Express* and other newspapers in western New York charged 50 cents for their Sunday paper.

The special introductory offers to subscribers and advertisers prompted the *Courier* to sue the *News,* claiming that it was violating the Sherman Anti-trust Act. On November 9, 1977, a U.S. District Judge agreed that it might be the case and granted injunctive relief that stopped short of spiking the new Sunday paper.

"They bought a lawsuit when they bought that paper," said Al Marshall, "But I never did believe they could lose."

Munger knew a good buy when he saw it, and his keen sense of what legal points could be lost or won served especially well when he and Buffett acquired the *Buffalo Evening News.* They knew full well that launching a Sunday newspaper would not be easy and in fact, might instigate an old fashioned newspaper war.

Despite the best efforts of Munger and lawyers he recruited to help, the injunction remained in place for two years. A Los Angeles friend of Munger and Marshall, Ernest Zack, was hired to help with the legal battle in Buffalo, which was so difficult and trying that Zack became exhausted. When Zack got so weary or frustrated that he complained, Munger admonished him, "Oh, it's good for you."

During the drawn out legal and business siege, people began to notice that Munger, 52, was having difficulty with his vision. "You would work with Charlie, go to his office and talk to him about whatever the situation was, Charlie was very good at reading documents," said Bob Denham. "A lot of people don't read them well, but it became difficult for him. He would struggle through, and as reading oriented as Charlie is, he must have been very concerned."

Even so, said Denham, "He was pretty stoic. I think he found it quite frustrating. He *didn't* take it out on other people."

Finally Munger had to admit he was not able to read paperwork the way he once did, and warned his colleagues not to count on him to discover errors the way he used to. He told Denham that the responsibility for carefully reviewing documents was now his.

At a relatively young age, Munger learned that he was developing rapid and severe cataracts. While the eye damage could have been from over-exposure to the bright California sunshine without the benefit of sunglasses, Charlie suspects that the more likely cause was using a sunlamp when he was a very young boy. For some reason, Munger said, he became enamored with the lamp and used it extensively without eye protection, unaware of the possible future consequences.

Despite his worsening health problems, Munger continued conferring on the telephone, and to Buffett the situation didn't seem all that serious—at first. Buffett was amazed that Charlie didn't complain about his problems.

"It was awful," recalled Molly Munger. "This horrible thing happened to him. He practically ran the boat into the dock, he couldn't see. He was afraid of being blind. But finally he had to [have the surgery]. He was losing his vision."

In the meantime, although it took five difficult years, the problems at the *Buffalo News* began to be resolved. An appeals panel reversed the injunction decision, finding no evidence of actual injurious intent.

"The original judge thought giving away the newspaper for four weeks, or whatever, violated rules of the Marquis of Queensbury," said Ron Olson. "The overturning judge said he could find nowhere in case law the Marquis of Queensbury. Charlie was confident and ready to stand by the lawyers as it played out."

Both the *Courier* and the *News* continued publishing at a financial loss. In 1979 the *News* was $4.6 million in the red, a large amount of money for two small operators from Nebraska and California. Charlie recalled, "I went through the calculations personally—I figured out exactly how much my share would cost me and exactly how much the Munger family could afford to lose."[2]

The United States experienced a serious recession in the early 1980s, which made a bad situation even worse. The *Courier-Express,* which in the midst of the territorial battle was sold to the Cowles family of Minneapolis, finally raised a white flag and folded on September 19, 1982.[3]

Even with lighter competition for readers and advertisers, profits came slowly for the *Buffalo News.* The Buffalo area lost 23 percent of its manufacturing jobs in the 1980s with the closing of many Bethlehem Steel operations. Unemployment in Buffalo during that time ran more than 15 percent, and one retailer after another went out of business, thus depressing advertising lineage. Between 1981 and 1982, operating profits dropped by half, and the outlook for the next few years appeared no brighter. Buffalo was hit harder than most American cities by the recession, but the economy wasn't the only problem. Newspapers everywhere were losing ground to television and other news media.

Munger, who all the while struggled with the possibility of total blindness, insisted that Blue Chip shareholders hold management responsible for lost opportunity costs far in excess of reported losses. In 1981, he wrote to Blue Chip Stamps shareholders: "We would now have about $70 million in value of other assets, earning over $10 million per year, in place of the *Buffalo Evening News* and its current red ink. No matter what happens in the future in Buffalo we are about 100 percent sure to have an economic place lower than we would have occupied if we had not made our purchase."[4]

In time however, Munger proved wrong as a forecaster. Buffalo's economy started to turn around, which boosted newspaper profits. The U.S.-Canada free trade agreement also helped revive Buffalo, which is now the U.S. center for many Canadian companies. *News* profits rose and rose.

Buffett was at the forefront of the *News* episode, highly visible in the struggle to resolve competition and problems with the Newspaper Guild. Munger remained mostly behind the scenes, but he was in constant contact with his partner to discuss business and legal strategies.

"Charlie was very much involved in the purchase of the *Buffalo Evening News,*" said Stanford Lipsey. Lipsey had been the editor of the Omaha weekly newspaper, *The Sun,* which Buffett owned. Under Lipsey's direction, the *Sun* won a 1973 Pulitzer prize for its exposé of Boys Town. Lipsey began going to Buffalo during its darkest hours to help the publisher and editor, and he finally stayed to run the paper.

Though the newspaper went through trying times, said Lipsey, "I've never seen Charlie get angry. If Warren and Charlie believe in the principle of something, they don't deviate from it, even if it's not popular with the individuals around them."

The *Buffalo News* is the last remaining metropolitan daily newspaper in Buffalo and serves a 10-county area of western New York with eight daily and three Sunday editions. About 80 percent of the population read it on Sunday and 64 percent on weekdays, putting the *News* among the top 50 newspapers in the country as far as market penetration is concerned. The *Buffalo News* claims a significantly higher percentage of space for news than any major market daily. With a daily circulation of nearly 300,000, the company now brings in around $157 million in revenues and $53 million in pretax profit. It is said to be the most profitable newspaper in the United States, delivering a 91.2 percent return on assets.

Despite an avid early interest in newspapers, Buffett and Munger say they are no longer the bulletproof franchises they used to be, since technology such as television and the Internet has changed the way people get their information and has dimmed newspaper prospects. In fact, says Munger, the Internet will increase competition and make it hard for all companies to show a profit.

Before success came to the *Buffalo News,* Wendy Munger remembers her father as a good looking, well-dressed man with excellent vision. "I had this movie star father—I just want people to know he didn't always wear thick glasses. That was only after his surgery."

Though the problems of the *Buffalo News* were resolved in his favor, Charlie lost an eye and he lost his mother.

When it became obvious he would lose his vision to cataracts, in 1978, Munger underwent what he described as an old-fashioned cataract operation at the Good Samaritan Hospital in Los Angeles.

"This all happened 25 years ago," said Munger. "A new and better operation had been invented, but I didn't pay attention—I just went along with the doctor that recommended the old one that he knew how to do. The new type of surgery had a complication rate of no more than 2 percent while the (surgery) I had had a 5 percent complication rate. The man who did the first operation? I won't tell you his name. A perfectly nice guy. Our family eye doctor. I made the mistake—the fault was mine."

After the surgery, Munger fell victim to a rare and devastating complication.

"I developed an epithelial downgrowth," he explained. "A few cells of the outside of the eye got inside the eye, which is virtually impossible with the new operation. When that happens, the cells from the outside just proliferate. They take over the interior of the eye and raise the pressure, and that kills the optic nerve."

The condition is similar to cancer, except that the growth does not spread outside the eye. Munger was in such agony that he decided there was one thing worse than a blind eye, and that was a blind eye that hurt. In 1980 Munger had the doctors eviscerate, or scoop out, the innards of the left eye and cover the eyeball with a glass eye.

"You cannot believe the pain and suffering from an evisceration. I was like a wounded animal for several days. I was in so much pain and had so much nausea that when the nurse came in to give me a bath I couldn't stand for her to bathe me," said Munger.

While all this was going on with his left eye, a cataract was slowly growing on his right eye as well. Munger knew for sure he didn't want to repeat the experience he was now going through. Charlie decided to adopt a strategy with absolute minimum risk for the right eye.

"I told the doctor to just get the clouded lens out of there, and I'll use cataract spectacles. Don't put in a new manmade lens," said Munger. Cataract eyeglasses were commonly worn by older people when Munger was a child.

"You almost don't see cataract glasses anymore. I may have the last pair on earth," he said. Munger keeps a file folder on his desk full of medical reports, his own notes written on a yellow pad, and other details of the event.

Except for his new bottle-bottom glasses, Munger says, "Life didn't change a bit. I lack peripheral vision, my straight ahead vision is excellent." Charlie had the sight in his right eye tested in 1999, and with his glasses, he had 20/15 vision.

Despite his blind left eye, Munger drives, and has learned how to change into lanes on his blind side by counting the cars in the rearview mirror, and knowing after which one there will be a gap. He drives a Lexus with a powerful engine because it gives him the ability to move quickly when he needs to. He tends to make what out-of-state drivers call California stops—slowing down to a near-stop at a sign, then zooming out when the way seems clear. That may not have anything to do with his vision.

His former partner Al Marshall insists Munger was never a good driver even when he had excellent eyesight because Charlie usually was thinking about something other than driving.

"He used to carry a gallon of gas in the trunk, which wasn't safe at all," said Marshall, "because he could never remember to put gas in the thing."

When the Mungers and the Marshalls were vacationing in Hawaii, Charlie was driving a rental car down a small back road, talking, gesturing, and looking around at everything as he drove. Al looked up and saw that a bridge ahead of them was washed out. "Stop," he shouted to Charlie, who didn't slow down a bit. "Why?" Charlie asked. Marshall was so frightened he couldn't find the words to explain, but Munger finally noticed the problem and screeched to a halt just before going over the edge.

"When he lost his eyesight, he handled it in a pragmatic fashion," recalled Otis Booth. "He got some books on braille to see if that would work for him."

When he figured out he would have enough vision to read well, Charlie gave up all thoughts of braille.

Even so, said Hal Borthwick, "It's not pleasant for a man who loves to read. He's a voracious reader. In every one of our houses there will be three, four, five books stacked by his chair and three, four, or five more stacked by the bed. He has certain things he wants to read. He's not a fiction reader so it's either a business book or a biography or a history or science book. It's always based on facts."

Though Munger plays golf, travels, and reads constantly, there are times when the glass eye becomes a real inconvenience. Booth says that when Charlie went to the Department of Motor Vehicles to get his driver's license renewed, he was required to take an eye exam.

"He told the person at the desk that he was blind in one eye," explained Booth. "The examiner said he'd have to have a doctor's letter on that. Charlie said, 'Hell, I can prove it to you right here. It's a false eye. I'll take it out and lay it on the counter if you like.' The examiner still insisted on a doctor's note until Charlie demanded to speak to a supervisor. It took about a half hour to sort out."

DURING A TIME WHEN SO much was happening, Charlie's mother passed away. Toody Munger lived on for fifteen years after her husband died. She and Dorothy Davis, Dr. Ed Davis' widow, spent much of their time together and especially enjoyed traveling.

"Mother and Toody went to France once," said Willa Davis Seemann. "By the time they got home they were rather sick. They took turns pushing each other around the airport in wheel chairs."

Molly said that her grandmother strove to maintain her intellectual edge and to keep up with times as they changed. "Grandma Toody and I went out to dinner with her other Omaha widow friends. One said, 'This summer, I think it's time to reread Tolstoy.' She was not a grandmother that you remember for cookies or anything—you remember what she said. My cousin Rodger was a hippy. She was taking one of her widow-ladies tours of Europe, which she did a lot. She'd say to a new friend, 'Does yours bake bread?' If the woman said yes, their eyes would light up and they knew they both had hippy grandsons."

At Toody's funeral, Charlie looked out on the faces of his Aunt Oofie, and Toody's good friends. He remembered his father and his grandparents, the Russells, and he realized that his mother's had been a "blessed life."

CHAPTER FOURTEEN

CHARLIE MUNGER GOES TO WAR WITH THE SAVINGS AND LOAN INDUSTRY

If you mix raisins with turds, they are still turds.

Charlie Munger, Berkshire Hathaway annual meeting, May 2000

Wesco Financial, once simply the parent company of a small Pasadena-based savings and loan institution with the plain-wrap name of Mutual Savings, was a source of contention for Charlie Munger and Warren Buffett almost from the moment they bought it. Over time however, Wesco Financial, like its majority owner Berkshire Hathaway, was transformed into an entirely different business from what it was originally. Berkshire is the big canvas on which Buffett—with the help of Munger—paints his large masterpiece. Wesco is a smaller work on which Munger—with the help of Buffett—has made his own colorful imprint.

Shortly after Blue Chip Stamps bought a modest number of shares in Wesco in 1974, Buffett and Munger waged a battle to stave off an unacceptable acquisition by another California thrift. That was followed by a Securities and Exchange Commission investigation into the way Buffett, Munger, and others were structuring business deals (see Chapter Ten). The SEC investigation was a hassle, but in the end, Berkshire Hathaway was transformed into a holding company of some substance, and that was good.

Then, following a deep rift between Munger, powerful members of a savings and loan trade organization and federal regulators, Wesco was completely remade into a holding company similar in structure to Berkshire.

Since 1976, Wesco and its owner Blue Chip Stamps, have been buried within the structure of Berkshire. Nevertheless, said Buffett, "Blue Chip Stamps still owns our Wesco stock. Because it came that way. We now have what we owned in the 1970s, 80.1 percent."

By following the ownership thread, it is clear that since Berkshire owns 100 percent of Blue Chip and because Buffett is Berkshire's largest shareholder, owning more than 35 percent, he controls Wesco. Yet, as is the case with the other Berkshire companies, Buffett does not participate directly in the management of Blue Chip or of Wesco, though he serves as a director of Wesco-Financial Insurance Company (Wes-FIC) and Precision Steel Warehouse, wholly-owned subsidiaries of Wesco.

It is Munger who is Wesco's chairman. He lives in the same area where the company is headquartered and even more important, he is well liked by Betty Peters, whose family founded the company. The Peters family still own about 1.3 percent of Wesco's outstanding stock.

The chairman's job pays Munger nothing, though he does earn $100,000 per year as vice chairman of Berkshire Hathaway and chairman of Blue Chip Stamps. In addition, Charlie now collects director's fees from Costco Wholesale Corporation. He once earned director's fees from Salomon Inc. and U.S. Airways Group, companies in which Berkshire Hathaway held large equity positions.[1]

In recent years, Wesco's annual meeting has become a royal court where Charlie holds forth on his own, beyond the wide and bright circle of light cast by Buffett at the Berkshire shareholders' event. For a long time, Wesco held its annual meeting in a tired, 1950s-style cafeteria at the seedier end of Pasadena's glamorous Colorado Boulevard. Each year the crowd at the meeting got larger and each year the long, narrow banquet room, with its fading floral wallpaper and dingy carpet, seemed more cramped.

The 1997 Wesco meeting, which takes place in May about two weeks after Berkshire Hathaway's, was attended by 100 or so people. "Typical group of gluttons (for punishment) and masochists—when you attract that crowd it gets bigger every year because nobody ever leaves," grumbled Munger.

Charlie was correct. In 1997, the cafeteria went out of business and Wesco's 1998 meeting was moved. The room at Pasadena's McCormick & Schmick's seafood restaurant was again too small to hold the crowd. In 1998, the crowd more than doubled and in 1999, 500 to 600 people attended the gathering. There are many faithful: Individual investors like Mr. and Mrs. Anwar, from Virginia; the Kilpatricks from Alabama; Jolene

Crowley from El Cajon, California, and others who return again and again. Many analysts, investment advisors, and institutional investors also show up.

"I want to apologize for the elaborateness of this room," Munger told the shareholders at McCormick & Schmick's. "Many of you have come to our annual meeting when we held it in the cafeteria in the basement of the old Mutual Savings Building. And then we moved it to a rather modest room in a building we own which was leased to a cafeteria. But they gave up the ghost—and that building is now vacant."

Munger explained that it would have cost more to clean the building up and move furniture into the vacant restaurant than it cost to rent a room for a few hours.

"But I know that many of you are disappointed to see our annual meeting held in such an elaborate room—even if your heavy attendance has established a new record for occupancy per square foot," he joked.

Charlie clearly is the star of the Wesco show, and at the 1999 meeting shareholders stayed in their chairs for three hours plying the 75-year-old capitalist with questions. But Munger didn't become a sensation over-night. He began to catch the attention of the business world—along with Berkshire and Wesco shareholders—in the 1980s.

While Warren wrote the famous chairman's message for the Berk-shire Hathaway annual report, Charlie wrote Wesco's message. Wesco's report was published independently, then parts of it were reprinted in the back of the Berkshire document. Munger used the early chairman's letter to do two things. First, he described the evolution of Wesco after it was merged into Berkshire. At the same time, he began warning share-holders, and indeed any one else who was willing to listen, of an approaching tempest in the savings and loan industry. With the backing of Buffett, he eventually made a bold public statement that got the thrift industry's attention but did not influence its leaders to act differently.

The history of savings and loan associations (often called thrift insti-tutions, thrifts, or S&Ls) goes back hundreds of years in the United States, but the thrifts became crucially important when returning World War II veterans rushed out to buy houses. From the post-war housing boom right up to the mid-1980s, the savings and loan business was a thriving indus-try, especially in California.

For most of their history, government regulators allowed thrifts to pay a higher rate of interest than banks were allowed to pay on passbook accounts, certificates of deposit, or other savings accounts. In return, the S&Ls were required to lend out most of their money as home mortgages. They were barred from making business loans or providing most other fi-nancial services. In the early 1980s, however, several things happened.

Brokerage houses and mutual fund companies—called nonbank banks—started offering money market accounts at an unregulated market interest rate, and the administration of President Ronald Reagan, with the intention of reducing government's role in business, started deregulating the thrift industry. The first step was enlarging the industry's lending and investment powers.

Though Munger is no champion of government regulation, he thought that the timing and the coordination of deregulation was dangerous. Charlie was irked over the increase in deposit insurance and some changes in rules for S&Ls, especially since the thrift's new competitors, the nonbank banks, operated under few regulations. There is no deposit insurance for their money market funds and fund owners, unlike thrifts, are not required to maintain branch offices. Costs to operate money market funds, Munger noted, were more than 50 percent lower than the annual costs of the most efficient thrifts. These nonbank banks were skimming the cream off what had once been the S&L's source of funds, forcing thrifts into a serious profits squeeze. At the same time, deposit insurance gave S&L operators the sense that they could take more risk in their attempts to ease the pressure.

In his 1983 letter to shareholders, Munger wrote that "an agency of the U.S. government (the Federal Savings and Loan Insurance Corporation) continues to insure savings accounts in the savings and loan industry, just as it did before. The result may [from expanded loan and investment powers] well be bolder and bolder conduct by many savings and loan associations. A sort of Gresham's law (bad loan practice drives out good) may take effect at fully competitive but deposit-insured institutions. If . . . 'bold conduct drives out conservative conduct,' there eventually could be widespread insolvencies caused by bold credit extensions come to grief."[2]

Munger and Buffett began to divert both Wesco and Mutual Savings away from the thrift business, preparing Wesco for what was to come. Wesco purchased 100,000 newly issued shares of Series A Cumulative convertible Preferred Stocks of Salomon Inc. on October 1, 1987, at a cost of $100 million. The investment was part of a $700 million transaction, in which Berkshire purchased $600 million and Wesco bought the remainder. In addition to the 9 percent dividend, each preferred share could be converted into 26.3 shares of Salomon common on or after October 31, 1990. The way the contract worked, Wesco and Berkshire would make a profit on the conversion if the shares traded at or above $38.[3]

As fate would have it, on October 19, 1987, the stock market experienced its worst day in recent history, Black Monday. Salomon was badly hurt by the crash, and its shares fell to as low as $16.62. Fortunately, by the end of 1989 Salomon common had recovered to $23.38.

In 1988, Munger and Buffett moved Mutual Savings another step away from its traditional role as a thrift. After a three-hour discussion, the pair decided to beef up Mutual's small stake in the Federal Home Loan Mortgage Corporation, commonly called Freddie Mac.

Freddie Mac provides liquidity in the mortgage market by pooling and packaging home loans into securities that are sold to investors. The company thus earns fees and "spreads," while side-stepping most interest-rate-change risk. Additionally, the company insures mortgages. Freddie Mac was created by the government in 1938 to make home ownership more affordable by creating a secondary market for home loans. Over the years, the character of Freddie Mac changed. Under a charter drafted by Congress in the midst of a 1970 credit crisis, ownership was limited to participating lenders, the S&Ls. Later Freddie Mac converted to private ownership largely held by institutional investors. It began trading on the New York Stock Exchange in 1988.

Freddie Mac is one of only two federally chartered companies that package and sell mortgage-backed securities. The other is the Federal National Mortgage Association, commonly called Fannie Mae. The implicit federal backing for Freddie Mac gave Munger and Buffett the competitive edge that they like.

Wesco—through Mutual Savings—bought 28.8 million shares of Freddie Mac for $72 million at a time when Freddie Mac shares could be lawfully owned only by an S&L. It was the maximum investment in Freddie Mac then allowed by law. It was an investment that built a castle wall around Wesco during the later collapse of the thrift industry. By the end of 1999, the Freddie Mac holding had a market value of $1.38 billion.[4]

"Our experience in shifting from savings and loan operation to ownership of Freddie Mac shares tends to confirm a long-held notion that being prepared, on a few occasions in a lifetime, to act promptly in scale, in doing some simple and logical things, will often dramatically improve the financial results of that lifetime," said Munger. "A few major opportunities clearly recognizable as such, will usually come to one who continuously searches and waits, with a curious mind, loving diagnosis involving multiple variables. And then all that is required is a willingness to bet heavily when the odds are extremely favorable, using resources available as a result of prudence and patience in the past."[5]

When a similar opportunity arose to buy Fannie Mae shares, Buffett and Munger faltered. Buffett said they should have taken a large stake in Fannie Mae as well.

"My biggest lost opportunity was probably Fannie Mae. We owned a savings and loan, and that entitled us to buy 4 percent of Freddie Mac stock when it first came out. We did this and should have followed the same reasoning and bought more Fannie Mae stock. What was I doing? I was sucking my thumb."

BY 1989, THE ATMOSPHERE IN the S&L industry had become stultifying. Thrift institutions were folding all over the country and the administration of President George Bush had put in place a massive bail-out mechanism. Munger likened the process to "a Chevy Chase movie of extreme duration," and he cut no slack for industry leaders who, with their self-serving positions and lobbying in Washington, sought to save their own skins by perpetuating a bad situation.[6]

"Charlie and I really thought what was going on was awful. We wanted no part of it. We both had a certain fervor," said Buffett.

Like most S&Ls in the early 1980s, Mutual Savings belonged to the powerful trade and lobbying organization, the United States League of Savings Institutions. Munger shocked both the thrift industry and everyday citizens who kept their life savings in S&Ls, with a flaming letter to the U.S. League protesting the group's unwillingness to back S&L reforms.

The letter was dated May 30, 1989.[7] It follows:

Gentlemen:

This letter is the formal resignation of Mutual Savings and Loan Association from the United States League of Saving Institutions.

Mutual Savings is a subsidiary of Wesco Financial Corporation, listed ASE, and Berkshire Hathaway Inc., listed NYSE, which are no longer willing to be associated with the League.

Mutual Savings does not lightly resign after belonging to the League for many years. But we believe that the League's current lobbying operations are so flawed, indeed disgraceful, that we are not willing to maintain membership.

Our savings and loan industry has now created the largest mess in the history of U.S. financial institutions. While the mess has many causes, which we tried to summarize fairly in our last annual report to stockholders, it was made much worse by (1) constant and successful inhibition over many years, through League lobbying, of proper regulatory response to operations of a minority of insured institutions dominated by crooks and fools, (2) Mickey Mouse accounting which made many insured institutions look sounder than they really were, and (3) inadequate levels of real equity capital underlying insured institutions' promises to holders of savings accounts.

It is not unfair to liken the situation now facing Congress to cancer and to liken the League to a significant carcinogenic agent. And, like cancer, our present troubles will recur if Congress lacks the wisdom and courage to excise elements which helped cause the troubles.

Moreover, despite the obvious need for real legislative reform, involving painful readjustment, the League's recent lobbying efforts regularly resist minimal reform. For instance, the League supports (1) extension of accounting conventions allowing 'goodwill' (in the financial institutions' context translate 'air') to count as capital in relations with regulators and (2) minimization of the amount of real equity capital required as a condition of maintenance of full scale operations relying on federal deposit insurance.

In the face of a national disaster which League lobbying plainly helped cause, the League obdurately persists in prescribing continuation of loose accounting principles, inadequate capital, and, in effect, inadequate management at many insured institutions. The League responds to the savings and loan mess as Exxon would have responded to the oil spill from the Valdez if it had insisted thereafter on liberal use of whiskey by tanker captains.

It would be much better if the League followed the wise example, in another era, of the manufacturer which made a public apology to Congress. Because the League has clearly misled its government for a long time, to the taxpayers' great detriment, a public apology is in order, not redoubled efforts to mislead further.

We know that there is a school of thought that trade associations are to be held to no high standard, that they are supposed to act as the League is acting. In this view, each industry creates a trade association not to proffer truth or reason or normal human courtesy following egregious fault, but merely to furnish self-serving nonsense and political contributions to counterbalance, in the legislative milieu, the self-serving nonsense and political contributions of other industries' trade associations. But the evidence is now before us that the type of trade association conduct, when backed as in the League's case by vocal and affluent constituents in every congressional district, has an immense capacity to do harm to the country. Therefore, the League's public duty is to behave in an entirely different way, much as major-league baseball reformed after the "Black Sox" scandal. Moreover, just as client savings institutions are now worse off because of the increased mess caused by League short-sightedness in the past, client institutions will later prove ill-served by the present short-sightedness of the League.

Believing this, Mr. Warren E. Buffett and I are not only causing
Mutual Savings to resign from the U.S. League of Savings Institutions;
we are also, as one small measure of protest, releasing to the media,
for such attention as may ensue, copies of this letter of resignation.

Truly yours,
Charles T. Munger

The U.S. League was clothed in the righteousness of the majority, and
was fortified by friends in the administration. Jim Grohl, spokesman for
the League, told the *Washington Post* that he wouldn't debate Munger's
letter, but added, "I think we have represented the views of our membership. I can assure you we have more resignations from members who
think the League is not pressing hard enough to change the Bush plan."[8]

Incidentally, Munger's fury at the S&L industry did not mean he opposed the concept of deposit insurance, as did some government critics.
Quite the contrary in Munger's case: "I want banking insured. Bank pan-
ics are for the birds."[9]

That same year Munger resigned Mutual Savings from the League,
congress proposed legislative reforms to the industry.

The next year Munger wrote: "When Wesco's annual report went to
press last year, Congress was mid-course in considering revisions to the
savings and loan laws. But it was clear that associations were shortly to
be 're-regulated' into some mode less likely to cause a fresh torrent of
deposit-insurance losses, borne by taxpayers. Provoking that legislative
action was a previous torrent of losses which now seem likely to exceed
$150 billion. These losses were caused by a combination of (1) competi-
tive pressure on the 'spread' between interest paid and interest received
put on associations and banks when federal deposit insurance is provided
to entities free to pay any interest rates they wish in order to attract de-
posits, (2) loose asset deployment rules for associations, (3) admission
and retention of crooks and fools as managers of associations without regulatory objection, (4) general real estate calamities in certain big regions,
and (5) continuous irresponsible protection and enhancement of un-
soundness by the savings and loan lobby and certain members of Congress
beholden to the most despicable savings and loan operators."[10]

Munger took some pride in the idea that Mutual Savings contributed
to tough legislative action by his dramatic and widely printed resignation
letter from the U.S. League of Savings Institutions. Just as he had on the
issue of legalized abortions, Munger had taken off on a divergent path
from his friends in the Republican party. The U.S. League leadership was
heavy with California supporters of President Reagan. As is traditional,

the Federal Home Loan Bank Board was headed by a presidential appointee. In this case, it was a man who formerly worked for California S&L baron Gordon Luce, an old friend of Reagan's, and a major Republican party contributor.

At the same time Munger was haranguing the government and industry leaders over the S&Ls, he helped deal with legal problems at the *Buffalo News.* The surgery on his left eye went awry and he had to learn to live with limited vision. The year he wrote the scathing letter resigning from the S&L League, 1989, his beloved oldest sister Mary died after years of suffering from Parkinson's Disease.

In Wesco's 1989 annual report, Munger said Mutual Savings expected to stay in the S&L business if all went well, but if not, it would get out of the business all together. Despite his optimism that legislative reform would be for the better, it was not. Munger's frustration with the S&L business grew. He described some of the new instruments then being purchased by S&Ls as nothing short of ridiculous.

"As we select mortgage-backed securities, we will probably not be buying any complex instruments. Despite our love of comedy, we are going to avoid the newest form of 'Jump Z tranches in REMICS.' This refers to a particular contractual fraction—the 'Z Form'—of a pool of mortgages, now subdivided by obliging issuers, advised by obliging investment bankers, into two new contractual fractions: (1) the 'sticky Jump Z' and (2) the 'non-sticky Jump Z.' At this rate, subdivision will soon get down to quarks. We are deterred from buying such securities partly by our hatred of complexity. We also dread the prospect of state and federal examiners, none of whom has a PhD in physics, reviewing, one after the other, our choices for soundness and billing us on a cost-plus basis to reflect value thus added. Some of the wonders of modern finance go on without us as we yearn for a lost age when most reasonable people could, with effort, understand what was going on."[11]

The U.S. League, which in 1989 had about 2,800 S&Ls as members, eventually collapsed, and Munger's gloomy predictions regarding the cost of deregulation came to pass. Ultimately, the savings and loan crisis became one of the greatest financial scandals in the nation's history. It took nearly a decade to resolve and some analysts claim it cost taxpayers $1 trillion, or $4,000 for every man, woman and child in the United States.[12]

BUT BEYOND THE ABSURDITY OF IT ALL, Munger realized that the new federal law would have a negative impact on Mutual Savings, a company that was a far different animal from most S&Ls, and had been for quite some time.

Under the re-regulation of S&Ls, Mutual Savings would be forced to dispose of a portfolio of high quality preferred stocks of companies that paid a dividend yield of 10.8 percent per year. The portfolio was carried on the books at a value of $41.1 million at the end of 1989. The sale of the securities would bring Mutual a profit of about $8.7 million, but deprive it of a remarkably high yield from the investments.

Under the new law, Mutual would need to sell its convertible preferred stock of Salomon Inc. which had a tax-advantaged dividend rate of 9 percent per year. The securities had been acquired for $26 million, and though Munger felt that a profit would be realized on the sale of those securities as well, he preferred to play out the Salomon hand in his own way.

The law required that Mutual Savings hold 70 percent of its $300 million in assets primarily in real estate loans. Additionally, deposit insurance premiums would be increased. ". . . by the mid-1990s the new premium rates will reduce Mutual Savings' annual earning power by about $200,000 from the level which would have occurred if it were still paying at the 0.083 percent-of-deposits rate which was in effect for years, instead of the new rate of 0.23 percent," Munger told shareholders.[13]

In 1992, Mutual Savings gave up its S&L charter, liquidated many of its assets, and in 1993 Wesco became a financial holding company not regulated under the S&L laws. Munger explained that the S&L took up a lot of his time in relation to the capital that was involved. About $300 million in capital was transferred to Wesco-Financial Insurance Co., which did business from Berkshire's National Indemnity offices in Omaha. Wes-FIC writes supercatastrophe insurance or "supercat" coverage. Wes-FIC kept Mutual Savings' Freddie Mac stock, however, Mutual Savings had previously sold its $92 million loan portfolio and its $230 million in deposits to CenFed Financial Corp. CenFed took over the operation of Mutual Savings' two offices.

By the time Wesco dedicated most of its assets to the insurance business, Berkshire had built one of the world's largest property-casualty insurance organizations in terms of capital. It seemed like a good business for Wesco and a good fit for Munger and Buffett. "So why shouldn't we do more of what works well for us and what's less complicated," Munger asked.[14]

THOUGH MUNGER EASED WESCO OUT of the S&L business, he was not fully convinced that it would be an easy go as a holding company, since it had become so difficult to find good acquisitions.

"To Wesco, which does not engage in leveraged buy-outs, making good acquisitions was always tough," said Munger. And that game has become increasingly like fishing for muskies at Leech Lake, in Minnesota, where Munger's earliest business partner, Ed Hoskins, had the following conversation with his Indian guide:

> "Are any muskies caught in this lake," asked Hoskins.
> "More muskies are caught in this lake than in any other lake in Minnesota. This lake is famous for muskies.
> "How long have you been fishing here?"
> "Nineteen years."
> "How many muskies have you caught?"
> "None."[15]

"Wesco continues to try more to profit from always remembering the obvious than from grasping the esoteric," said Munger. "It is remarkable how much long-term advantage people like us have gotten by trying to be consistently not stupid, instead of trying to be very intelligent. There must be some wisdom in the folk saying, 'It's the strong swimmers who drown.' "[16]

Nevertheless, some of the businesses acquired by Wesco did not perform well. Such was the case with New American Electric, a company discovered by Glen Mitchel, a Caltech electrical engineer and a friend whom Munger believed had good business abilities.

Charlie suggested Mitchel buy the business, and agreed to go into it with him. Charlie was short of cash at the time, so he and Rick Guerin invested in the electrical supply company through the New America Fund. For years New America Electric, which sold electrical equipment to Southern California home builders and mobile home parks developers, was a cash cow.

It was still a cash cow when New America Fund liquidated. At that time Munger gave Mitchel three choices: (1) distribution of New America Electric shares to New America Fund shareholders, which would turn New America Electric into a small publicly traded company, dominated by Mitchel; (2) sell New America Electric in its entirety in any way Mitchel wished; or (3) have Wesco buy 80 percent of New America Electric at a price approved by Buffett, 70 percent coming from New America Fund and 10 percent coming from Mitchel, leaving him with 20 percent. Mitchel selected the third alternative. However, business conditions soon changed and Mitchel's choice appeared far from optimal for Mitchel, bad for Wesco, and good for New America Fund shareholders like Munger.

The next year California went into one of its periodic real estate nose dives and the company lost about 30 percent of its value.

"It was the worst recession in Southern California since the Depression. New America Electric got clobbered," said Munger. "Wesco sold it at a moderate loss. It wasn't as if I knew it was going to result in a loss to Wesco. If so, I would have never done it. It was very embarrassing."

BESIDES THE FREDDIE MAC STOCK and some preferred shares, all that remains from Wesco's Mutual Savings days is a small real estate subsidiary, MS Property Company, that holds tag ends of assets and liabilities with a net book value of about $13 million. MS Property manages office buildings in downtown Pasadena and a small shopping center in Upland, California. It was under Wesco's property segment that Munger developed "Mungerville," or Montecito Sea Meadow in Santa Barbara.

As it has evolved today, Wesco can be divided into an investment segment, the securities in its insurance subsidiaries, and its business portion. In one year, 47 percent of Wesco's net income came from realized gains on securities it held.

At the end of 1999, Wesco's consolidated balance sheet contained $2.8 billion of marketable securities, stated at market value. The largest holding was Freddie Mac, with a value of $1.9 billion. This holding is the 28.8 million shares of Freddie Mac purchased in 1988 for $71.7 million. The second and third largest holdings were shares of The Coca-Cola Company and The Gillette Company, with a combined value of $800 million. Like Berkshire, Wesco has held preferred stock positions in Travelers, U.S. Airways, and small equity positions in American Express and Wells Fargo.

Wesco's business segments fall into two major categories—insurance and industrial. The company has four major subsidiaries: Wesco-Financial Insurance Company (Wes-FIC, the Omaha-based supercat re-insurer), the Kansas Bankers Surety Company, Precision Steel, and Cort Business Services Corp.

At the end of 1999, the Wes-FIC subsidiary held $2.5 billion in investment assets. Munger called it "a very strong insurance company with very low costs . . ."[17] Nevertheless, Munger often has warned shareholders that "supercat reinsurance is not for the faint of heart. A huge variation in annual results, with some very unpleasant future years for Wes-FIC is inevitable."[18]

As part of its on-going search for appropriate acquisitions, Kansas Bankers Surety Company was purchased in 1996 for $80 million in cash. Founded in 1909, the Topeka, Kansas, company insures about 1,200 banks, including 70 percent of the banks in Nebraska. Originally the KBSC served mainly as a deposit guarantee company.

Though it seems completely out of character for Wesco, since 1979 it has owned Precision Steel, a steel products supplier with locations in Franklin Park, Illinois, and Charlotte, North Carolina.

Wesco acquired Cort Business Services, owner of Cort Furniture Rental, in February 2000, for $467 million cash.

In 1999, Wesco had a 5-year-revenue growth rate of 11.8 percent, and an earnings per share growth rate of 27.64 percent. Total return for 1999 was 19.6 percent; the total return for the previous three years was 58.7 percent; and the 5-year total return was 27.5 percent. Berkshire Hathaway itself doesn't pay dividends, but Wesco Financial, like most of the companies partially owned by Berkshire, does pay them.

"Wesco's dividend policy is that which the minority shareholders prefer," explained Munger, referring to Betty Peters. "At least the ones we know who invited us in. So, we are just deferring to the wishes of the very much minority shareholders. Now you can say, 'that's eccentric,' and you're right."[19]

Buffett explained further, "At Berkshire, incidentally, we have about three or four 80 percent-plus owned subsidiaries where the balance is owned by a few people, as opposed to Wesco, where the minority interest is owned by a great many people. In each case, we tell the owners of the 20 percent or less interest that they set the dividend policy. It's up to them. We have no tax consequences to us in terms of dividend policy, they have the tax consequences. They have a lot of other considerations within families and all of that, and they set the dividend policy."[20]

Since Berkshire owns such a large percentage of the shares and the founding family owns a fairly substantial block, Wesco is thinly traded— averaging 1,300 shares per day on the American Exchange. There are about 5,000 shareholders.

Though Munger does not approve of the practice, many investors pore over Wesco's Form 10-Q filing for insight into Buffett's investing style at Berkshire Hathaway. To investors trying to mimic Buffett this seems to be logical, since Berkshire owns many of the same stocks that Wesco holds.[21]

Analysts sometimes call Wesco a miniature, or "tourist class" version of Berkshire Hathaway, much the same, but cheaper, since Wesco's price tends to fluctuate between $220 and $350 per share, compared to $40,000 to $90,000 per share for Berkshire A. Blue Chip bought its first Wesco stock at about $6 per share and paid around $17 for stock it bought later.

Munger does not like the comparison of Wesco to Berkshire and warned: "Wesco is not an equally-good-but-smaller version of Berkshire Hathaway, better because its small size makes growth easier. Instead, each dollar of book value at Wesco continues to provide much less intrinsic value than a similar dollar of book value at Berkshire Hathaway. Moreover, the quality disparity in book value's intrinsic merits has, in recent years, been widening in favor of Berkshire Hathaway."

Though it was never their intention to do so said Munger, "what we have created at Berkshire and Wesco is, to some extent, a cult. And you can say it's a nice cult and you like the people who join—and we do feel that way. But to some extent, we have followers who are unusually interested in what we do and feel comfortable about investing with us. I think it's had effects on the stock prices of Wesco and Berkshire."[22]

Just to keep everyone's thinking straight, Munger departs from the philosophy of Berkshire Hathaway and in the annual report he calculates Wesco's intrinsic value for shareholders. At the end of 1998, Munger said Wesco's intrinsic value was $342 per share. At that time, Wesco was selling for $354, about 4 percent above intrinsic value.[23]

Munger has no compunction about telling shareholders when the stock is overpriced. Back in 1993, he said, "An orangutan could figure out that the stock is selling miles above the value of the company if it were liquidated. I keep telling people this, but they keep buying the stock."[24]

In June 1999, Munger told shareholders that their equity was worth $294 per share, a decline from the year earlier. The change was based on the fluctuating price of the publicly-traded equities that Wesco owns, which in turn affects Wesco's unrealized gains from these holdings. At the close of 1999, Wesco was trading near its 52-week low of $253, disappointing for investors who during the year saw the stock price soar as high as $353. Part of Wesco's decline could be attributed to its Freddie Mac holdings. After two consecutive years of stock price increases of greater than 50 percent, Freddie Mac's share price was driven back down by higher interest rates. The stock fell 30 percent over a 14-month period between December 1999 and February 2000.

The price dip didn't disturb Munger's equanimity. "I'm 76 years of age," he said. "I've been through a number of down periods. If you live a long time, you're going to be out of investment fashion some of the time."

Munger said it is appropriate to calculate Wesco's intrinsic value for shareholders, and not to do it for Berkshire shareholders, because the companies are quite different.

"Wesco is so liquid and its operating businesses so moderate in size that it's rather easy to make a computation as to its asset value. You can figure out what would happen if you just closed the place and mailed checks back to all the shareholders."

Partly because of the reflected glory of Berkshire, partly because Wesco has many of the same investment holdings that Berkshire does, and partly because of Munger's unusual personality, Wesco attracts its own cult following.

Munger protests at the silliness of it all, but he is willing to sit for hours answering questions posed to him by shareholders and the media. The audience seems to enjoy the discourse, staying until Munger is out of time and must leave for the board meeting that is scheduled directly after the annual meeting.

At the 1999 meeting, when the share price was fluctuating wildly, Charlie explained to Wesco shareholders that some corporate problems seem large at the moment, but in time, they will seem trivial. That is why long-term investing pays off. "Wesco once moved its account from Security Pacific to Bank of America where we had the account get out of balance and nobody at the bank could get it back in balance. We closed our account and let it run out and made some accounting adjustments. In five years, nobody will remember. . . ."

CHAPTER FIFTEEN

THE BLOSSOMING OF BERKSHIRE HATHAWAY

If you're going to learn to drive a car, it doesn't do any good just to know how to use the accelerator. There are four or five things you have to know before you understand the system correctly. I do think some things are way more important than others, and in the game we're in, understanding the advantages of scale, scale of experience, efficiency in the plant, scale of experience in leasing, other advantages of scale. [Take] Adam Smith's pin factory, I think that's a very important basic concept, but it's just one.[1]

Charlie Munger

C HARLIE MUNGER WAS CALLED UPON to testify in court when a small Los Angeles legal publication sued the Daily Journal Corporation for unfair trade practices. To demonstrate Munger's experience in evaluating the worth of a business, attorney Ron Olson first established that Munger was vice chairman of Berkshire Hathaway, chairman of Wesco Financial, and former chairman of Blue Chip Stamps. His testimony provided a thumbnail sketch of how Berkshire grew into a twenty-first century company.

Q. Mr. Munger, during the course of these several business associations, did you have occasion to buy and sell other companies?

A. Well, we've done way more buying than selling. Because we're successful, we just kept buying one company after another. By now I think we've bought well over a hundred. And maybe we've sold two. We don't like what we call gin rummy management where you're always buying and selling. We like to buy and hold.

Q. Would you give the jury a little bit of a feel for what's involved in analyzing a company before an acquisition is made?

A. Sure. You start with the accounting figures. But that's only the start. If you try and make judgments just based on accounting figures, you will make one terrible error after another. We've got to understand the accounting and the implications of the accounting and understand it thoroughly and also ask a lot of intelligent questions to enable us to judge what is really going on.

Q. Do these questions take you into an assessment of the direction of the general business climate for that particular industry or business?

A. Yes. We do some of that. But more, we like the quality of the individual business. If we admire a management enough, and we admire the way a company is run enough, we will occasionally buy one that's in kind of a lousy industry.

Q. So assessment of management is another factor that you take into account?

A. You bet.[2]

WHEN CHARLIE MUNGER AND WARREN BUFFETT MET, they were young, Munger in his mid-30s and Buffett in his late-20s and as Nancy Munger noted, they were men in a hurry. After they started working in tandem, success came much faster to both. Buffett handled the East Coast clients he inherited when Ben Graham and Jerome Newman closed their partnership and continued to recruit new investors, mostly from Nebraska. At the same time, Munger started steering California investors in Buffett's direction.

"Charlie recognized Warren's genius before anybody. If I had totally listened to Charlie about Warren I'd be a lot richer now," said Munger's former real estate and investment partner Al Marshall.

One person who did "totally" listen to Munger was Otis Booth, the man who came to his law office seeking help in buying a printing plant and ended up Munger's partner in two lucrative condominium construction deals. In 1963, Munger suggested to Booth that he go see Buffett.

"After I'd been in Charlie's partnership a year or two, he told me about Warren and showed me the record from 1957 on," recalled Booth. "In 1963 or 1964, I went back to Omaha, spent a night there and spoke to him about investments."

The two men sat up all night talking. "I wrote a check shortly after that. The partnership was open once a year. I think I wrote half that year and half the next—$1 million. I wrote $500,000 on the first check, but I had earnings on that, so the next year it was less than $500,000. I also had a million in Charlie's partnership," Booth said.

Buffett's partnership only lasted about five more years. In the late 1950s and early 1960s, Buffett began accumulating shares of a struggling old New England manufacturer of textiles, handkerchiefs, and suit linings. Contrary to popular belief, Berkshire Hathaway never did make shirts. Buffett bought his first shares from Tweedy, Browne, a New York investment firm with links to Ben Graham and a reputation for its strict value approach. Tweedy, Browne's offices near Grand Central Station, said Munger, is a place Buffett "used to hang out when he was young and poor."[3]

Buffett disbanded his partnership in 1969, explaining that the stock market had become overblown and it was too difficult to find bargain stocks. Shareholders received several recommendations as to what to do with their money. Buffett suggested that investors might want to participate in his friend William Ruane's well-respected Sequoia Fund (now closed to new investment), or they could do what Buffett was doing with his own money.

By the time he disbanded the partnership, Buffett had accumulated enough shares of Berkshire Hathaway to take control of the company, and he would be transferring the fund's prized assets and most of his personal money in Berkshire's corporate structure. It would be a leap of faith for investors, since it wasn't clear what Buffett intended to do with the company. For 20 years he tried to run it as a manufacturing plant while making other investments simultaneously. But Munger described Berkshire as "a small, doomed New England textile enterprise" and he was correct.[4]

Calling the purchase of Berkshire one of his worst financial mistakes, Buffett gave up trying to make it profitable as a manufacturer. In 1985, he liquidated the business and concentrated entirely on buying and holding other companies. Even the loyal early investors were surprised at how well the reconfigured Berkshire would do.

Otis Booth, Al Marshall, and Rick Guerin are just three of the people, most of them from the West Coast, whom Charlie brought into the Buffett family of investors. Booth lives today in a gated Tudor home in the Bel Air section of Los Angeles next door to Disney Chairman Michael Eisner. Booth's net worth is estimated at $1.4 billion. Guerin and his family live in a large Spanish colonial-style estate in Beverly Hills, with a sweeping view of mountains, tree tops, and Los Angeles. Marshall and his wife Martha are spending their retirement years in a golf course home in Palm Springs.

Between 1976 and 1986, a number of events transpired. Both Munger and Buffett had closed their partnerships, Blue Chip and its subsidiaries were merged into Berkshire, and life became simpler. As a holding company for insurance and other subsidiaries, Berkshire would not be subject to the same regulatory pressures to diversify as the typical mutual fund or pension fund. The company owned several cash-laden companies outright and its stock portfolio was heavily concentrated in a small group of select companies. Munger and Buffett had laid their groundwork and Berkshire Hathaway as we know it today was taking shape.

Even with simplification, so much was happening at once and so many deals overlapped, the pace of acquisitions was dizzying. Within two years after Munger and Buffett began consolidating, Berkshire's major stock holdings included American Broadcasting Companies Inc. (ABC), Government Employees Insurance Company (GEICO) common and preferred, and SAFECO Corporation. They soon bought outright the Nebraska Furniture Mart and Omaha's premier jewelry emporium, Borsheim's. There were stakes in the advertising agencies Interpublic and Ogilvy & Mather, and in the *Boston Globe*, all three of which were later sold.

Buffett had owned GEICO shares when he was in college, but later sold them. When he bought into the company again in 1976, GEICO had been mismanaged, one of its top executives had committed suicide, and the company was near bankruptcy. Despite Buffett's wish not to buy into companies that needed to be rescued, he saw fundamental advantages to GEICO's business and believed that with discipline and direction, it could survive and prosper. A similar decision had been made in 1963 with American Express, and that worked out well.

Between 1976 and 1981, Berkshire invested $45 million in GEICO, which by 1995 was worth more than $1.9 billion. Eventually Berkshire bought the whole company. Munger said there was no particular strategy involved, except to wait and watch for opportunities.

"Our rule is pure opportunism," said Charlie. "We do not have a master plan. If there is a master plan somewhere in Berkshire, they're hiding it from me. Not only do we not have a master plan, we don't have a master planner."[5]

In 1985, Munger and Buffett snatched Scott & Fetzer from the grasp of hostile suitor Ivan Boesky for $315 million. Scott & Fetzer is the parent of World Book Encyclopedia and Kirby vacuum cleaners.

In the second half of 1989, Berkshire cut three big deals that signaled once and for all that Berkshire was a sophisticated contender in the world of finance. A $1.3 billion investment was made in Gillette, USAir, and

Champion International. Buffett and Munger negotiated together with Gillette Chairman Coleman Mockler. In July 1989, Berkshire invested $600 million in Gillette's preferred stock, all of which later was converted into common shares. Gillette has the sort of folksy history that appeals to both Munger and Buffett. It was founded in 1901 as the American Safety Razor Co. by King C. Gillette. The company's first office was located over a fish market on the Boston waterfront. The company changed its name to Gillette Safety Razor Co. in 1904. Gillette dominates the worldwide market for razors with a 40 percent market share. In addition to the razor blade business, Gillette owns Liquid Paper, Paper Mate and Waterman pens, and Oral-B toothbrushes. In 1996 Gillette acquire Duracell batteries for $7.8 billion, the largest purchase Gillette ever made.

Gillette's earnings grew at an impressive 15.9 percent between 1985, but in the late 1990s it invested huge amounts of research and development funds in a new razor that sold well, but not quite as well as hoped. Its earnings eventually slumped and Gillette's subsequent poor stock performance was one contributor to a decline in Berkshire Hathaway's share price.

CONTRARY TO WHAT SOME ANALYSTS CLAIM, Berkshire Hathaway is not a closed-end fund. "No, it never was," said Munger. "We always preferred operating companies to marketable securities. We used float to buy other stocks. Berkshire has a lot of marketable securities—and big operating companies. We like that system. We generate all this cash. We started out that way, buying companies that throw off cash. Why should we change?"

Buffett had learned the basics of insurance when he was in graduate school studying under Graham, who at the time was chairman of GEICO. Buffett has used that expertise at Berkshire. Way back when Munger and Buffett were acquiring Blue Chip Stamps shares, Berkshire made its first substantial foray into insurance, purchasing National Indemnity Company in Omaha for approximately $8.6 million. Many of Berkshire's very large investments are made through National Indemnity.

During this activity, Munger kept agitating to buy better quality companies, ones with strong earnings potential for the long-term and ones he believed would be less troublesome to own.

"There are huge advantages for an individual to get into a position where you make a few great investments and just sit back," said Munger. "You're paying less to brokers. You're listening to less nonsense. . . . If it works, the governmental tax system gives you an extra one, two, or three percentage points per annum with compound effects."[6]

Warren Buffett, Charlie and Nancy Munger arrive at a Buffett Group gathering.

Starting with See's Candy, Munger nudged Buffett in the direction of paying up for quality. "Charlie was very instrumental in pushing Warren toward Coca Cola type investments—a franchise that will have carrying value for generations," observed Ron Olson. "That is consistent with how Charlie conducts his own life. He's not looking for a quick victory, but to long-term success."

In 1988, Berkshire started acquiring Coca Cola stock, and within about six months purchased 7 percent of the company. At an average price of $5.46 a share, it was a total investment of $1.02 billion. Buffett, an addict of caffeinated soft drinks, felt confident that Coca Cola was a quality company with superior long-term prospects. In fact, Buffett himself gave up Pepsi Cola in favor of Coke.[7]

"Many times, Charlie elevates Warren's thinking—such as going for a stronger franchise. They can converse on any level," said *Buffalo News* publisher Stan Lipsey. "When you have people that are thinking and living at that level, you not only get the intellectual exchange, you get ideas that are complementary."

Apparently Munger hasn't always agreed with Buffett when it came to personal investing, which at times worked to his advantage. When Buffett sold Berkshire's Capital Cities Communications stock in 1978 to 1980, he later regretted the sale. Munger, however, kept some personal holdings of Cap Cities, which performed exceptionally well.[8]

Despite their blazing success, Buffett and Munger tried numerous ideas that didn't pan out. Before they bought their *Washington Post* shares, Buffett and Munger called on Katharine Graham and asked her to participate in purchasing the *New Yorker* magazine. Graham didn't even know who these two guys from west of the Potomac River were, and she didn't think twice before turning down their proposal.

"People used to bring projects in all the time. I just thought about whether we wanted to be partners in the *New Yorker*. At the time I didn't. I thought it needed a new editor and I didn't know how to choose one. I sent them to see Fritz Beebe," said Graham.

The *New Yorker* was a lost opportunity, but probably not a huge loss. Failures and misfires were part of the record during this period. "Some major mistakes have been made during the decade, both in products and personnel," Buffett wrote in Berkshire's 1977 annual report. Yet, he added, "It's comforting to be in a business where some mistakes can be made and yet quite satisfactory overall performance can be achieved. In a sense, this is the opposite of our textile business where even very good management probably can average only modest results. One of the lessons your management has learned—and unfortunately, sometimes re-learned—is the importance of being in businesses where tailwinds prevail rather than headwinds."[9]

Throughout the 1980s and straight through to the end of the century, Buffett and Munger showed a knack for getting a good deal. When they buy a company, the management usually stays with it and the acquisition requires very little effort, except for collecting profits and allocating the capital to its highest and best use.

"Our chief contribution to the businesses we acquire," said Munger, "is what we don't do." What they don't do is interfere with effective managers, especially those with certain characteristics.[10]

"There's integrity, intelligence, experience, and dedication," said Charlie. "That's what human enterprises need to run well. And we've been very lucky in getting this marvelous group of associates to work with all these years. It would be hard to do better, I think, than we've done."

Writing for an insurance publication, John Nauss, a Chartered Property and Casualty Underwriter, observed: "Warren and Charlie commented that they simply get out of the way and let their managers focus on running their businesses without interference or concern about other factors. But they do more. They create, perhaps, the best operating environment for businesses that exist anywhere. This environment includes wise evaluations without extensive meetings and documents (we know the business) as well as capital access, focused compensation, and freedom to do one's best." These methods, said Nauss, deserve greater attention from the business community.[11]

BOTH CHARLIE AND WARREN SAY they set the example for Berkshire companies by keeping their own overhead costs at a minimum. Berkshires' headquarters are simple and the staff is small. The company's overhead ratio is $\frac{1}{250}$th that of many mutual funds.

"I don't know of anybody our size who has lower overhead than we do," Munger said. "And we like it that way. Once a company starts getting fancy," he said, "it's difficult to stop."

"In fact, Warren once considered buying a building on a distressed basis for about a quarter of what it would have cost to duplicate. And tempting as it was, he decided that it would give everybody bad ideas to have surroundings so opulent. So we continue to run our insurance operations from very modest quarters."[12]

At one time Berkshire was subpoenaed for its "staff papers" in connection with one of its acquisitions, but, said Munger, "There were no papers. There was no staff."[13]

But, as Munger so often says, what's right for Berkshire isn't necessarily right for all companies. "We've decentralized power in our operating businesses to a point just short of total abdication. . . . Our model's not right for everybody, but it's suited us and the kind of people who've joined us. But we don't have criticism for others—such as General Electric—who operate with plans, compare performance against plans, and all that sort of thing. That's just not our style." He added, "Berkshire's assets have been lovingly put together so as not to require continuing intelligence at headquarters."

Berkshire Hathaway is one of the best-performing stocks in the history of the market. Its shares have underperformed the S&P in only five of the past 34 years, and book value has never had a declining year. An investor who put $10,000 into Berkshire shares in 1965 would have been worth $51 million on December 1, 1998, versus a worth of $132,990 if the money had been invested in the S&P. In 1999, PaineWebber insurance analyst Alice Schroeder estimated Berkshire's intrinsic value at $92,253 per share. Using a more conservative approach, Seth Klarman of the Baupost Fund estimated Berkshire to be worth between $62,000 to $73,000 per share. At that time, the shares had retreated from their historic high in the $90,000 range, to around $65,600, and the price declined even lower before recovering.

Shareholders are understandably loyal to a company with such a record. Some families have invested with Buffett for two, three, and four generations. Not only did Dr. Ed Davis and his wife benefit from Berkshire Hathaway, so did the Davis children and their families. Willa and Lee Seemann have been with Berkshire since 1957. "People say the stock is so high—I say yea, and it's going higher. The way to make money is to get a damn good stock and stick with it," insisted Seemann.

JUST AS THE COLLECTION OF Berkshire holdings built over time, so has the crowd at the annual meeting. "I remember when the attendance at the Berkshire annual meeting was not much of anything," said Stan Lipsey. "Warren said 'we'll have a board meeting (actually, just a lunch), and said come on up,'" and that was about it.

Otis Booth attended the meeting in 1970, when by happenstance he was returning from the East Coast and Buffett suggested he stop in Omaha. "There were only six or eight people present, Fred Stanback, Guerin, Munger, and a few others. We all went out to dinner later," Booth recalled.

Around 1990, Berkshire, Buffett, and to some extent Munger, began developing a noticeable reputation. "I heard Charlie say for the first time he was getting worried about adulators—movie star, rock star-type adulators. That was more than 10 years ago, when we met at the museum," said Lipsey. At that same meeting, Lipsey got more of a glimpse into Munger's character. "I had rented a normal-sized car, then I noticed Charlie had rented a smaller one."

The number of people attending Berkshire's annual meeting grew from 250 in 1985 to more than 11,000 in 1999. Most of Omaha gears up for the Berkshire weekend. Gorat's, Buffett's favorite steak house, ordered an extra 3,000 pounds of tenderloins and T-bones to feed the 1,500 people who were expected to dine there.[14]

In the audience at the Berkshire Hathaway meeting are apt to be some impressive, though barely noticeable, people. Among them—former FCC chairman Newton Minnow; Microsoft founder Bill Gates, and sometimes his father Bill Sr.; Disney's Michael Eisner; Abigail (Dear Abby) Van Buren, and Chicago billionaire Lester Crown.[15]

The rise in attendance isn't entirely unwelcome. Buffett enjoys seeing the shareholders and goes out of his way to put on a good show. The Berkshire Hathaway business meeting only lasts five to ten minutes, but the question-and-answer period can last up to six hours, with as many as 80 questions posed by shareholders. At the meeting, it is Munger's designated role to play stoic straight man to Buffett's one-liners. Nevertheless it was clear that Munger's influence on Berkshire continued to be strong. In 1997, Berkshire's Los Angeles lawyer Ron Olson was named to the Berkshire board.

Buffett and Munger hold court, dispensing corporate wisdom—and as Charlie likes to remind people—facing the world as it really is. A shareholder once complained that there were no great franchises like Coca Cola left, meaning that Berkshire's style would be cramped in the future. Munger replied, "Why should it be easy to do something that, if done well two or three times, will make your family rich for life?"[16]

Munger, like Buffett, is a fan of Berkshire-owned products. He drinks Coca Cola, though not as much of it as Buffett does. Unlike Buffett, who is a teetotaler, Munger doesn't mind substituting his Coke with an occasional beer or glass of wine. At the 1994 annual meeting, Munger put in a plug for World Book Encyclopedias:

> I give away more of that product than any other product that Berkshire Hathaway makes. . . . It's a perfectly fabulous human achievement. To edit something that is user-friendly with that much wisdom encapsulated is a fabulous thing.[17]

While Munger can be as smug about the success of Berkshire as its investors are, he can't resist telling everyone why they're there.

"It's wonderful that we all come here each year," Charlie told a group of friends at his own dinner party the weekend of the Berkshire annual meeting. "But why do we really do it? Yes, it's fun. But it's also a way of subtly saying, I'm very rich. It's also a way of subtly saying, I'm very smart."

Munger then went on to say that it was becoming a problem to Berkshire that many original shareholders were getting older and dividing up the shares among their heirs. It makes the shareholder base grow to unwieldy proportions. Charlie suggested that everyone bring their unmarried children and grandchildren to the annual meeting and hold mixer dances so the Berkshire heirs could meet and marry one another, thus keeping the shares within fewer families. Just another one of Charlie's semi-bewildering jokes.

WHILE BERKSHIRE HATHAWAY WAS GAINING size and influence and Munger was growing wealthier, his family was blissfully unaware of what was happening to their lives. As far as Emilie Munger was concerned, her father was chairman of Blue Chip Stamps, and Blue Chip Stamps were something you got at a store and pasted in a book.

"I don't remember when Berkshire started growing to a point at which he was in a different league," said Emilie. "I think my parents were really private. They didn't want publicity. My dad was a creature of habit so everything was exactly the same. We never had a feeling we were growing up in some rich household."

Though Charlie was becoming a celebrity in Omaha, in star-strewn Los Angeles and on the rest of the West Coast, he didn't attract much attention.

"Over time," said Emilie, "nothing changed about the way we were perceived. Not until I was in law school in 1989. I realized some group over at the business school recognized my name."

The lack of interest the Munger children showed in their father's career, said Emilie "probably had something to do with coming of age in the 1960s and 1970s. I went to a fairly liberal college—almost an anti-business atmosphere. There was a lot of socialism. Evil corporate America. Our schools were more public service or public policy oriented. When Wendy and Molly went to school, it was really different."

If Emilie Munger's classmates had been inclined to study Berkshire and it's business practices, they no doubt would have been surprised that the company operates nothing like other corporate giants. Munger and Buffett have remained steadfast in keeping their own compensation low. Each takes $100,000 in salary, plus directors fees from various corporations not controlled by Berkshire. Munger's 1998 directors fees came to about $81,300. Their enormous wealth comes from their ownership shares of Berkshire, though that is more true for Buffett than it is for Munger. Buffett's proportional ownership is much larger, but Munger also follows a slightly different financial path.

"Charlie's family has 90 percent or more of its net worth in Berkshire shares," said Buffett. "My wife, Susie, and I have more than 99 percent."

Though Buffett says he almost never sells shares, Munger sometimes does. In fact between 1993 and 1997 he sold $25 million worth of Berkshire. Additionally, Munger has given away hundreds of shares, including a share to Robert Cialdini, author of the book *Influence,* just because he likes him and his work.

"I've given away a fair amount of Berkshire (stock) in the last couple of years," Munger said. "I gave away a lot . . . because I thought it was the correct way to behave. And I've sold some because I've had businesses of my own."[18]

THERE ARE LESSONS TO BE learned from his personal career and from the development of Berkshire Hathaway, and they are learnable, as long as people don't confuse simplicity with ease, says Munger, though he doesn't think everyone will learn them.

"People underrate the importance of a few simple big ideas. And I think to the extent Berkshire Hathaway is a didactic enterprise teaching the right systems of thought, the chief lesson is that a few big ideas really work. I think these filters of ours have worked pretty well—because they are so simple," says Munger.

Even so, Munger said of Berkshire, "I knew it would do well, but not this well."[19]

Munger's children say they continue to benefit from their father's example. "It's a rich lesson to learn," said Molly Munger. "If you just keep pressing on and don't let anything that happens get to you, your life is so much better."

CHAPTER SIXTEEN

BERKSHIRE IN THE 1990s— POWER BUILDING

The game of investing is one of making better predictions about the future than other people. How are you going to do that? One way is to limit your tries to areas of competence. If you try to predict the future of everything, you attempt too much. You're going to fail through lack of specialization.[1]

Charlie Munger

"ONE OF CHARLIE'S MAXIMS ABOUT practicing law is the best source of legal work is the work on your desk," said Robert Denham, the Munger, Tolles & Olson attorney who handles much of Berkshire Hathaway's legal work. Following that philosophy, said Denham, his working relationship with Charlie, Warren, and Berkshire has "grown organically."

In fact, Munger, Tolles and its foremost client Berkshire grew together through the 1970s and 1980s. Building brick by brick, Berkshire emerged in the 1990s with its corporate identity and its position in the business world secured. From that time on, Munger and Buffett often found themselves either on the spot or in the spotlight. At the start of the 1990s, Berkshire owned a remarkable collection of businesses and a strong portfolio of securities. Not only did the operating businesses bring in large amounts of cash, the Berkshire insurance companies were building substantial amounts of float—all money for Buffett and Munger to work with. Acquisitions continued apace, and for the most part the investments were in high quality companies.

"Charlie made me focus on the merits of a great business with tremendously growing earning power," said Buffett, "but only when you

176

can be sure of it—not like Texas Instruments or Polaroid, where the earning power was hypothetical."[2]

Buffett continued to practice some of the arbitrage techniques he learned from Ben Graham and occasionally made short-term investments. Berkshire bought RJR Nabisco junk bonds in 1989 through 1990, Wells Fargo Bank shares from 1989 through 1991, and in 1991 Berkshire acquired H.H. Brown Shoe Company, the leading North American shoe manufacturer, which in turn bought the Lowell Shoe Company.

In 1992, Buffett acquired 14 percent of the stock of General Dynamics, a company largely owned by his long-time friends, the Crown family of Chicago. General Dynamics' military business was badly wounded when the Cold War ended, and the management was drastically restructuring GD for its new, smaller book of businesses. Several things then happened in the world, including a civil war in Eastern Europe and a company-sponsored Dutch auction to buy back shares. GD's stock shot from Buffett's $11 purchase price to $43.50 and he later sold his shares at a substantial profit. The same year, Berkshire bought 82 percent of Central States Indemnity, a credit insurance company.

In 1993, Berkshire got FTC permission to raise its existing stake in Salomon Bros. to 25 percent, and the same year Berkshire expanded its shoe holdings by purchasing Dexter Shoe in a stock swap. In 1995, Berkshire added to its home furnishings and jewelry store business with the purchase of R.C. Willey Home Furnishings and Helzberg's Diamond Shops.

About this time Buffett and Munger began to draw fire from critics, the *Wall Street Journal* especially, for getting better deals on their investments than other investors would. The terms of the deals were particularly attractive in cases such as Salomon and USAir, where the investment was not acquired on the open market. In these situations, Berkshire was summoned by management as a white knight, either to save the company from a hostile takeover or to provide a desperately needed cash infusion. The deal was negotiated, often taking the form of preferred stock that had an interest rate component and a feature that allowed conversion to common stock at a specified price.

Munger defended such arrangements, saying that it is appropriate that Berkshire get terms not available to others, because Berkshire "brings more to the party than just our money." Munger said Buffett provides advice and expertise, in addition to "patient" capital that allows management to pursue long-term strategies. And, pointed out Munger, other shareholders also benefit when the stock in these companies rise.[3]

This acquisition list includes only some of Berkshire's purchases during the early 1990s, but they demonstrate a pattern. Berkshire was sticking to the admittedly broad range of industries Buffett and Munger knew best, but with a particular emphasis on the insurance field.

Perhaps even more important, during the last decade of the century, Munger and Buffett were able to pursue their preferred strategy of swallowing companies whole whenever possible. When Berkshire owns a company entirely, the two are free to allocate the company's profits as they see fit. The structure of Berkshire's holdings made a dramatic transition. At the beginning of 1996, Berkshire's stock portfolio accounted for 76 percent of its $29.9 billion in assets. By the end of the first quarter of 1999, the stocks represented only 32 percent of assets, which by then had reached $124 billion. During those three years, Berkshire spent $27.3 billion to buy seven companies.[4] At the 2000 annual meeting, Munger and Buffett explained that by owning companies in their entirety, they could minimize the impact of a whimsical stock market or Berkshire's share price.

Berkshire's approximately $36.6 million holdings in cash and equivalents and its AAA credit rating gave Munger and Buffett enormous buying power. PaineWebber insurance analysts Alice Schroeder and Gregory Lapin point out that Berkshire has become the "buyer of first resort" for business owners who want to continue to operate their companies, while at the same time freeing themselves from raising and allocating capital. The sellers also include privately or closely-held corporations where the major investors want the option of cashing out all or part of their equity at will. This is made possible when the owners swap their ownership for Berkshire shares with limited tax consequences, then later sell Berkshire stock when it meets their needs.

Berkshire prefers to pay cash, but when necessary, will do a stock swap. Many families with a large stake in a company insist on a tax-free transfer, lest they lose a large portion of their wealth to the Internal Revenue Service.

"It's not by accident that recent acquisitions at Berkshire Hathaway have been with stock. It's hard to make cash transactions in this market," said Munger.

"Berkshire's ability to instantly commit capital to ideas—no committee process or elaborate prospectus required—means that good investment ideas go to Omaha first," wrote Schroeder and Lapin. "We believe that (1) Berkshire generally approaches businesses it wants to buy only once, and (2) no one ever gets a better price from Berkshire the second time around. This also gives the company a strong advantage in buying businesses."[5]

HIGH QUALITY INSURANCE BUSINESSES WITH massive float continued to be the rocket fueling Berkshire's vertical ascent. As mentioned earlier, Buffett first started learning about insurance at Columbia University when he discovered that his professor, Ben Graham, was chairman of GEICO. Berkshire first entered the insurance business in 1967 with an investment of $8.6 million. By the late 1990s, the insurance capital had topped $10 billion.[6] Munger said the insurance companies have done well because of a conservative business approach. Asked at Wesco's 1993 annual meeting why Berkshire didn't write more insurance policies, considering its size, Munger replied:

> People are always saying to Berkshire, 'Gee, why don't you write a lot more volume in relation to capital? Everyone else is doing it. The rating agencies say that you can write twice as much in annual volume as you have capital ' And they look at our $10 billion in insurance capital and say, 'That's $20 billion a year. What are you doing writing only $1 billion?' But then . . . somebody else comes in and asks, 'Why did everybody get killed last year but you?' Maybe the questions are related.

Munger admitted that Berkshire's huge "supercat," or catastrophic event insurance unit, makes the company somewhat vulnerable, but he thinks they've become experts at evaluating the risk and dealing with it appropriately. A big loss from a California earthquake might cause an insurance loss as high as $600 million for the company, and that would be "irritating," Munger said. The 1994 Northridge, California, earthquake, produced a significant loss, though the company didn't say how much. Nevertheless, that year Berkshire's insurance division reported earnings of $129.9 million from insurance plus $419.4 million from investments.[7]

"If we have a real disaster—if you had Hurricane Andrew followed one week later by another one just like it—Berkshire would have a very unpleasant year," said Munger.

Both Munger and Buffett have repeatedly warned shareholders that as the company grows in assets, it will have more difficulty maintaining an earnings growth rate, and thus share price growth, at the levels of the past two decades.

"Size, at a certain point, gets to be an anchor, which drags you down," explained Munger. "We always knew that it would. You get $10 billion in marketable securities. Show me unbelievable compound rates when people get $10 billion."[8]

They did, however, find places to put their money. In August 1994, Warren Buffett had in his pocket about $2 billion from the sale of Capital Cities/ABC Inc. to Walt Disney Company. He began negotiating that same month with Louis A. Simpson, GEICO's co-chairman to buy the 50 percent of the insurance company Berkshire didn't already own. There were several thorny issues to be resolved, including how to fairly manage a stock trade when GEICO paid a dividend and Berkshire did not.

Negotiations continued for seven months and the New York investment banking firm Morgan Stanley was brought in to help set a fair price for GEICO. Using cash flow and other yardsticks, Morgan Stanley said GEICO's value could be as low as $50.80 or as high as $73.43 a share. Ultimately, Morgan Stanley suggested $70 as a fair price. Buffett said he wanted to talk to Munger about the deal. Later the same day, he offered $70 per share in cash to GEICO shareholders.[9]

It cost Berkshire $2.3 billion to buy the second half of GEICO at that price. With GEICO, Berkshire got the full-time services of Lou Simpson, who is believed by many to be Buffett's heir apparent. The shy, Princeton-educated Simpson had been in charge of investing GEICO's float and continues to do so after the acquisition. GEICO's fixed income portfolio is now managed from Berkshire headquarters. Simpson had been beating the market since at least 1980 and has an investment record nearly as good as Buffett's. In 1997, 1998, and 1999, however, Simpson's return failed to match the return on the Standard and Poor's 500, which meant that instead of earning a bonus, Simpson owed Berkshire money.

Simpson became known to investors in the mid-1990s when shareholders pressured Buffett, then in his mid-60s, to reveal his succession plan. Warren mentioned somewhat casually that there was plenty of backup, including Simpson. However, Munger says Buffett did not mean to imply that Simpson would replace him, merely that Simpson was immediately available if necessary. "We could have done the job of naming a replacement directly and not in some crazy, indirect way," Munger insisted.[10]

A few years after the GEICO purchase, Berkshire surprised the insurance world and nailed down its position as an insurance leader with a $22 billion acquisition of General Reinsurance (Gen Re). This huge acquisition was described as a "watershed event" in Berkshire's history by some analysts, and Buffett himself said, "We are creating Fort Knox."[11]

Berkshire Hathaway's stock was trading near an all-time high when in 1998 Buffett acquired the reinsurance giant in a stock swap deal.

"Warren's timing is uncanny," said Otis Booth. "He bought out Gen Re when Berkshire's stock was trading at around $80,000 in a stock-for-stock merger."

Munger points out, however, that Gen Re's stock, too was trading at a high price. These overall high valuations in the market, however, were about to go through some adjustments.

In the Gen Re transaction, a substantial number of institutional investors were added to Berkshire's mix of shareholders, since 70 percent of Gen Re was held by mutual funds, insurance companies and pension plans.

Berkshire had trending in that direction, but now it was primarily a property-casualty insurer, with 79 percent of its revenues and operating earnings from insurance. Based on premiums, it is the fourth largest U.S.-based casualty insurance company. With revenues of $4 billion, GEICO is the seventh largest auto insurer in the United States, and the eighteenth largest insurer overall. But Gen Re focuses on insuring the risks on insurance companies themselves, thus it's name, General Reinsurance. Based on premiums and surplus, Gen Re is the largest direct-writing reinsurance provider in the United States and third largest in the world, with 1997 revenues of $8.3 billion. Added to that, National Indemnity, headed by Buffett's bridge-playing friend Ajit Jain, is the most prominent supercat underwriter in the nation.

The purchase of Gen Re gave Berkshire a net worth of $56 billion, the highest of any company in the United States, and a stock market capitalization of $120 billion. At the start of 1999, Schroeder and Lapin estimated Berkshire's intrinsic, or actual per-share value at $91,253 (for B shares, that would be $3,041 per share). And of course, Berkshire's insurance float kept growing. It is estimated that Berkshire's float from all of its insurance operations in 1998 was just under $23 billion, and would escalate to nearly $53 billion a year by 2008.

However, there was a set-back. Almost immediately after Berkshire acquired Gen Re, it was discovered that the insurance company had made an underwriting error that would affect its short-term profits. But Munger and Buffett were undaunted. Their experience told them that long-term, the re-insurer remained an excellent purchase.

THE PUBLIC HOLDS MUNGER AND Buffett to exceptionally high standards. They get more attention for their difficult deals than they do their trouble-free deals.

Such was the case when in 1990, Buffett and Munger bought a $358 million stake in USAirways preferred stock that could be converted into a 12 percent ownership of the airline. Both men joined the airline's board of directors. USAir's motive in selling the shares to Berkshire was to bring much-needed funds into the company and at the same time make itself less vulnerable to an unwelcome takeover by someone else.

USAir, cobbled together from mergers over time of Lake Central, Mohawk, Piedmont, and Pacific Southwest Airlines, had made itself a contender for top national carrier. Then, after an impressive start, USAir ran into serious problems.

Munger and Buffett had stepped into a real mess. At Berkshire's 1991 annual meeting, Munger describe an airline as "marginal cost with wings." Charlie's gripe was against the now defunct Eastern Airlines which brought other carriers down with it as it fought for survival. He believed a bankruptcy judge should have shut Eastern down earlier than he did. Munger explained that once an airline files for bankruptcy, it is then operating debt free, thus it can be more competitive than a solvent one.

Just as S&L deregulation had unsettled that industry, airline deregulation was underway, leading to a scramble for industry dominance. In addition to competing with Eastern's low fares, USAir suffered a series of fatal crashes between 1991 and 1994 which devastated both employee morale and passenger loyalty. In its eerily scientific objectivity, the National Transportation and Safety Board described a 1994 USAir accident in Pennsylvania in which 132 people died, as "an uncontrolled descent and collision with terrain."[12]

In 1994, USAir stopped paying dividends on preferred shares. That same year, Berkshire wrote down its investment in the company, taking a $269.5 million pretax charge on the books. In 1995, Berkshire's stake, which was acquired for $358 million, was valued at only $86 million.

Lawsuits, operating problems, and especially labor union troubles were so intractable that the pair resigned from the board after two years. Munger and Buffett stepped down in 1995 after the airline failed to win cost-saving concessions from its unions.

When an investor asked Munger to explain the economics of Berkshire's involvement in USAir, Munger replied, "I'm glad you've given me the opportunity to display my small share of humility. . . . We did not display our greatest brilliance."

In 1996, Buffett tried to sell the USAir shares, but luckily, he was unsuccessful. The very next year, USAir reported the best quarterly profits in the airline's history and, although it was as difficult as turning the Titanic away from the iceberg, USAir made a reversal.[13]

"When Charlie and I left the board, the fortunes of USAir went abruptly upward," quipped Buffett, suggesting that things work better if they stay away.[14] USAir finally was able to pay preferred dividends in arrears, and on February 3, 1998, USAir redeemed Berkshire's $358 million in preferred stock.

"It was a humbling experience. To sit there and watch that net worth melt away—$150 million, $200 million—to watch a lot of lovely money that used to be yours and see it melt away. . . . And all those unions that could only think about reality from their own point of view. And the idiot competition—including bankrupt competitors who stiff-armed their creditors while they lost money ruining our business. It was a very unpleasant experience," Munger recalled. "All that said, it's a very leveraged business. So when the industry turned, it turned beautifully—for USAir included. . . . It worked out fine for Berkshire. But we're not looking for another experience like it."

BUFFETT HAS ALWAYS SAID THAT the airline industry has been great for travelers, but a disaster for investors. And yet he is attracted again and again to aviation-oriented stocks. The Berkshire investment that has puzzled people the most is its 20 percent stake in PS Group Holdings. The relationships surrounding this investment go back to when Munger was operating out of the old Pacific Coast Stock Exchange and he introduced Buffett to his friend Rick Guerin. Guerin had participated in the acquisition of Blue Chip Stamps, See's Candy, and other investments with Munger and Buffett.

Guerin was a major shareholder and a director of Pacific Southwest Airlines. PS Group is the residual company from PSA after it was sold to USAir in 1987. With assets of $700 million, PS Group's main business was leasing out the airplanes that USAir would not buy when it acquired the airline. Some of those aircraft were leased back to USAir. PS Group also had ownership in a travel agency, an oil and gas exploration concern, a waste-recycling company, and a fuel trading and distribution company.[15]

In 1990, Berkshire acquired a 11.04 percent stake in PS Group, for $18.68 million. The 603,275 shares were purchased for an average price of $30.96. Four months after the original purchase, Buffett increased his ownership to 22.5 percent.[16]

Some experts believe that Buffett bought the shares to bail Guerin, vice chairman of PS Group, out of a tight spot. Over the years, Guerin had his financial ups and downs. At one point he was forced to sell 5,700 shares of Berkshire at a relatively low price to pay off bank debts.[17]

"Warren bought his shares—about 20 percent of PS Group—because a broker called from New York and said he had them," said Guerin. "They looked cheap. He trusted me to be sensible. But PS Group is a meaningless asset to Berkshire, only about $20 million on the books. You can't even find it. It's been one of his worst investments, and mine, for various reasons."

Munger's former law partner Chuck Rickershauser also was involved in PS Group. "We took money from the sale of the airline and invested it in things that ranged from bad to terrible," said Rickershauser.

Berkshire still owns the shares, and though business started looking up for PS Group when USAir recovered its health, many of PS Group's problems are unresolved. Earnings for PS Group have been spotty, following several disappointing attempts to diversify by investing its cash.[18] In 1999, one PS Group board member and major shareholder, Joseph S. Pirinea, resigned and protested the company's management policy. Pirinea suggested the board put the company up for sale: "Just look at the company's book value per share—$13," said the Seaford, New York, accountant. "The stock sells for $8."

WHEN BUFFETT ACQUIRED A PRIVATE JET to ease the burden of business travel, Munger continued to take commercial flights and chided Buffett for his extravagance. Buffett dubbed his business jet the "Indefensible," in reaction to Munger's jabs, but said he had been seriously considering naming the plane the Charles T. Munger.

After Berkshire became the owner of the pilot-training company FlightSafety International in 1997 for $1.5 billion in stock and cash, Munger changed his tune. He told shareholders: "Prompted by Al Ueltschi (the company's founder), we are changing the name of the company plane from 'the Indefensible' to 'the Indispensable,'"[19]

FlightSafety International, which gained notoriety in 1999 as the school from which John F. Kennedy, Jr. took flying lessons, is Berkshire's largest noninsurance business. The company was founded in 1951 by Ueltschi, a pilot who mortgaged his home to start the business. Based in Flushing, New York, FlightSafety provides high-technology training to operators of aircraft and ships, using sophisticated simulators and other training tools. With 500 employees across the country, FlightSafety has about 90 percent of the training market, secured by long-term contracts. Customers generally are airlines, corporations, and the government. Those clients include Airbus, Bell Helicopters, Boeing, British Aerospace, Raytheon, Sikorsky, Learjet, Lockheed, Cessna, Gulfstream, and other aircraft companies. With 1997 net income of $84.4 million, FlightSafety represented 28 percent of Berkshire's after-tax earnings from businesses other than insurance.

THE 1990S WERE A MUSCLE-BUILDING time for Berkshire, and while some of the investments the company has made are brilliant, many of them also seem predictable. The exception came in 1998. Buffett showed that he was still on the prowl for undervalued assets, when it appeared that someone was making a move on the silver market. Speculation ran rampant, accusations flew, but nobody suspected that the orders for silver were originating in Omaha.

Berkshire never discloses its investments until required to by law, but turmoil was swirling in the silver commodities market, including threatened law suits against some silver traders and complaints to regulators that certain traders were manipulating the market. Buffett and Munger stepped forward and admitted that they'd been accumulating a large stash of the precious metal. Buffett revealed that the company had purchased 129,710,000 ounces of silver between July 25, 1997, and January 12, 1998.

"Over 30 years ago," said the company press release, "Warren Buffett, CEO of Berkshire, made his first purchase of silver in anticipation of the metal's demonetization by the U.S. government. Since that time he has followed silver's fundamentals but no entity he manages has owned it. In recent years, widely published reports have shown that bullion inventories have fallen very materially, because of an excess of user-demand over mine production and reclamation. Therefore, last summer Mr. Buffett and Mr. Munger, vice chairman of Berkshire, concluded that equilibrium between supply and demand was only likely to be established by a somewhat higher price."

At the 1998 Berkshire shareholders meeting, Munger explained that the company's $650 million purchase of about 20 percent of the world's supply of silver may have had an impact on the silver market, and it represented an uncharacteristic Buffett investment, but it meant very little to Berkshire's bottom line.

"This whole episode will have about as much impact on Berkshire's future as Warren's bridge playing. It is close to a non-event."

Munger issued his usual warning that just because Berkshire bought silver, or convertible preferred shares of airline stock, or did anything at all, didn't mean everyone else should do it.

"It would be a huge mistake to assume that Berkshire Hathaway is the right model for all America. It would be an absolute disaster if every single corporation in America suddenly tried to turn itself into a clone of Berkshire Hathaway."[20]

They paid around $4.60 to $4.80 per troy ounce for the silver in the summer of 1997. By February 1998, the price was up to $7 per ounce, its 9-year-high, but by the end of the year it was trading at around $5 per ounce, and the price has been relatively flat since then. Munger would not say what Berkshire's position in silver was at that time, but said that based on the current price, it was "perfectly obvious" that their expectations of silver price performance had not yet been realized.

MUNGER AND BUFFETT CAN STILL startle the investment world now and then, and as he did in the past Munger sometimes goes forward with his own ideas, even if Buffett isn't fully aboard. Such was the case with Costco, the Issequah, Washington-based warehouse store.

"I admired this place so much that I violated my rules [against sitting on outside boards]," said Munger. "It's hard to think of people who've done more in my lifetime to change the world of retailing for good, for added human happiness for the customer."[21]

Munger contends that by selling quality merchandise very close to cost, the stores built such a loyal customer base that it qualifies as a franchise. "If you get hooked on going to Costco with your family, you'll go for the rest of your life," he said.[22]

One of the reasons Munger likes Costco is because of Jim Sinegal, the company's president, whose office has no walls separating him from passing employees. Sinegal, chairman of Costco, studied at the feet of Sol Price, the San Diego, California, entrepreneur who originated the warehouse store concept. Price first opened the California-based Fedmart stores, then sold the chain to a German company, who apparently didn't understand the concept and couldn't keep the stores going. Price then took the plain-wrap-shopping concept a level higher with his Price Club warehouse stores. Price Club eventually was acquired by Costco, which now is the second-largest warehouse store chain behind Wal-Mart's Sam's Clubs.

Charlie absolutely crows at the story of Costco's paper towels, a story that to Munger represents an admirable example of business ethics. Costco produces its own line of Kirkland products, which it guarantees to be as good or better than the top selling product in its field. When Costco's paper towels didn't live up to the promise, they were withdrawn until a suitable towel could be sold.

"He truly believes in our business," says Sinegal, adding that the 76-year-old Munger has never missed a board meeting. "He loves it."

Buffett was asked why he hadn't bought more Costco shares, considering that Munger owns shares and is on the board of directors.

"Yeah, you hit on a good one here," Buffett replied. "We should've owned more Costco, and probably if Charlie had been sitting in Omaha, we would've owned more Costco. Charlie was constantly telling me about this terrific method of distribution, and after 10 years or so I started catching on to what he was saying, and we bought a little of Costco at Berkshire.

"We actually negotiated to buy more. I made the most common mistake that I make . . . We started buying it, and the price went up, and instead of following it up and continuing to buy more. . . . If Costco had stayed at $15 a share or so, where we were buying it, we would've bought a lot more. But instead it went to 15⅛ and who could pay 15⅛ when they'd been paying $15—it wasn't quite that bad. But I have made that mistake a lot of times, and it's very irritating."[23]

In February 1999, Munger made a related investment when he and several family members bought 8 to 9 percent of San Diego-based Price Enterprises Inc. Price Enterprises is a real estate investment trust formed with real estate retained from the old Price Club retail empire. It owns 31 shopping centers, some of which are anchored by Costco stores. The Munger group holds around 2 million of Price's 23.7 million preferred shares.[24]

Buffett also makes independent investments for his own account. Such was the case in the summer of 1999 when he bought a 5.3 percent stake in Bell Industries, a small California electronics business. In January 2000, a month after it was disclosed that Buffett bought shares in the company, he quietly sold for a profit of $1 million—a 50 percent return on investment.

BUFFETT AND MUNGER HAVE WARNED that Berkshire Hathaway, like so many other businesses, could go through a negative cycle. They've said this for so long that shareholders and analysts alike stopped believing them. They were, however, telling the truth. In 1998, Berkshire reported that its earnings slipped 24 percent from 1997, as gains from investments fell by more than half. That didn't mean Berkshire actually lost money. Net earnings were just down, $1.902 billion or $1,542 per share in 1997, compared to $2.489 billion or $2,065 per share for the previous year.[25]

Throughout its history, Berkshire's short-term earnings have been volatile—partly because insurance results are notoriously bumpy and partly because Munger and Buffett are willing to forego short-term results for longer-term gains. At the end of the century, Gen Re was being reorganized to better fit the Berkshire philosophy, and GEICO was being primed for a growth spurt.

Berkshire's share price declined 19.9 percent in 1999, the first time in nearly a decade, and the price kept falling in the early part of 2000. But so be it. Munger tells investors to conduct their financial affairs so that no matter what crazy things happen in the markets, they can stay in the game. He cautioned that if you can't afford for your Berkshire Hathaway stock (or any stock, for that matter) to drop 50 percent, you probably shouldn't own it. The share price decline could tarnish the pairs image with the public, but any wane in his and Buffett's personal popularity might come as a welcome relief. Both men are constantly badgered to make speeches, give personal advice, or contribute money to hundreds of different charities.

Nevertheless, in 1999 Berkshire was still a powerful company. Operating revenues gave it a rank of 75 on the Fortune 500. When measured by earnings, excluding investment gains, it ranked fifty-fourth. But some investors were worried that in the last year to start with the number one, Berkshire would have a substantial earnings decline. Net earnings were strong, although at $1.5 billion they were less than half 1998 net earnings. Per-share book value rose only .5 percent and relative to the S&P 500, results were down 20.5 percent.

Overall and for the long-term, Munger is optimistic about the future of Berkshire Hathaway, for very simple reasons. "Basically, we have a wonderful bunch of businesses. We have float that keeps increasing and a pretty good record of doing well in marketable securities. None of that has gone away." Indeed, in the first quarter, 2000, Berkshire's net income rose by 49 percent.

As the company has grown and taken shape, the relationship between Munger and Buffett has changed somewhat. In the 1970s and 1980s, they conferred several times every day.

"We don't talk as often," says Buffett. "We talked about more prospective ideas 25 years ago. There was a time when we averaged well over once a day. They were long conversations. The hospital is his main occupation now—Harvard School and Mungerville. Those aren't things for us to talk about. Charlie is just a fraction less involved in Berkshire than I am, but if anything big comes along and is specific, then we talk. He understands the business and the principles very well. Charlie doesn't have his ego wrapped up in Berkshire the way I do, but he understands it perfectly."[26]

Though Buffett is nearly 70 years old and Munger is six and a half years his senior, they show no signs of retiring.

"Warren likes the game," said Munger. "I like the game. And even in periods that are thought of as a tough times for other people, it's a lot of fun."[27]

CHAPTER SEVENTEEN

SALOMON
BROTHERS

Charlie says as you get older you tolerate more and more in your old friends and less and less in your new friends.

Warren Buffett.

WHEN WARREN BUFFETT GOT THE call that something was amiss at Salomon Brothers, it was 10:30 P.M. and he was standing at a noisy pay phone kiosk inside a Lake Tahoe restaurant. Charlie Munger, Berkshire Hathaway's vice chairman and a Salomon board member, received the message a few hours earlier as he was having dinner with his family at his summer cabin in Minnesota.[1]

Ordinarily, nothing interrupts Munger's time at the lake. The summer of 1991 was different. Charlie's swift reaction to the telephone call told the family that something serious was afoot.

"He doesn't show that he's under pressure to his kids," said Wendy Munger. But "he was totally absorbed by it and engaged, and it was the first time we ever saw him in a suit on Star Island."

This was the beginning of the most traumatic and public of Berkshire's troubles. The news was out about an illegal $12.2 billion Treasury notes "short squeeze" at Salomon, a New York investment banking firm in which Berkshire owned a considerable stake of preferred shares.

At the core of the widely reported episode was managing director Paul W. Mozer, a 34-year-old bond trader who in December 1990 and February 1991, made Treasury securities trades above the legal limit allowed for any one institution. Additionally, Mozer made secret and unauthorized trades in the accounts of some Salomon clients, then switched the transactions onto Salomon's own books.

Munger first heard of the situation on Thursday, August 8, from Salomon's president Thomas Strauss and its inside attorney Donald

Feuerstein. From the very first telephone call, Munger harbored suspicions that Salomon's official story was incomplete.

Buffett was having dinner at Lake Tahoe with the executives of one of Berkshire's subsidiaries when he talked to Strauss and Feuerstein. From the sketchy details and matter-of-fact tone, the matter didn't strike Buffett as an extreme crisis. It was Saturday before Buffett called Munger at Star Island, and only then did he realize how serious the infraction was. Salomon's lawyer had read to Munger their talking points, an internal document Salomon executives would use during media interviews regarding a news release that was about to be distributed. The talking points noted that "one part of the problem has been known since late April." Munger objected to the use of the passive voice, and demanded to be told who exactly knew.[2]

Though Munger challenged the wording of the talking points, the attorney explained that management and its lawyers were worried that different wording would threaten the firm's funding, its ability to roll over the billions of dollars of short-term debt that became due daily. This was dangerous because Salomon was highly leveraged, with only $4 billion of equity. In addition to the short-term debt, Salomon was relying on $16 billion in medium-term notes, bank debt, and commercial paper.

In her account of the Salomon affair in *Fortune* magazine, Carol Loomis wrote, "So Salomon's play was to tell its directors and regulators that management had known of Mozer's misconduct, but to avoid saying this publicly. Munger didn't like it, finding this behavior neither candid nor smart. But not considering himself an expert on 'funding,' he subsided."[3]

Munger was indignant at the attempt to brush over personal culpability, but perhaps because Charlie and Warren thought highly of Salomon's Chief Executive Officer John Gutfruend and had a congenial relationship with him, Munger admits that "Warren and I didn't see John's downfall" that first evening.[4]

Nevertheless, Munger was certain from the very outset that Salomon had stepped in a pile of horse manure. After all, Treasury securities, a $2.2 trillion business, is the foundation of the United States financial system. Salomon is a primary dealer in U.S. government treasury securities, one of only about 40 companies with the privileged status that allows them to buy bills, notes, and bonds from the federal government and resell them to customers. Individuals in America and abroad, businesses, and other governments invest in U.S. Treasury securities because they trust the U.S. government and its public finance system. However, the system itself operates on a delicate balance of trust, and some experts feared that the Salomon breach of conduct would ruin the reputation of

American securities markets worldwide and raise the government's cost of debt financing.[5]

Munger and Buffett continued to communicate about the problem, and planned a board meeting by conference call the next Wednesday, August 14. During that conference call, the board was read a second press release, which included three pages of details. The board members exploded in unified objection to a phrase stating that management had failed to go to the regulators for nearly four months due to the "press of other business." That lame excuse, the board felt, would not fly. The wording was changed, and in time, Munger and Buffett learned that management had met the previous April and agreed that something criminal had occurred and it should be reported to regulators immediately. For some inexplicable reason, nobody in the group did so.[6]

By late summer, the *New York Times* and the *Wall Street Journal* were broadcasting the story on their front pages and tension escalated. The securities markets reacted with a run on Salomon's own corporate securities. On Friday, Charlie donned a suit and caught a flight from Bimidji to New York for one of the most hectic episodes of his life.

SALOMON WAS FOUNDED IN 1910 and became one of the largest, most profitable and most admired brokerage houses in the United States. Buffett and Munger's connection with Salomon went back many years during which Salomon performed investment banking and brokerage services for Berkshire. Berkshire bought into Salomon in 1987, when the firm became the target of a hostile takeover by corporate marauder Ronald O. Perelman, chairman of Revlon Inc. Gutfruend dodged that bullet by approaching Buffett and asking that Berkshire take a financial position to stave Perelman off.

Bob Denham, Berkshire's main lawyer, remembers the weekend in September when he first became involved with Salomon. Denham got a telephone call on a Saturday morning. "I walked in the door from coaching a soccer game when they called to say they'd struck a deal to buy," said Denham. "They asked if I could work on it right away. I went to the office and got others in to work with me. An agreement was signed on Monday. That deal was more compressed than usual, but it is typical of working with Charlie and Warren, because they worked so closely together. They're two of the smartest and most creative businesspeople America has produced. They are always thinking of novel ways to slant investments. There is a high level of trust. They never try to undercut. They seldom disagree. If they do, they talk it out."

In the fall of 1987, Berkshire allocated $700 million of Berkshire's cash, the company's biggest investment to that time, to Salomon redeemable convertible preferred stock. The preferred securities paid 9 percent and were convertible after three years into common shares at $38. At that time Salomon's common stock was trading at around $30. If not converted, the shares would be redeemed over five years beginning in 1995. The deal also provided for a seven-year "standstill" during which Buffett agreed not to purchase any more Salomon shares.

In effect, Berkshire got a 12 percent stake in Salomon and became the company's largest shareholder. The deal was structured so that Berkshire's $700 million would be used to buy out a 12 percent stake in Salomon owned by Minerals and Resources Corp., Ltd. (Minorco) a subsidiary of the giant South African conglomerate Anglo-American Corp. Gutfreund worried that the Minorco interest would fall into the hands of Perelman or some other unfriendly takeover artist.[7]

The move angered some shareholders, who thought they should have had the opportunity to consider Perelman's proposition. Furthermore, some Salomon officers considered Berkshire's deal a sweetheart arrangement that took advantage of Gutfreund at a vulnerable time. But shareholders also got considerable benefits from the deal between Gutfreund and Buffett. The transaction increased Salomon's capital, provided a financial cushion for losses, and put Gutfreund into a relationship of his own choosing.[8]

As part of the deal, Buffett and Munger got seats on Salomon's board of directors.

"We had some pretty good foresight," said Munger. "When we bought big positions in ABC and in Salomon, Warren suggested I go on ABC's board. I said, 'you never will need me (there).' Salomon could get into enough trouble that it would need both of us.'"

Wall Street veterans were surprised and puzzled at the Salomon investment, since Buffett and Munger often made disparaging remarks about the quality of work in the brokerage and investment industry as well as the high salaries and lavish lifestyles enjoyed by top executives. In Berkshire's 1982 annual report, Buffett scolded investment bankers for providing whatever advice would bring them the most income: "Don't ask your barber whether you need a haircut," he wrote.[9]

Buffett explained later that he knew the Salomon investment wouldn't be one of his famous "three baggers," but he was having a hard time finding suitable investments for his cash holdings, and he'd had good experiences working with Salomon in the past, especially from 1976 to 1981 when Berkshire was purchasing the first half of GEICO.[10]

Nevertheless, there were always differences of perception between Buffett's and Munger's ideas of how business should be conducted, and those of Wall Street regulars. Salomon felt the sting of the Midwesterner's conservatism.

"When they went on the Salomon board, Salomon had a star chef on call," recalled Charles Munger, Jr., "The first time Warren sat down with a Coke and a hamburger, some changes in culture had been introduced."

Even before the Treasury scandal, there were early rumors that Buffett and Munger were unhappy with Gutfreund, but in Berkshire's 1987 Annual Report Buffett tried to lay those stories to rest: "We have no special insights regarding the direction or future profitability of investment banking. What we do have is a strong feeling about is the ability and integrity of John Gutfreund, CEO of Salomon, Inc."[11]

He said Gutfruend had at times advised clients to stay away from deals, even in cases where Salomon would have reaped huge fees. "Such service-above-self behavior is far from automatic on Wall Street," said Buffett.[12]

Gutfruend impressed Warren and Charlie when in 1987 Salomon took a large trading loss, and then in a restructuring laid off 800 employees. That year Gutfreund declined a bonus worth about $2 million. Again in 1989, when profits were down, he took a $500,000 pay cut to $3.5 million.[13]

By the 1990s, however, Buffett and Munger had become uneasy about the chaos and lack of attention to procedure that seemed to be inherent in Salomon's culture. For example, they were disturbed that at board meetings, directors were given out-of-date balance sheets.[14]

Those concerns rose to the top in August 1991, when under pressure from federal regulators, Salomon made its disclosure regarding irregularities and rule violations in connection with its Treasury securities bids. The government probe was initiated after other firms complained that Salomon had seized more than its legal share of the $12.26 billion in notes, then squeezed competitors by driving up the prices.

Paul Mozer at one point claimed that he'd been unfairly accused of misdeeds, and that he was guilty only of one "spur of the moment" decision to flout the rules of a single Treasury auction in February 1991. Mozer insisted he had been used as a scapegoat. He told the *Wall Street Journal* that when he made the trades he was just trying to accommodate a request by Salomon's government arbitrage trading desk to bid for $1.5 billion worth of notes, even though Salomon would be bidding for much more than government rules allowed.[15] To prevent big players like Salomon from cornering the market, the Fed had issued a rule in 1990 barring a single firm from bidding for more than 35 percent of the Treasury securities offered in any one auction.

Later investigations and court cases showed that Mozer had been involved in more than one incident of illegal trading in 1990 and 1991. Apparently afraid that he was about to be found out, Mozer disclosed some trading infractions to Salomon's vice chairman John Meriwether as early as April. The reactions of Gutfreund and Salomon's president Thomas Strauss, when they learned of the problems, dug Salomon in even deeper.

"What happened was Meriwether came to Gutfruend and said, hey, I have this problem, and it's my responsibility to report it to you," said Munger. "Meriwether, the supervisor, in essence was washing his hands of it, protecting himself by disclosing it to Gutfruend—handing the problem up. But Meriwether also added, 'I hope you can figure out a way to save this fine young man (Paul Mozer).' Gutfreund talked to the general counsel, who told him to immediately report to the Feds and throw himself on the mercy of the Federal Reserve Bank of New York. Gutfruend was indecisive—'How can I save my profit center, this employee, etc., etc.' He procrastinated and didn't level with the board until the Fed threatened him—and then he still didn't fully disclose. The general counsel should have told him, 'Hey, if you don't do as I say you'll lose your job, your reputation, your standing in the community, your wife will be mad at you, and your kids will be embarrassed to admit you're their dad. Tell the truth, tell it fully, tell it fast.' He would have had to cashier the trader, but he got cashiered anyway."

Considered a bond-trading wizard, John Meriwether was deeply involved in the technical movements of the market. One of the highest paid executives at Salomon, he is reported to have been compensated $89 million in a year in which Gutfreund earned only $3.5 million.[16] While Meriwether, Strauss, and Mozer let Salomon down, Gutfruend's behavior was most bewildering, even disappointing to Munger and Buffett.

"To Charlie Munger, Gutfreund evoked all that was noble in Salomon's tribal culture, particularly its willingness to lay its capital on the line. He had a grandeur that the newer breed of executive lacked," wrote financial author Roger Lowenstein.[17]

Gutfruend was known as a tough-willed operator, and served at Salomon's helm for 13 of the 38 years he'd been with the company. A gruff man who had little tolerance for the media, Gutfruend was credited with building Salomon into an investment banking power house. He told recruits at Salomon to come in each morning "ready to bite the ass off a bear."[18]

But rather than acting boldly, in this case, Gutfreund engaged in what Charlie described as a "thumb-sucking response." When the board met that August and learned Gutfreund had been withholding information critical to the operation of Salomon as an on-going business, his credibility with the board of directors was destroyed.[19]

MUNGER FLEW FROM MINNESOTA TO New York and met Buffett on Saturday, August 17. The two immediately went into talks with Gutfreund and other Salomon top managers that lasted until 11 P.M. Full disclosure of the events and the players remained a top priority.

"Charlie insisted that they get the whole truth out," said Buffett. "We didn't know what would happen. He worked on Saturday from about 3 P.M. through Sunday," said Buffett, "then went to Washington with me on Monday."

Buffett and Munger immediately called in Munger, Tolles & Olson's top guns, Ron Olson and Bob Denham. They would help deal with complex legal issues and a cadre of irate federal regulators ready to file criminal charges. Olson says that Munger's contribution to getting matters under control was "most important because it was made early, on August 18. He was there for the critical board meeting. In the middle of the day, the decision to waive attorney client privilege between the Salomon board and previous lawyers had a lot to do with why Salomon wasn't criminally indicted. Buffett and Munger made that decision together. We would give them everything we had as fast as we could get it. In the end, they decided not to indict. We built the confidence that the new leadership would clean the place up, that they were not rotten to the core, not involved in the problems."

It wasn't until after Buffett and Munger met with Securities and Exchange Commission chairman Richard Breeden, that they began to get a bigger picture. They eventually learned that Gutfreund had received a letter from Gerald Corrigan, the president of the Federal Reserve of New York, who said that the bidding irregularities called into question Salomon's continuing business relationship with the Fed, and Corrigan demanded a comprehensive report within ten days of all "irregularities, violations, and oversights" Salomon knew to have occurred. It was disturbing that Salomon's directors had to learn of the letter on their own.[20]

"He gave it to outside lawyers but didn't send a copy to the directors," recalled Munger of Gutfreund. "Warren and I went into that crisis without knowing all the facts. We got mildly nebulous responses. If we'd known, we would have worked it differently."

The message from the Federal Reserve Bank of New York to Salomon was clear said Munger. "Old management, your time is over. We can no longer trust you. We can't have you being a prime dealer. We paid attention to our sovereign, and our views changed as our cognition improved." As for Gutfreund's failure to paint a complete picture for the board, "we had no option of forgiveness."[21]

Gutfreund and Thomas W. Strauss, the firm's president, both resigned on August 18, 1991. It was a tragic come down for Gutfreund, the man *Business Week* once called "King of Wall Street."

SALOMON WAS TEMPORARY SUSPENDED FROM trading and nearly shut down by the government, prompting Salomon's own lawyers to start working on a back-up bankruptcy plan. In a single week, Salomon's share price plummeted from above $36 per share to under $27. The run on Salomon's own debt securities forced the company to take the unprecedented move of halting trading in its own securities. To stop the carnage, it would be necessary to convince the public that Salomon wasn't on the rocks. Ron Olson and Bob Denham played central roles in helping Salomon get through the scandal with minimal damage.

"At least five authorities—The SEC, the Federal Reserve Bank of New York, the U.S. Treasury, and the U.S. attorney for the Southern District of New York and the antitrust division of the Department of Justice—had important concerns about Salomon," Buffett wrote in Salomon's 1992 annual report.[22]

The implications of not resolving the legal issues effectively would have been dire, said Buffett. "If we had declared bankruptcy, and we were close, $1 billion in transactions would not have cleared that should have cleared. There was drama, personality, and terror. It was like a (doomsday) machine."

Senator Daniel Moynihan went to New York to ask if he could be of help, since there were 9,000 jobs in New York at risk. Berkshire also owns the *Buffalo News* in the state Moynihan represents. "We said to Moynihan, the New York Fed chairman (Gerald Corrigan) is a dominant man with his nose out of joint," explained Munger. "He will resent political interference. We asked Moynihan to go back to his office and stay out of it, which is what he did."

While Warren dealt with management issues and communications with the pivotal players, "Charlie was able to step back and think about broader legal issues," said Denham. "Thinking rapidly and intensely about strategy. At the end of the week in New York, the decision was made that the general counsel of Salomon should resign. Saturday morning Warren called and asked if I could be the general counsel."

The resignations of Gutfreund, Strauss, and the general counsel were not enough to satisfy the regulators. It would be necessary to appoint new management, someone regulators and the public would believe was completely ethical and trustworthy. Buffett was the obvious candidate, but Munger told him he would be crazy to take the job, a warning that did not stick.[23]

"When Warren realized the problem, he volunteered, which they took him up on," said Munger. "He had a good reputation. Nick Brady (Secretary of the Treasury) backed off a little, enough of a signal. Based on Brady's backing off, we know it gave us credibility."

After Buffett and he traveled to Washington, DC to testify before Congress about the scandal, Munger decided to go home and thereafter served as a long-distance advisor, except when he needed to be present as a Salomon board member. "Charlie thought I was doing what I could," said Buffett. "It was sort of out of our hands. We sort of behaved and hoped they wouldn't kill us."

Even after he returned to California, Munger stayed connected, said Denham. "Afterward, we talked about issues and strategy. Charlie was a very involved director. He had real ideas about the best way to approach things."

Serving on the Salomon Board was an intense experience, but the fact that Munger was in his late 60s did not seem to matter, explained Lou Simpson, who also was a director.

"Health and age do not slow Charlie down at all," observed Simpson. "He got off the plane (from Los Angeles) and came directly to Salomon meetings and was sharp as a tack. The Salomon meeting was an afternoon meeting, then another meeting the next morning, then the next day Charlie was on his way home."

"A lot of the time we would all stay at the Millennium on the West side. We'd have a board dinner, and walk back," recalled Simpson. Occasionally Nancy Munger would come along and she and Charlie visited their son Barry, a freelance photographer who lived in Manhattan's Tribeca neighborhood. When Nancy made the trip, the Mungers stayed at the Carlyle on the upper East side.

"There was not a lot of socializing at Salomon," said Simpson. "It was pretty businesslike. There were lots of problems and considerations we had to deal with. A dramatic time in everyone's life. I'm sure that Warren and Charlie got a lot more than they bargained for."

Simpson served on Salomon's board for five years, four of them as chairman of the audit committee where Munger served as a committee member. "He was a very active, questioning member," said Simpson. "The audit committee at Salomon was pro-active, a probing group of people. We had three-hour meetings at least. Charlie, to a lot of people in management, was a pain in the rear. He seized on tough issues and came back to them. There were a lot of issues that were difficult—accounting, management, derivatives, risks involved. You want in a group of people someone who points out that the emperor has no clothes. Management will present the positive side. It's harder to get people who will point out the pitfalls, risks, and so on. I suspect people thought Charlie was a crank. Things would be going well, then he'd say—'but you've got this issue of off-the-balance-sheet items. And commissions.' To understand the operations of a business is exhausting, very intense. I remember many many flights between here and Los Angeles, five- to six-hour flights. He spent the whole time reading and re-reading audit material. He added a lot of value in just questioning practices and the way to think about these practices."

Munger also helped keep the team energized. "I felt I had just about wrung myself out in the case," recalled Ron Olson. "Then I would run into Charlie. He'd say, 'You can take it.' "

Buffett gives Olson and Denham credit for the final Salomon settlement, a relatively light penalty of $290 million and no criminal charges. Salomon also was allowed to keep its prestigious and lucrative status as a primary dealer in government securities.

As part of the legal settlement, Salomon admitted that in several 1991 Treasury auctions, it improperly bid for substantially more than the 35 percent of an issue that any one firm is permitted to seek. Salomon also admitted submitting bids in the names of customers who had not authorized the company to make bids on their behalf, thus allowing Salomon to buy more securities than it was allowed. Paul Mozer was suspended from his job in August and later pleaded guilty to lying to the Fed. He served four months in prison.[24]

As for the final resolution, "The shareholders came out very well in that situation, better than they had any reason to expect, if they knew the real facts," said Simpson.

Though many at the company thought the settlement was a near-miracle, Salomon wasn't out of trouble yet. Difficult, ongoing management issues remained, not the least of which was the question as to who would run the company after Buffett.

Buffett and Munger, who are among the lowest paid top corporate executives in the United States, were displeased with Salomon's compensation system. Buffett pointed out that 106 people in the securities unit had each earned $1million or more in 1990, even though the division's overall results were below average that year. "Employees producing mediocre returns for owners should expect their pay to reflect this shortfall," Buffett wrote in the company's quarterly report.[25]

When Buffett took the helm at Salomon, however, Munger became even more tolerant of his use of a corporate jet, "The Indefensible." Munger said that if any CEO is entitled travel by private airplane, it is Buffett. "It's the most deserved jet in corporate America."[26]

BUFFETT STAYED ON THE JOB AT Salomon Brothers for nine long and exhausting months, but he didn't intend to do the job indefinitely. There were rumors that a Wall Street insider such as Fund America CEO John Byrne or former Federal Reserve Chairman Paul Volcker would be named to the post when he stepped aside. In 1992, Buffett caught the financial community off balance when he named the Texas-born Bob Denham as chairman and chief executive officer.[27]

When the Salomon story first broke, Denham had moved to New York on three days notice to serve as an outside counsel. When it was necessary to replace Salomon's general counsel, Denham took the job. Finally he realized it would be a very long haul and purchased an apartment in Battery Park City. It was not an easy assignment for Denham, whose wife was a high-level academician in California. Rebuilding Salomon was a daunting task and some issues, such as the granting of excessive bonuses, were never resolved to Munger's and Buffett's full satisfaction.

"The problems at Salomon proved more difficult and it was a closer thing, a closer call than I thought going in," said Denham. "It became clear to me that this is hard enough working away from home, and it could have a bad ending—not career enhancing. But after government issues were resolved, it was clear the company would survive. The time as CEO was terrifically interesting and challenging in a lot of ways. There were more good times than bad times and it had a good conclusion."

Denham's wife moved to New York to join him, and in 1997, Denham's job was finally completed. Salomon was sold to Travelers Group Inc. for $9 billion, and Denham went back to Munger, Tolles & Olson.[28] When he returned to Los Angeles, his wife, who had been a faculty member at Fordham University in the interim, was named president of Pacific Oaks College and Children's School.[29]

Berkshire's stake in the Salomon sale turned into a 3 percent ownership of Travelers worth $1.7 billion. In 1998, Travelers merged with Citicorp, forming the world's largest financial service firm. Together they offer banking, securities sales, and insurance services.

Salomon came out of the difficult period in fine shape, and in time, most of the company's top executives landed on their feet. On the day Gutfreund fell from power, his lawyer met with Buffett and Munger in California in an attempt to negotiate a severance package. Though Buffett and Munger say they still like Gutfreund, a dispute arose over how much departure money he was entitled to receive. Salomon's board offered Gutfreund $8.6 million, but he asked for a lot more—some reports say as much as $55 million. Gutfreund went to battle with Salomon over benefits, stock options, and legal fees that he said the firm owed him. No luck. An arbitration panel ruled against him, leaving him with no severance, options, or bonuses. Nothing at all.[30, 31]

Under an agreement with the SEC, Gutfreund agreed to pay a $100,000 civil penalty and was barred from running a securities firm without special approval from the SEC. "I didn't do anything illegal and wasn't charged with doing anything illegal," he told a *Business Week* reporter.[32]

After leaving Salomon, Gutfreund established his own office, where he became an advisor and investor in companies with capitalizations of $50 million or so. A member of the controversial Trilateral Commission, he still moves in high circles.[33]

As for John Meriwether, he eventually was suspended from the securities industry for three months and was fined $50,000 for his role in the Salomon incident.[34] When Meriwether was ready to return to Salomon, Deryck Maugham, whom Buffett tapped to run the investment banking business, offered him a job with less responsibility than he'd previously had. Meriwether rejected the offer, and led a group of Salomon defectors to create a new hedge fund based in Greenwich, Connecticut, informally dubbed Salomon North, or the Dream Team.

Salomon's atmosphere, even under Gutfreund, had been contentious and that did not entirely change.[35] Traders and Wall Street insiders were critical of the way Denham and Maugham ran the company, especially their attempts to limit in Salomon's extremely high salaries and bonuses for traders, compensation that grew faster than the company's earnings did.

Some disgruntled employees left Salomon, including the core members of Meriwether's former team, who joined him at his new company, the glamorous but ill-fated Long Term Capital Management.

LTCM was a highly sophisticated attempt to use the Black-Scholes risk model, a formula commonly favored by commodity traders, plus other mathematical models, to allow LTCM to safely and profitably trade in international markets. Meriwether assembled a team that included two of the professors who developed and refined the formula, Myron Scholes and Harvard professor Robert Merton, along with former Federal Reserve officer David Mullins and of course, the crack traders from Salomon.

The minimum investment in LTCM was $10 million, but because of the team's towering credentials and contacts, they quickly raised $3 billion. The returns in LTCM's first three years were fabulous: 20 percent in the first, 43 percent in the second, and 41 percent in the third.

Then in 1997, the fourth year, returns fell to 17 percent. That same year a real estate crisis erupted in Thailand and rapidly spread throughout Asia, and in August of the next year, Russia defaulted on its international debt, which created worldwide panic in financial markets. LTCM's mathematical models failed so badly that it lost $500 million in a single day. In September, Meriwether sent a letter to investors saying the fund had lost $2.5 billion or 52 percent of its value that year.[36] Though the fund held some valuable assets, because LTCM was highly leveraged, it was trapped when margin obligations came due. According to some accounts, the fund's global investment positions amounted to $1.25 trillion, frighteningly close to the annual budget of the United States government. It became clear that if LTCM collapsed, there would be reverberations around the globe.[37]

The LTCM problems erupted when Buffett was on a wilderness trip with his friend Microsoft founder Bill Gates. Never much of a technical person, Buffett's only contact with the outside world was a satellite telephone. Munger was on vacation in Hawaii and making telephone connections by satellite was problematic, so they never actually discussed a bail-out offer Buffett made to LTCM.

Buffett offered to buy the ailing LTCM portfolio for $250 million and recapitalize it with $3 billion from Berkshire Hathaway, plus $700 million from the insurance giant AIG and $300 million from the investment banking house Goldman Sachs. None of LTCM's contingent liabilities would be picked up and there would be no management position for Meriwether and his team. Meriwether rejected the offer, and not long afterward was rescued through pressure from the Federal Reserve Bank by a consortium of 14 commercial banks who themselves had something to lose if LTCM went under. The 14 contributors put up $3.6 billion. Meriwether and his people held on to a 10 percent stake in the company and would run it under the supervision of an oversight committee. With enough capital to allow the investments to play out, Meriwether was able to work his way through the difficulties and by mid-year 1999 was back on his feet.[38] He repaid the banks, and a few weeks later quietly closed the fund. Some original investors, however, never got their money back.

Though he remained at arm's length from the LTCM drama, Munger had an opinion about it. "The hedge fund known as Long Term Capital Management recently collapsed through overconfidence in its highly leveraged methods, despite IQs of its principals that must have averaged 160," he said. "Smart, hard-working people aren't exempted from professional disasters of overconfidence. Often, they just go aground in the more difficult voyages they choose, relying on their self-appraisals that they have superior talents and methods."[39]

THE SALOMON AFFAIR FIRMLY ESTABLISHED Munger and Buffett as voices of integrity in the business world, but it also showed how tough they could be. Corporate leaders, no matter how deeply entrenched they may seem, shouldn't mess with Buffett and Munger when they're on the war path of righteousness.

"When the final chapter is written, the behavior evinced by Salomon will be followed in other, similar cases," said Munger. "People will be smart enough to realize this is the response we want—super prompt—even if it means cashiering some people who may not deserve it."[40]

Among the many lessons to be learned from the Salomon episode, said Munger, is that when serious problems arise, the reaction of top management must be both swift and thorough.

"It was a huge mistake for John Gutfreund not to go to the New York Fed when he saw that Mozer was in trouble," said Munger. "The Fed would not have called for Gutfreund's head. *Face* your big troubles. Don't sweep them under the rug."

As well-publicized as Salomon's debacle was, Munger says the same sort of thing is likely to happen again in the future. "Warren and I will never stop criticizing some aspect of investment banking culture. It's hard to have people floating around in a miasma of billions without an occasional regrettable act."[41]

THE DAILY JOURNAL CORPORATION— A MODEST MEDIA EMPIRE

In my whole life nobody has ever accused me of being hum-
ble. Although humility is a trait I much admire, I don't think
I quite got my full share.[1]

Charlie Munger

THE LOS ANGELES FEDERAL COURT HOUSE, across the street from the
Dorothy Chandler Music Center, is a famous edifice. It often is used
as a movie or television backdrop and was seen daily on television during
the O.J. Simpson murder trial. In the summer of 1999, the Daily Journal
Corporation, publisher of the legal newspaper the *Los Angeles Daily Jour-*
nal, was in court there facing an unfair trade practices suit brought by
the tiny *Los Angeles Metropolitan.* On most days of the trial, an artfully-
dressed older man wearing extremely thick glasses sat in the spectators'
gallery watching the proceedings. Finally Charles T. Munger, chairman of
the *Daily Journal* Corporation, was called to the witness stand.

Ronald Olson, Munger's attorney, knowing Charlie's personality, had
warned his client to limit his testimony to simply answering the questions. At first Charlie did fairly well, but gradually he slipped into the per-
sona he occasionally displays at the Berkshire Hathaway annual meeting
and shares every year at the Wesco Financial Corporation gathering. Charlie began to wax philosophical about his life, his work, and his fascination with newspapers and the news business. The plaintiff's attorney,
Thomas Girardi, objected, asking the judge: "And what would the court

think about asking Mr. Munger if he could reply directly to Mr. Olson's questions? This is beyond the pale."

Girardi insisted that he'd practiced law long enough to know what was going on. "This obviously is an orchestrated attempt—Munger has his chair turned toward the jury, trying to be cute: 'I lost money here, I lost money there.' This is totally wrong."

The judge instructed Olson to keep his client strictly to the business at hand.

"I'll do the best I can," said Olson.[2]

About an hour later, the plaintiff's attorney again had enough of Munger and complained to the judge:

> He's a real smart guy, I know it, Ron knows it, the court knows it. And I think it's totally inappropriate the way he's behaving. And it's forcing me as a lawyer to have to jump up every time that he goes on his diatribe. He's yet to answer one question directly out of the 42 questions that have been asked so far.[3]

The judge seemed perplexed at what to do, since it was becoming clear that Charlie's way was Charlie's way, and he might not *have* any other method of answering questions. Finally the judge simply asked that Mr. Munger avoid hearsay, and the trial continued.

A half hour later, in the middle of testimony regarding how much the *LA Metropolitan* might be worth if sold, Munger was still on the witness stand. Suddenly he let out a howl.

"Ow, Ow, ouch, ouch, ouch."

The eyes of the judge, the attorneys and the jury were riveted on Munger as he writhed and struggled with some sort of pain.

"I've got a cramp in my leg," he finally explained. "It's the beauty of getting old."

The opposing attorney demanded—in vain—that the judge call a break in the proceedings, no doubt worried that Munger's plight would make the jury more sympathetic to his newspaper's cause. The judge allowed the witness to stand up for a moment and work out the cramp. Finally Charlie declared the pain gone and himself ready to continue.

"When you get as old as I am, it will happen to you," he proclaimed to everyone present in the courtroom.[4]

IT WAS JUST ANOTHER DAY in court for the Daily Journal Corporation, and an all too familiar experience for Munger.

"Berkshire has practically no litigation," said Munger. "But if you take our legal newspapers, I don't think a year passes without litigation. Discrimination, sex, old age, race. It is very litigious. The *Metropolitan*

News is suing us now regarding the foreclosure business. It gets to be a bit of a sewer."

Munger's interest in journalism and the business of newspapers goes back to his childhood in Omaha when his father was the chief outside counsel to the *Omaha World Herald.* Among the Munger family friends were both the managing editor and city editor of the newspaper.

"He loves newspapers," said Molly Munger of her father. "He loves to read the newspapers in Minnesota. Getting daddy's newspaper (at Star Island) is a big deal."

A passion for print media is something that Munger and Buffett share. That fascination, along with the good economics that once existed in the industry, prompted their investments in the *Washington Post* and the *Buffalo News.* But Berkshire only has a partial ownership in the *Washington Post.* Actual control of the newspaper is in the hands of Katharine Graham's family. When the small Los Angeles legal publication, the *Daily Journal,* came on the market, Munger saw a chance to own his own newspaper and expressed interest immediately. Here would be a newspaper where he could have a vastly greater influence, and one in his own city to boot.

In 1977, Munger asked Stan Lipsey, who ran the *Buffalo News* for Berkshire, to take a look at the *Daily Journal* and give him an appraisal. Lipsey told Charlie that the *Daily Journal,* which was then printed on newsprint that was even broader than a broadsheet, was sadly outdated in its style and content and needed modernizing.

Munger had heard that the newspaper was for sale from a member of his breakfast group at the Pacific Coast Stock Exchange. Chuck Rickershauser, one of Munger's former law partners, had been hired by the *Daily Journal*'s prior owners to sell the paper as part of a settlement of an antitrust case.

"Because I was having breakfast with Charlie daily and wanted to pick his brain, I asked him how to conduct the sale. He said, 'I would like to be a bidder.' We had some connection, so I got him another lawyer."

As it turned out, Munger was the high bidder for the newspaper. The *Daily Journal* was bought for about $2.5 million through the New America Fund. In May of 1986, when Munger and Guerin liquidated the New America Fund, the Daily Journal Corporation became an over-the-counter public company with several thousand shareholders.

The newspaper's stock was distributed to New America Fund shareholders in proportion to their holdings in the fund. Among those getting stock were Otis Booth and some of Charlie's old Omaha friends such as Lee and Willa Davis Seemann. Munger and Guerin ended up the largest shareholders, with exactly the same amount of ownership held within their respective families.

"But since I had this legal-judicial background that he didn't, I was the logical one to be chairman," said Munger. "And we made him the vice chairman."[5]

Al Marshall, Munger's partner at Wheeler, Munger, became secretary of the corporation.

Munger owns about 6 percent, his children have another 6 percent, and his grandchildren hold an additional 6 percent of the shares, giving the family control of about 18 percent of the newspaper.[6] The shares are held within a limited partnership called Munger, Marshall & Co., which also includes stock held by Marshall, Booth, the Seemanns, and a few other original New America Fund investors. In all, Munger, Marshall & Co. controls 34.5 percent of the Daily Journal Corporation, Guerin interests hold almost 18 percent and the general public owns the remaining 48 percent.

Gerald Salzman, president of the company, says there are approximately 1,700 shareholders of record, though the shareholder pool gradually declines. "The board has a policy of buying on the open market from time to time. One year we bought 12 shares, another year we bought several thousand."

Over the years, Munger and Guerin's investing interests have diverged and though they remain friends, "The only thing we're in together now is the Daily Journal Corporation," said Guerin.

After acquiring the newspaper, prompted in some cases by opportunity and in other cases by a need to protect their territory, Munger and Guerin began building a chain of legal publications and businesses related to legal publishing. In time, the Daily Journal Corporation became more than a big city legal rag, it turned into an empire—a small regional empire, to be sure, but an empire nonetheless.

"Charlie was always an aspiring media mogul. He didn't get very big," said Al Marshall.

In 1988, the Daily Journal Corporation bought the *San Jose Post-Record,* the *San Jose Advocate Journal,* and the *Santa Cruz Record.* The acquisitions continued and by 1997 the company owned 18 newspapers with a total paid circulation of about 35,000. The flagship newspaper, the *Los Angeles Daily Journal* had a circulation of 15,000.[7] The company acquired the *California Lawyer* from the California State Bar. The publication has about 700 paid subscribers and the magazine is sent free to California attorneys. In addition to California, the company now has operations in Arizona, Colorado, Nevada, and Washington state. Counting all its publications, the company has 100 reporters and 350 total employees.

California is one of the better venues in which to be engaged in the legal publishing business. With more than 105,000 lawyers, the state is home to one-seventh of all U.S. attorneys.

Guerin and Munger feel the 112-year-old newspaper has improved from being weak to a paper that now sometimes scoops the respected *Los Angeles Times* on stories.

Munger says he is particularly proud of the paper's daily profiles of judges: "The truth of the matter is I like judges. If judges don't do their work well, then civilization doesn't work well."[8]

Despite the improvements, the *Daily Journal* remains a paper that only an attorney could love. Even at that, many attorneys complain that too few resources are allocated to the paper and its news coverage is skimpy. Another small Los Angeles newspaper, the *New Times,* described the paper as "the embodiment of journalist sobriety. It prides itself on being a local newspaper of record, even if, to some, that also means being hopelessly dull. Indeed, the *Journal* seems permanently stuck in safe mode."[9] The newspaper, groused the *New Times,* doesn't even write its own editorials, but rather reprints editorial material from other publications.[10]

A reporter who jumped ship to join a competing paper described Munger and Salzman as aloof, and wanting to forge closer relationships between advertising and editorial, an alarming prospect to dedicated journalists. "They have a trade rag mentality. They don't want to publish anything controversial or anything negative about law firms."[11]

Compared to the mainstream *Los Angeles Times* or the entertainment-oriented alternative newspapers in its circulation areas, the *Daily Journal* and its sister newspapers do on many days seem bland. The news stories are wrapped around pages and pages of court dockets and other information upon which attorneys rely. Yet among legal newspapers in California, the *Daily Journal* is the one against which most legal publications measure themselves. Other legals have tried to imitate the *Daily Journal*'s court calendars, descriptions of court rules, and its daily appellate reports.

If the *Los Angeles Daily Journal* is more of a tool for lawyers than a journalistic lollapalooza blockbuster, the *California Lawyer* is livelier than it's sedate name implies. When the Daily Journal Corporation first bought the magazine, it was published in cooperation with the State Bar. In 1993 some lawyers complained that the news of their professional organization was being printed along with stories that were critical of lawyers and their behavior. The joint-publishing arrangement was terminated and the State Bar again began publishing its own magazine.

The *California Lawyer* prints stories related to all aspects of law and law enforcement in California, a state in which there are plenty of knock-your-socks-off stories. The magazine's cover frequently splashes titles such as "Bienvenidos, Felons: It's a good time to be a fugitive in Mexico," a page-turner about the crackdown on U.S. bounty hunters across the

Mexico-California border, accompanied by an eye-popping photo essay of Tijuana's notorious La Mesa prison. Another 1999 issue recapped a sex-and-favors-for-testimony scandal in the San Diego District Attorney's much heralded gang unit. A writer of lurid true-crime tales would be wise to subscribe to the *California Lawyer* for story leads.

As far as the business aspects of the Daily Journal Corporation go, Al Marshall, the corporate secretary, says they are frightful. "Nobody else could stand the heat. It's not that profitable, and he's always being sued." Marshall pointed out that neither Munger nor Buffett like investing in newspapers as much as they once did.

While the *Daily Journal* has been a source of satisfaction, it continues to be an irritation. Competition among the legal newspapers in California is intense for the lucrative legal advertisement business, and, as noted earlier, the *Daily Journal* has had to defend itself in one lawsuit after another. While Munger concedes that he is in the newspaper business more for personal satisfaction than for profit, he is keenly competitive and hangs on tenaciously when he thinks his company's economic base is threatened or being unjustly attacked.

CHALLENGES HAVE COME FROM EVERY direction for Munger's chain of newspapers. One of the most alarming threats came in 1986, shortly after the Daily Journal Corporation became public. That fall Steven Brill, a chubby, suspendered young man who had accumulated a group of eastern legal publications, thus earning the title of "the Rupert Murdoch of the legal publishing world," called at the offices of the Daily Journal Corporation.[12] Brill, who later made a national name for himself in television and magazine publishing, sauntered into the business offices and asked if the business was for sale. He'd like to buy it. "We have no intention of selling at any price," declared Munger.[13]

Brill, who was 36 at the time, moved north and acquired the stodgy 3,200-circulation *San Francisco Recorder* for around $9 million. Since 25 percent of the *Daily Journal*'s subscribers were in the Bay Area, the move brought Munger to full attention. Brill then began raiding the *Daily Journal*'s newsroom. After pumping up his writing staff, Brill sent them out to dig up stories of dissatisfaction and misconduct, or other juicy tidbits in the legal community. He also promised readers he would expand coverage to Los Angeles and the southern regions, and hinted that he might start a Southern California paper within three years "so that you won't have to look anywhere else for all the California legal news you can use."[14]

A newspaper war was underway. The Daily Journal Corporation garnered forces by snapping up smaller San Francisco-area legal newspapers, redesigning popular features and shoring up coverage in the northern part of the state. Working with Daily Journal President Gerald Salzman, Munger bought the *San Francisco Banner* and the *Marin County Reporter,* which together had a circulation of only 800. The Journal already owned the *Sacramento Daily Recorder* and the Oakland-based *Inter-City Express.*

When asked if the Daily Journal's expansion in the Bay Area was a response to Brill's arrival, Munger said, "It's always hard to know what your motivations are when they are mixed. We had been thinking for a long time of doing a better job in San Francisco."[15]

Munger added that he was not worried about Brill, "because we've coexisted with the *Recorder* with respectable profits for many decades. I don't expect the whole thing to escalate into insanity."

"STEVEN BRILL—HE'S BRAVE, EGOCENTRIC, brilliant, and has done a yeoman's service for good journalism," said Charlie Munger more than a decade later. "There's a lot of competition in San Francisco. He sold out and is gone."

Brill told the *Wall Street Journal* in 1997 that it had been maddening to go up against someone too rich to care if he lost "bales of money." Brill added, "If Charlie spent even 20 percent of his time running his legal papers, we probably would have been crushed."[16]

Munger's reply no doubt was delivered with a chuckle, but in print, it sounded harsh. "Why would I want to crush a gnat?"[17]

Steve Brill's company had been predominantly owned by Time Warner Inc., and eventually Brill and a Time Warner subsidiary jointly created *Court TV.* When Ted Turner merged Cable News Network into Time Warner, Turner, who once had come up against Brill as a cable television competitor, began to play a role in Time Warner activities. Soon afterward Time Warner bought Brill out.[18]

Brill sold his shares of his legal publishing empire and his interest in *Court TV* to Time Warner for about $20 million. His next project was the $20 million 1998 launch of *Brill's Content* a print and online magazine covering and critiquing the news media. Brill's first issue contained a controversial story claiming that independent counsel Kenneth Starr had admitted leaking information about the presidential Whitewater investigation to reporters.[19]

Later, as consolidation continued in the publishing industry, Brill's former publications, which included the San Francisco newspaper, the *American Lawyer* and several law journals in other parts of the country, were sold by Time Warner to the investment banking firm Wasserstein and Perella for $300 million.

In 1996, the *Wall Street Journal* reported that the *San Francisco Daily Journal* had cost the Daily Journal Corporation $2 million a year for the preceding 10 years, a high price for outlasting Brill. Munger disagrees with the numbers and maintains he will never close the paper down.

THE DAILY JOURNAL CORPORATION HAS been sued on various theories by a swarm of small California newspapers, up and down the state, including the 100-plus-year-old *San Diego Daily Transcript.* Jeff Barge, publisher of a start-up Seattle newspaper, in 1996 claimed that Salzman traveled to Seattle and feigned an interest in purchasing his newspaper, *Washington Law,* but after obtaining its trade secrets, started a competing publication and engaged in predatory pricing. Salzman said he didn't acquire Barge's newspaper because the publisher was nearly bankrupt and was in arrears in turning over employee withholding taxes and other money to the Internal Revenue Service. And anyway, said Salzman, Barge stopped publishing before Salzman launched the *Washington Journal.*[20] The Seattle suit was filed in several courts around the country, and has been dismissed in all, over the objections of the plaintiff.

Most contentious of the *Daily Journal's* competitors has been another gnat, the 2,000 circulation *Los Angeles Metropolitan News,* run by attorney Roger M. Grace. Thus far, the *Daily Journal* has prevailed in most, though not all, of the lawsuits.

Part of the rivalry between the *Met News* and the *Journal* stems back to 1986, the year the *Journal's* longtime editor, Robert E. Work, died quite suddenly. Rather than promote Work's second in command, Munger gave the job of president to Gerald L. Salzman, the newspaper's accountant and chief financial officer. The offended number two man, John Babigian left two years later to become the *Metropolitan News'* vice president and general manager.

Babigian accused the company of age discrimination, which Munger denied. As for choosing Salzman, "That's an accident of Salzman being so talented and so honest," said Munger.[21]

Salzman, a baldheaded man with large, expressive eyes, seems trustworthy and competent in the business arena, but he is not a fire-in-the-belly journalist. He has been with Munger since he and Guerin took control of the New America Fund. An accountant with a Big Eight accounting firm, Salzman left consulting to join the Fund to help with the financial details. Later he consulted with the Munger, Tolles law firm. As he is prone to do, Munger decided to stick with a known, tested, and trusted person when choosing a new chief executive officer for the Daily Journal

Corporation. Additionally, Salzman owns about 1 percent, or between 16,000 and 17,000 shares, of the company.[22] Salzman's wife is the company's personnel director and three of the Salzman children, including the *Daily Journal*'s webmistress Sherrie Salzman, work there.

The entire company is something of a family deal. In 1982, Emilie Munger worked at the *Daily Commerce,* an afternoon real estate adjunct to the *Daily Journal.* She did reporting, editing, and page layout before returning to Stanford to earn her law degree. Barry Munger, a professional freelance photographer in New York, also did a stint with the company.

The *Metropolitan News* is particularly critical of the 1990 Daily Journal acquisition of the California Newspaper Service Bureau, specialists in placing public notice advertising in publications throughout the state. The Bureau gets a block of legal notices, usually from some government agency, then places all the ads in its own newspapers—if the Daily Journal has a publication in the proper jurisdiction. When there is none, the legal notice is placed in another newspaper for a 15 percent commission. Clients for the service include Fannie Mae, Child Services for the County of Los Angeles, and other agencies that are required to place legal ads.

Alleging predatory practices in one of its suits, the *Metropolitan* charged that the *Journal* priced its legal notice ads below cost in Los Angeles specifically to drive the *Met News* out of business. The *Metropolitan News* further claimed a *Daily Journal*'s deal with Fannie Mae, the mortgage giant, and other agencies to carry legal notices in California at less than cost, violated state law prohibiting so-called "loss leader" tactics in advertising. Munger said the suit's charges were erroneous because the *Daily Journal* does not subsidize the profitable Fannie Mae account. Some of the offenses in the suit carried treble damages that legal experts said could have pushed the *Journal*'s liability to more than $30 million.

The *Metropolitan News* case ended in a hung jury in January 1998, after a three-week trial. Grace said Munger's "arrogant" and "dismissive" behavior on the witness stand was a great boon to his case. Nevertheless, Munger said he would testify again in the retrial. "We won't lose," he responded. "The *Daily Journal* did nothing that violated any laws."[23]

Still, reported the *National Law Journal,* "Mr. Munger acknowledged that the paper beefed up its defense team when the case went to court for retrial in June 1999. Ronald Olson, the biggest name to come out of Mr. Munger's firm, will be overseeing partner Bradley S. Phillips, who was in charge the first time around."[24]

The second time, the *Daily Journal* successfully defended itself against the charges. The jury voted eleven to one in favor of Munger's newspapers. However, within a few weeks, the *Metropolitan News* not only appealed the ruling but filed an additional suit.

In the meantime, the *Metropolitan News-Enterprise* has made controversies between itself and the *Daily Journal* the subject of oversized headlines in its own newspaper and on its Web page. In most cases, the stories emphasize Munger's wealth and include a photograph of Charlie in which he seems to be smirking.

"Since the time in early 1997 when the Metropolitan News Company added Munger as a defendant in its action against DJC for unfair business practices, Munger has accumulated more than $1 billion," wrote publisher Roger Grace. "And yet, the 75-year-old magnate seemingly has as his mission, if not obsession, the crushing of MNC—which, I regret to say, is considerably smaller than Munger's competing company."[25]

The *Met News* did win a major victory in the newspaper war in 1998, when the City of Los Angeles put up for bid the bulk of its legal-notice business, which for 50 years had gone to the *Journal.* The $450,000 annual contract went to the *News.* The *Journal* hired an attorney to try to overturn the council decision in court, but Superior Court Judge Robert H. O'Brien ruled in favor of the smaller paper, throwing out the *Journal's* suit.[26] Judge O'Brien has since been reversed after an appeal by the Daily Journal Corporation.

IN PART BECAUSE OF LEGAL wrangles, and in part because of changes in the culture and in the economics of the business, newspapers aren't as lucrative as they once were. For one thing, the nature of news has changed. As television and the Internet expand, readership is declining. Those problems aside, the legal advertising business has always been cyclical, rising during a recession when bankruptcies, foreclosure, and liens are more prevalent. In a long, strong economy, a legal newspaper invariably suffers a decline in revenues.

Legal advertising still provides the base for profits at Munger's papers, but they are a slowly shrinking revenue source due to a trend toward fewer required legal notices. For example, nonprofit organizations once had to advertise their status annually, but the law no longer makes that demand. A number of government agencies across the nation are seeking changes in the law to allow them to put pro-forma advertisements on the Internet. Courts are giving those requests serious consideration.

As a precautionary measure, said Salzman, "We try to be as independent of legal advertising as possible." The Daily Journal-owned newspapers have tried to beef up their display, or commercial advertising lineage, and the company has expanded into new but associated lines of business.

In addition to its two magazines, *California Lawyer* and *House Counsel,* the Daily Journal does significant trade in printing court rule books, judicial profiles and other guidebooks, directories and manuals related to the legal industry.

Recently, the company bought Choice Information Systems, a company that provides software for case management to court systems. The Daily Journal changed the company's name to Sustain Technologies, Inc. Sustain Technologies, which looks like the Daily Journal's most promising new enterprise, created a software program for the joint justice system for Toronto and the Province of Ontario and so far has placed similar software in court systems in three countries and nine U.S. states.

Because of new businesses, and some centralization of its California publishing activities, the Daily Journal Corporation is nearly doubling its office space by constructing another building adjacent to the Los Angeles office.

Despite the operating difficulties, the Daily Journal has increased in net worth substantially since Munger and Guerin acquired it for $2.5 million in 1977. It has been estimated that the modest media chain now is worth about $65 million. Revenues in its 1999 fiscal year were $37 million, up from the previous year. Its net income was $1.9 million, down 40 percent from the year before, due to a year of extremely heavy litigation expense.

Though there has been interest from potential buyers, Munger says the *Daily Journal* is a vehicle that allows him to be "socially constructive" and has interesting financial prospects. Guerin says he and Munger are in the business both for love of journalism and for the money the company earns. "A combination of both. We're lucky enough to be in things because we want to be. None of us (Charlie, Warren, or himself) have to do anything we don't want to do. Charlie and I love owning it. It's great fun. We think we're serving the justice system, if you will. It does make money and is gaining in value every year. We try to make it better," said Guerin.

He then added, "Money is not everything to Charlie. We do hope we've advanced civilization an inch."[27]

While Munger keeps close tabs on what's happening at the *Daily Journal,* he says he spends 5 percent or less of his time at the newspaper. Although he tries to be available as needed, his main job is to stay out of Salzman's way and let him run the company.[28]

"I'm plenty active though," said Munger. "I don't have a good half speed. I'm quite active in the newspaper but not on the editorial side."

Each fall the company has a breakfast meeting with the board of directors and all of the publishers, editors, and heads of the sections.

Munger and Guerin attend to get reports on what the company's managers anticipate and plan for the year ahead. Salzman said that Munger and Guerin both make a considerable contribution to the discussion. "Rick can get to the real issues as fast or faster than Charlie can. It's pretty fast. I don't have a lot of educating to do."

THE DAILY JOURNAL OFFICES ARE just beyond Los Angeles's Japan town in an industrial area where many high action and car chase scenes are filmed, including sequences of the Batman movies. The 10-year-old Daily Journal corporate and editorial offices are pleasant, modest, and within easy striking distance of the courts and various government buildings. In the entry area flows a fountain, full of field stones and brass sculptures of sea otters. If Munger had his way, the foyer would display a nice bronze statue of his hero, Benjamin Franklin.

During his lifetime, Franklin worked as an editor, author, legislator, scientist, inventor (Franklin stove and bifocals), diplomat, Revolutionary War hero, and was a founding father of the nation. "Franklin's story can scarcely ever be told often enough," Munger told a Rotary Club audience in Santa Barbara. "Born into poverty and obscurity, his father was a tallow chandler—he worked with rancid fats. He was the fifteenth of 17 children, only went to school two years. He died 84 years later and perhaps was the most famous man in the world, if not, close."[29]

Munger's love of Benjamin Franklin, said Guerin, sometimes clouds his common sense. "When we built the new Daily Journal Corporation building—we found out later that there is a requirement that you spend 3 percent of the cost of the building for art or make a contribution to the city's art fund. Charlie said, 'let's commission a head of Ben Franklin, looking affable and wise, and engrave his great sayings on the pedestal.' I said, 'Charlie, that's horse manure. Our employees don't want to be preached to.' I said, 'Let's do something cheerful.' He thought about it for a while and said, 'I think you're right.' We commissioned an artist to do sea otters and a fountain."

But that wasn't the end of Franklin for Charlie. "Having the idea of a Ben Franklin bust already in his mind, Charlie commissioned an artist to do about 20 copies," said Guerin. "I took one. He took one for his office. He gave the Marlborough School and the Harvard School copies. Then he gave copies to other people as gifts."

CHAPTER NINETEEN

DOING GOOD AT GOOD SAMARITAN HOSPITAL

The early Charlie Munger is a horrible career model for the young, because not enough was delivered to civilization in return for what was wrested from capitalism.[1]

Charles T. Munger

IT WAS RELUCTANTLY THAT ANDREW LEEKA traveled the fearsome freeways, right through the writhing core of Los Angeles, to meet with the board of directors of Good Samaritan Hospital regarding the position of president. The traffic wasn't what worried Leeka.

Good Samaritan is one of Los Angeles' oldest and most relied upon hospitals and although Good Sam had a reputation in the Southern California medical community for delivering quality care, it also was known for having constant financial problems and high turnover among staff and management. In fact, recalled Leeka, contention and disorganization were such that, "This place was like Bosnia."

Part of the problem, Leeka's contacts told him, was chairman of the board Charles T. Munger, who held an executive committee meeting every few weeks and gave the chief administrator very little peace. Nevertheless, following his heart more than his head, Leeka reported to a small conference room on the hospital's first floor, where the executive committee had gathered. Suddenly the door burst open, and Munger strode in and seated himself at the head of the table.

"Charlie came in and I don't think he really looked up to see me," recalled Leeka. "He said 'well, this hospital has a lot of problems and they are thus, thus, and thus.' He went on for 35 to 40 minutes. Finally he asked me a question, but didn't give me a chance to answer."

A few minutes later Munger stood up, and Leeka stood as well, extending his hand to shake. Munger simply ignored him, turned, and strode out the door through which he'd entered.

"I said to the other board members, 'I don't think he liked me.'" The members in unison replied, "No, no, he loved you.'"

"Then why didn't he shake my hand?" asked Leeka.

"He couldn't see your hand," explained one of the board members. "He's blind in that eye."

Despite that explanation, Leeka felt sure he was out of the running, and remained doubtful about wanting the job anyway. It would seem that Leeka and Munger had little in common. Leeka could hardly be described as an Ivy League type. As an undergraduate, he attended a school near his home, the University of California at Riverside, a slightly scruffy but academically competent school on the smoggy eastern edge of the Los Angeles basin. Leeka then earned an MBA and a master's in health care administration at California State University Northridge, and went on to spend 16 years in nonprofit hospital administration. He owns a show-quality Harley-Davidson motorcycle and holds a black belt in Karate. The only apparent connection between the two men is that Leeka also was born in the Midwest and knows and cares about hospitals.

Leeka had several other job interviews scheduled the week he went to Good Sam. But before he could leave that day, he was asked to stay and meet certain key staff members. Leeka was pressed to cancel an afternoon appointment, then urged to return the next day for more interviews.

Soon afterward he met with Munger again, who got right to the point. He wanted to hire Leeka, this would be the deal, the salary, and so forth. The offer was generous. What was Leeka's answer?

"I said, usually something of this magnitude I like to discuss with my wife," Leeka recalled. Munger said nothing; he simply stared at Leeka. After an awkward silence, Leeka relented. "In this situation, I don't think I need to."

"Good," said Charlie. "That's why I'm hiring you."

Despite Munger's idiosyncratic behavior, Leeka knew right away that he liked Munger, and felt that he could learn a lot from him.

"Health care is such a tough business," said Leeka, "you just have to believe in it. I fell in love with the hospital itself. I felt I belonged here."

It didn't take long for them to agree that Munger would hold executive committee meetings less than once a month, after which Munger walked out and left Leeka to do his job. Micro managing, any more than he has to, isn't Munger's style, though he never hesitates to call employees at his various enterprises and share ideas as they occur to him. Munger was only holding biweekly meetings because he felt it was necessary.

Munger was asked to join the board by the Episcopal Bishop of Los Angeles and by a personal friend, Dick Seaver. "I had enough sense to know it would be like tar baby. Once you got in, you would become stuck," said Munger. But it is Charlie's philosophy that a first-rate man should be willing to take at least some difficult jobs with a high chance of failure. And just as he decries making money "with lily white hands," he believes that giving time, talent, and risking his reputation is just as important as contributing money.

He involves himself in community causes to ease his guilt over having accumulated so much money, to clear his own conscience for having more wealth than he thinks he deserves. John Maynard Keynes "atoned for his portfolio management 'sins' by making money for his college and serving his nation," said Munger. "I do my outside activities to atone, and Warren uses his investment success to be a great teacher."[2]

Munger has given some of his Berkshire stock, a few hundred shares each to Good Samaritan Hospital, Planned Parenthood, Stanford University Law School, and the Harvard-Westlake School. Both Charlie and Nancy Munger spend hours each month on community work, most of it in Los Angeles. In addition to his long stint with Planned Parenthood, Charlie has served on the boards of the Harvard-Westlake School, the National Corporation for Housing Partnerships, and other groups over the years. The Housing Partnership was a 1980s private-public attempt to increase the inventory of low-income housing in the United States. But Munger grew impatient with the way the work was going and eventually resigned from the board.

It is Munger's habit to choose just two or three public causes that seem important, then concentrate on making a difference there. Just as he and Buffett stay within their "circle of competence," or areas that they truly understand when selecting investments, Charlie has developed a circle of competence in his charitable work. He has focused primarily on reproductive choice, health care, and education.

Nancy Munger, who herself is a devoted watercolor painter, has added the arts to her circle. She serves on the board of the renowned Huntington Library, Art Collection, and Botanical Gardens in San Marino, about 10 miles from downtown Los Angeles. The Huntington specializes in Anglo-American civilization and contains an immense research library plus one of the most comprehensive collections in the United States of British and American art of the eighteenth and nineteenth centuries. The Huntington is home to the famous duo, *Blue Boy* by Thomas Gainsborough and *Pinkie* by Thomas Lawrence. The Mungers have helped fund a major 1999 to 2000 exhibit commemorating the 150th anniversary of the Gold Rush and California's statehood.

Munger takes seriously the obligation of the fortunate to support the needs of society that cannot be met by market capitalism. Moreover, he argues that it is unfair for top officers of a company to allocate money to their favorite causes, while the real owners, the shareholders, have little or no voice in the matter. In 1981, Munger came up with a novel corporate charity plan for Berkshire Hathaway. For each of its roughly one million shares (then trading at $470) Berkshire would contribute $2 to a charity of the shareholder's choice. For example, a person who owned 1000 shares could designate $2000 to go to the Salvation Army or the American Red Cross, or whatever other nonprofit the person selected. The plan was extremely popular with Berkshire shareholders, many of whom have much of their wealth tied up in the company. The charitable giving plan allows them to donate money without cashing in their stock, an anathema to many long-time Berkshire shareholders.

Munger's feeling about public service no doubt is related to his upbringing. Stan Lipsey, publisher of the *Buffalo News,* was born in Omaha and lived there until he went to Buffalo to take charge of the newspaper. "In Omaha, you get up in the morning and say, 'What am I going to do for my city today?' There is a value system, structure of the family, a culture where it is expected that you serve your city," said Lipsey.

Some of Munger's charitable work has had contentious elements to it, especially his activities with Planned Parenthood, and in recent years, Charlie's service on the board of the not-for-profit Good Samaritan Hospital.

Good Samaritan, a massive stack of white buildings, sits in a neighborhood that once was one of Los Angeles's most refined. Not far from the Ambassador Hotel where Bobby Kennedy was assassinated, Good Sam's neighborhood, to put it politely, is in transition. "I don't think it's yet found its destiny," said Munger's stepson Hal Borthwick.

An area that used to be dominated by high-priced department stores, restaurants, and apartments now has many empty buildings. It has evolved into part of Korea Town, although many of the residents are in fact Hispanic or low-income Caucasians. Many are elderly. Yet Good Sam, with its 408 beds, 650 physicians, 550 nurses, and 1,800 employees, is well-rooted in the Los Angeles community and many old families of solid financial standing still receive their care there. Nancy Munger was born at Good Sam, as was her son Hal and his son after that. It was the hospital where Charlie underwent the cataract surgery that went awry, leaving him blind in one eye.

The hospital was established in 1885 when Sister Mary Wood of the Episcopal Church founded a nine-bed nursing ward. The following year,

St. Paul's Episcopal Church entered into an agreement with the California Diocese to assume control of the facility, then known as the Los Angeles Hospital and Home for Invalids. From early on, Good Sam has trained nurses and interns studying at the University of Southern California (USC).

Soon after he joined the board, Munger came to believe that the facility was mismanaged because the board always backed decisions of the medical staff and these decisions frequently protected the economic interests of certain doctors, rather than that of the patients or of quality medicine.

"The existing chairman did not agree with me. I proposed a resolution reversing a ruling of the organized medical staff on the ground that the staff was endangering the health and safety of our patients. With some doctors on the board voting yes, it passed 17 to 2," said Munger.

After the board vote, the chairman resigned. "He was an able man," said Munger, "and understandably was reluctant, as a layman, to reverse what purported to be medical decisions." Because Charlie had started the trouble by pushing for reform, he felt obligated to accept the job of chairman.

The problems that set the whole episode off occurred in the cardiovascular department, which then was rife with political intrigue, turf protection, and not enough attention to medical issues. Before he took his contrarian position on the medical procedure that would be followed, Munger studied, with the help of a physician friend, the mortality and morbidity rates for different systems of surgical care. It seemed clear to him that the medical staff had made wrong decisions, choices Munger felt were motivated by "old guard" physicians against the more progressive staffers.

"Hospitals are not unlike universities in the sense that you have these tremendous struggles for ownership, possession and control," explained Hal Borthwick, whose wife now serves on Good Sam's board. "Basically Good Samaritan had kind of a community practice for a number of years with a number of people that . . . I'm not saying they were without ability, but there was no particular reason to go to Good Samaritan, other than your doctor practiced there. Charlie recognized that for the hospital to survive it had to have virtues of critical mass and of excellence."

As Munger pressed toward those goals, said Borthwick, there were bad feelings and damaged relationships. "The breakage was not unlike the breakage that you get in a takeover of a company, and you do things differently from the previous management. A lot of people trained in their old ways can't adjust and they have to leave."

After a long, bitter battle with other board members and some staff doctors, Munger and his supporters prevailed. "Ten years later, I hate having had to go through the heartache and tragedy, but I love many of the people I now work with," said Munger.

Munger personally has recruited many physicians to the hospital staff, which is unconventional for a lay chairperson of a large nonprofit hospital. Charlie is intrigued by the technology of medicine and gets a big kick out of working with the doctors.

By the time Leeka took charge of the medical center, good relations existed between the staff and the board, but the business side was still a mess. The hospital had such a large backlog of uncollected bills that in the first year of his administration, Good Sam took a staggering $20 million bad-debt write off. But from then on things got better. Leeka had become accustomed to Munger's personality and they clearly were on the same team.

"I see people who just don't understand him," said Leeka. "They think he's zoning out. He's not. He's sitting there looking at cash flow, return on investment three years out, then back filling to see how he can make it work."

Leeka says that Munger insists on running the hospital with one purpose in mind—serving the community in the best way possible. "There are tricks a hospital can do to squeeze extra revenue from low-income and Medi-Cal billings, but Munger won't allow that," said Leeka.

Following the Northridge earthquake, said Leeka, other hospitals in the area tried to maximize the funds they got from the Federal Emergency Management Agency by claiming every old crack in their cement was caused by the earthquake. After the Good Sam buildings were examined and it was decided there was no significant damage, Munger would not file a FEMA claim.

"He won't do anything just for money," said Leeka. "He'll go into a business (health care special services) even if he knows it will lose money, if it is the right thing to do."

Good Samaritan is now a base for various specialty practices that draw patients from all over Southern California, the western states, and even from abroad. These specialties include California's largest cardiology program; Southern California's second largest cardiothoracic surgery program; new treatments for brain disorders; women's health services, including obstetrics, gynecology, neonatal intensive care, urogynecology, breast cancer and fertility services; orthopedic surgery, especially joint replacement and pelvic reconstruction; opthalmological care, including a very large retinal surgery practice; an oncology program; an advanced digestive diseases program, and one of the largest kidney stone treatment units in Southern California.

Perhaps the most gratifying sign of the hospital's turn around was when it was chosen one of the best hospitals in the country by *U.S. News & World Report* in the July 27, 1998, issue.

There are still many physicians in the area who do a slow burn over Munger's reorganization tactics. Nevertheless, Good Sam is on far better medical ground than it has been. However, its financial condition is still shaky, despite substantial cash reserves. Although there has been progress, Munger said that there are always a lot of questions and "ifs" at a major inner-city hospital. Even with the best laid plans, long-term success isn't guaranteed.

"I have a lot of respect for Good Samaritan Hospital, but it's a very tough hand to play," said Hal Borthwick. "And if you ask Charlie why he does it, one of the things he'll say is that he doesn't want all the hands that he plays in life to be easy ones."

In the decade that he's been chairman, Munger has become a familiar figure at the hospital. Leeka says staff members all have their favorite "Mungerisms," stories or aphorisms or jokes that Charlie has told, perhaps more than once. Each year, Nancy and Charlie attend a dinner at the hospital's institutionally plain auditorium to hand out 5, 10, and even 40-year pins to faithful employees. One year Leeka asked Charlie to come to the podium to say a few words. Charlie clambered to the stage, but went to the wrong microphone, one that was not turned on. He began talking, but the audience could only hear a muffled mumble.

Nancy shouted "Charlie, the mike's not on," several times, but Charlie paid no attention. The engineers rushed around behind the scenes for several minutes trying to get power to the microphone, which they finally accomplished. The sound boomed into the auditorium just as Munger wrapped up. "Thank you for working at Good Samaritan," he said, and turned and left the stage.

A BREEZE RUSTLES THE NORWEGIAN pines and Cass Lake laps a little more aggressively than usual on the shore on the beach in front of the Munger house. Charlie is at the head of the breakfast table, as a small group of family members polish off eggs, turkey bacon, and rewarmed homemade biscuits from last night's dinner.

Charles, Jr. came in late the evening before to join his wife and three children at Star Island. He's a late arrival, flying in from Sacramento, California, where he was working with a state commission on rewriting the kindergarten through twelfth-grade science and math curriculum for California schools. The conversation is focused on education as Charles, Jr. explained what his committee of college professors is trying to accomplish.

Charlie, Sr. has some ideas on higher education that he would like to express, but at the same time 2-year-old Nan, Barry Munger's daughter, also has something to share. As the adults talk right on, she sits at her grandfather's side and at the top of her lungs sings the alphabet song, from A all the way to "now I've said my ABCs, tell me what you think of me."

As if in duet with the little girl, Charlie, Sr. is saying that he'd like to create a true liberal arts college in which students have no major and few elective courses. They would have a set curriculum in which they learn enough about math, sciences, economics, history, and so on, to be truly well-educated for today's world. No specialization would be allowed until graduate school. The problem with many of today's young people, Munger argues to his unconvinced offspring, is that they specialize too early and never learn some subjects they can't live well without. They don't know enough about the world. As if to prove her own versatility, the laughing toddler Nan has moved on to "Twinkle, Twinkle Little Star." Same tune as the alphabet song, different words.

THE MUNGER CHILDREN RECEIVED A public school education until they reached middle school (except the youngest, Philip, who attended private school beginning in the fourth grade). All five sons graduated from Harvard-Westlake, a private school in Los Angeles that was named around 1900 when the founder, formerly from Boston, wrote to Harvard University, and asked permission to use the name Harvard for his new secondary school in Los Angeles. Emilie Munger, like her mother, went to Marlborough School, and Molly and Wendy, who were living in Pasadena with their own mother, attended Westridge School. Molly eventually departed and enrolled herself in public school.

The entire family is passionate about education. Nancy Munger has been a trustee both for the Marlborough School and her college alma mater, Stanford University. In 1997, Nancy and Charlie Munger donated $1.8 million to the Marlborough School's Campaign for a New Era in Excellence.[3] They also gave a major capital gift to the Green Library at Stanford and funded a Munger Chair, or professorship at Stanford Law School, so that business can be taught within the law school curriculum.

Charlie has served as a trustee for Harvard-Westlake for more than three decades. He is an active trustee and for part of the time was chairman. He's so fond of the school that he hopes some day his memorial service will be held in the chapel there. At the school, Munger has been able to blend his dedication to quality education and his admiration of science and architecture. He and Nancy donated more than $7 million to build the Munger Science Building and Charlie himself was involved in almost every aspect of the building's design. Before Harvard School and Westlake merged, Munger believed the science laboratories were too limited. After the merger, there were twice as many students studying science in the upper grades. Munger declared that it would have been educational malpractice not to have expanded the science facilities.

"The problem with most buildings is that they don't build enough flexibility into them. We tried to assure that the science facility will work, and work well, for the better part of a century. I see no reason why it should become obsolete," Munger said at the dedication ceremony.[4]

The state-of-the-art building is nestled on a hillside overlooking Coldwater Canyon. It includes a dozen customized laboratory-classrooms, a conference room, a computer center and a theater-style lecture hall with each of the 110 seats wired to accommodate laptop computers. Some of the features of the building might not be obvious to a casual observer. Benches in the biology, chemistry, and physics labs, for example, are different to accommodate the different kinds of lab work. While Munger left many of the decisions on the building to the teachers, he insisted on top of the line ventilation and heating systems, and that the building far exceed current earthquake standards.

Charlie spends hours reviewing the architectural plans for buildings at the school. On one occasion, Munger asked an architect to make a change in the school's auditorium to put a slope in the floor, but the architect said that it couldn't be done. Munger pushed until the architect found a way.

Oddly, the architect did not seem to be offended by Munger's persistence. "No, he doesn't offend people." said Otis Booth, who also serves on the Harvard-Westlake board. "He has a great ability to turn a phrase and make things amusing."

Although most of Munger's time and money has gone to support the exclusive private schools his children attended, he is sympathetic to the plight of public schools.

"I'm a product of the Omaha public schools. And in my day, the people who went to private schools were those who couldn't quite hack it in public schools. And that's still the situation in Germany today. The private schools are for people who aren't up to the public schools. I prefer a system like that. However, once a big segment of that system measurably fails, then I think we have to do something different. You don't just keep repeating what isn't working."

Munger said he would favor the school voucher concept if the vouchers were given only to poor people. "The better off people don't need them, since they already can afford choice and are exercising it. It wouldn't bother me at all if vouchers were only for people otherwise destined for failed schools. But I think we have to do something in our most troubled schools to change our techniques. I think it's insane to keep going the way we are."

Charlie's conservative—even puritanical views—emerge when he contemplates the state of higher education today. He is especially offended by the "victim" mentality that he says is fostered in U.S. colleges.

"You could argue that the very worst of all academic inanity is in the liberal arts departments of the great universities. You can see the reason if you ask the question, 'What one frame of mind is likely to cause the most damage to an individual's happiness, his contribution to others, and the like—what one frame of mind will be the worst?' The answer, of course, would be some sort of paranoid self-pity. I can't imagine a more destructive frame of mind. Yet whole university departments want everyone to feel like a victim. And you pay money to send your children to these places. And this is what they teach them!" said Munger. "It's amazing how these pockets of irrationality creep into eminent places."

Then Munger adds a little midwestern Zen, what he calls "the iron prescription: every time you think some person, or some unfairness is ruining your life, it is you who are ruining your life."

As he did that August morning at Cass Lake, Munger often muses over ways to improve undergraduate education. His views are largely derived from reviewing his own education and from watching his own eight children—and now his grandchildren—attend a variety of schools. "Our education was far too uni-disciplinary," claimed Munger. "Many problems, by nature, cross many academic disciplines. Accordingly, using a uni-disciplinary attack on such problems is like playing a bridge hand by counting trumps and ignoring all else. This is bonkers, sort of like the Mad Hatter's tea party. But nonetheless, too much of that thinking remains in professional practice and, even worse, has long been encouraged in isolated departments of soft science, which I define as everything less fundamental than biology."[5]

Munger is not impressed by the notion that the scope of knowledge has become so massive that few people can become truly multidisciplinary, and still have enough time in life for a career. "You don't have to know everything," insists Munger. "A few really big ideas carry most of the freight."[6]

Certainly Munger's concepts of the big ideas do not coincide with those of many academics. He says, for example, that mastery of both psychology and accounting should be required of lawyers, rather than taught as mere elective courses. Munger claims that most people would be better off if they were trained for their professions the way pilots are taught to fly: "They learn everything that is useful in piloting, and then, must retrain continuously so that they can cope promptly with practically any eventuality," he explained.

"Like any good algebraist," said Munger, "the pilot is made to think sometimes in a forward fashion and sometimes in reverse; and so he learns when to concentrate mostly on what he wants to happen and also when to concentrate mostly on avoiding what he does not want to happen."[7]

Munger says his own life is an example of that process. When he went to Harvard Law School, "I had taken one silly course in biology in high school, briefly learning, mostly by rote, an obviously incomplete theory of evolution, portions of the anatomy of the paramecium and frog, plus a ridiculous concept of 'protoplasm' that has since disappeared. To this day, I have never taken any course, anywhere, in chemistry, economics, psychology, or business. But I early took elementary physics and math and paid enough attention to somehow assimilate the fundamental organizing ethos of hard science, which I thereafter pushed further and further into softer and softer subjects, using it as my organizing guide and filing system in a search for whatever multidisciplinary worldly wisdom it would be easy to get."[8]

Thus, his life became a sort of accidental educational experiment, continued Munger. "What I found, in my extended attempts to complete by informal means my stunted education, was that, plugging along with only ordinary will but with the fundamental organizing ethos of science as my guide, my ability to serve anything I loved was enhanced far beyond my deserts. Large gains came in places that seemed unlikely when I started out, sometimes making me like the only one without a blindfold in a high-stakes game of 'pin the donkey.' For instance, I was productively led into psychology, where I had no plans to go, creating large advantages."[9]

"I'VE TRIED TO IMITATE, in a poor way, the life of Benjamin Franklin," Munger said. "When he was 42, Franklin quit business to focus more on being a writer, statesman, philanthropist, inventor, and scientist. That's why I have diverted my interest away from business."[10]

One of the important lessons from Munger's life, said his daughter Emilie, is: "Don't just take for your own family and hoard it. He gives a lot to institutions, especially educational institutions. He cares about it—not just giving money, but time and intelligence to solving problems."

Easy for a daughter to say about her father. But Munger's friend Otis Booth, who also is from a generation not used to the frivolous expression of emotions, sees through the crusty outer layer that shrouds Munger's personality. "It is not readily apparent, but he has an immense, high level of compassion and understanding. It's way back inside of him. It is publicly manifested in his charitable work. He does not wear his heart on his sleeve, but he nonetheless has a large heart."

CHAPTER TWENTY

ELDER STATESMAN AND CONSCIENCE OF THE INVESTMENT WORLD

The values that guide his personal life guide his public life. You live life simply. You live it in the middle of the field, and you don't cut corners.

Ronald Olson

CHARLIE MUNGER OFTEN QUOTES THE late Nobel laureate physicist Richard Feynman, who said the first rule is to not fool yourself, and you are the easiest person to fool. Munger can be merciless if he believes he has caught someone in an act of silly self-deception.

Pity the poor professor who gets caught up in a debate with Munger on the academic treatment of investment policy. Such was the case at The Benjamin Cardozo School of Law in New York City in 1996 when, due to the death of a close friend, the scheduled moderator was unable to attend. Charlie Munger was asked to step in.

Charlie told the audience: "The accidents of mortality have given you a Baptist bumpkin suddenly put in charge of a bunch of Catholic archbishops who are going to debate revisions of the Catholic mass, in Latin. But I figure I could moderate such a convention."[1]

It was the panel's assignment to discuss the research of Professor William Bratton of the Rutgers-Newark School of Law, which dealt with the corporate decision to pay dividends to shareholders rather than reinvest profits. Munger soon nailed Bratton with what he considered a flawed assumption in the research.

Munger: I take it that you believe that there is no one-size-fits-all dividend policy and that you're with the professor (Jill E. Fisch of Fordham University School of Law) who said yesterday that there wasn't any one-size-fits-all scheme for corporate governance?

Bratton: On that simple proposition I am entirely in concord with Professor Fisch.

Munger: But you say there is some vaguely established view in economics as to what is an optimal dividend policy or an optimal investment?

Bratton: I think we all know what an optimal investment is.

Munger: No, I do not. At least not as these people use the term.

Bratton: I don't know it when I see it . . . but in theory, if I knew it when I saw it this conference would be about me and not about Warren Buffett. [Laughter from the audience]

Munger: What is the break point where a business becomes suboptimal in an ordinary corporation or when an investment becomes suboptimal?

Bratton: When the return on the investment is lower than the cost of capital.

Munger: And what is the cost of capital?

Bratton: Well, that's a nice one [Laughter] and I would . . .

Munger: Well, it's only fair, if you're going to use the cost of capital, to say what it is.

Bratton: I would be interested in knowing, we're talking theoretically.

Munger: No, I want to know what the cost of capital is in the model.

Bratton: In the model? It will just be stated.

Munger: Where? Out of the forehead of Job or something?

Bratton: That is correct. [Laughter]

Munger: Well, some of us don't find this too satisfactory. [Laughter]

Bratton: I said, you'd be a fool to use it as a template for real world investment decision making. [Laughter] They're only trying to use a particular perspective on human behavior to try to explain things

Munger: But if you explain things in terms of unexplainable subconcepts what kind of an explanation is that? [Laughter]

Bratton: It's a social science explanation. You take for what it's worth.

Munger: Do you consider it understandable for some people to regard this as gibberish? [Laughter]

Bratton: Perfectly understandable, although I do my best to teach it. [Laughter]

Munger: Why? Why do you do this? [Laughter]

Bratton: It's in my job description. [Laughter]

Munger: Because other people are teaching it, is what you're telling me. [Laughter][2]

The audience laughter points are essential in this exchange, lest it sound like a food fight at a junior high school cafeteria. The bantering was done in a good-natured tone, but the point of the exchange was quite serious. Later, to make sure his comments were not misunderstood, Munger made amends:

> I don't want my remark about the cost of capital to be interpreted as meaning that I think the great bulk of Professor Bratton's paper is wrong. I think it's profoundly right. When he talks about agency costs in corporations and the discipline caused by levels of debt and the discipline caused by dividend conventions, I think he is profoundly right. And to the extent that those are the conventional academic explanations, I think it's wisdom he's giving. It's just the cost of capital thing that always makes me go into orbit. [Laughter][3]

Although he did not say so then, Munger has his own idea of how the cost of investment capital should be measured. Buffett has explained that at Berkshire, the cost of capital is measured by the company's ability to create more than $1 of value for every $1 of earnings retained. "If we're keeping $1 bills that would be worth more in your hands than in ours, then we've failed to exceed our cost of capital," Buffett said.

A STUDENT ONCE ASKED CHARLIE MUNGER if he and Buffett were fulfilling their responsibility to share his wisdom:

> Sure: Look at Berkshire Hathaway. I call it the ultimate didactic exercise. Warren's never going to spend any money. He's going to give it back to society. He's just building a platform so people will listen to his notions. Needless to say, they are very good notions. And the platform's not so bad either. But you could argue that Warren and I are academics in our own way.[4]

Both Charlie and Warren are at a phase in their lives when they can choose their activities, concentrating only on those things that seem to have meaning and that interest them. Munger has done some public speaking to law classes at Stanford and the University of Southern California, and to organizations when asked by special friends. He, like Warren, prefers to talk to young people, to students who are still learning about life and who have time to implement some of the concepts that the two of them consider important.

Charlie's speeches are always informally presented, but as was sometimes the case with Ben Graham, his ideas occasionally go over the heads of the listeners. His method is to present major themes, such as advising listeners to identify the few big ideas that make a difference and try to live by them. Although he talks about what those ideas might be, he does not offer a succinct formula, or a simple list of directions, leaving his listeners with the sense of insufficient guidelines. But occasionally he'll cut right to the bone and lay out a perfect nugget of personal or financial wisdom.

Some of his lessons are quite practical and apply to life in general and to financial matters in particular: To those whom much is given, much is expected. Always live below your financial means so that you will have money to invest. Invest in such a way so as to avoid the possibility of falling into a negative position—primarily, by limiting the amount of debt you use.

"If you want to get smart," Munger said, "the question you have to keep asking is 'why, why, why?' And you have to relate the answers to a structure of deep theory. You've got to know the main theories. And it's mildly laborious, but it's also a lot of fun."

From physicists, Munger has learned to solve a problem by seeking the simplest, most direct answer. The easiest way invariably is the best way. From mathematicians Munger learned to turn problems upside down or to look at them backward—invert, always invert.

Munger used this method, inversion, to capture the attention of his youngest son Philip's graduating class when he gave the commencement address at Harvard School in 1986. Munger told the students that his prescriptions for life were based on a Johnny Carson speech explaining the things a person should do to ensure a miserable life. These included ingesting chemicals in an effort to alter mood or perception, and allowing oneself to indulge in envy and to wallow in resentment. He cited the example of a youthful acquaintance who became an alcoholic, and spent the rest of his life fighting off all sorts of demons. All or any of Carson's three behaviors will guarantee an unhappy existence. Then Munger added four practices that he believes also will help guarantee failure. Be unreliable; learn everything from your own experience rather than learning from others; give up trying after your first, second, or third reverse of fortune; and finally, give in to fuzzy thinking. ". . . ignore a story they told me when I was very young about a rustic who said, 'I wish I knew where I was going to die, and then I'd never go there.' "[5]

BERKSHIRE HATHAWAY AND WESCO INVESTORS listen carefully to maxims about life, but they literally crowd the doorways to hear Munger and Buffett talk about investment issues. A frequently asked question is, how do you learn to be a great investor?

First of all, you have to understand your own nature, said Munger. "Each person has to play the game given his own marginal utility considerations and in a way that takes into account his own psychology. If losses are going to make you miserable—and some losses are inevitable—you might be wise to utilize a very conservative pattern of investment and saving all your life. So you have to adapt your strategy to your own nature and your own talents. I don't think there's a one-size-fits-all investment strategy that I can give you."[6]

Then, says Munger, you have to gather information. "I think both Warren and I learn more from the great business magazines than we do anywhere else," said Charlie. "It's such an easy, shorthand way of getting a vast variety of business experience just to riffle through issue after issue covering a great variety of businesses. And if you get into the mental habit of relating what you're reading to the basic structure of the underlying ideas being demonstrated, you gradually accumulate some wisdom about investing. I don't think you can get to be a really good investor over a broad range without doing a massive amount of reading. I don't think any one book will do it for you."

Each year at the Berkshire annual meeting Munger recommends a wide range of reading material. These include *Value Line* charts, Robert B. Cialdini's book *Influence* on how people are persuaded to buy products and take other actions, and recently, Robert Hagstrom's book, *The Warren Buffett Portfolio: Mastering the Power of the Focus Investment Strategy.*

Munger explained that a person's reading should not be random: ". . . you have to have some idea of why you're looking for the information. Don't read annual reports the way Francis Bacon said you do science—which, by the way, is not the way you do science—where you just collect endless data and then only later do you try to make sense of it. You have to start with some ideas about reality. And then you have to look to see whether what you're seeing fits in with proven basic concepts.

"Frequently, you'll look at a business having fabulous results. And the question is, 'How long can this continue?' Well, there's only one way I know to answer that. And that's to think about why the results are occurring now—and then to figure out the forces that could cause those results to stop occurring."

This is the method of thinking that helps Munger and Buffett spot a company that has a franchise on a certain product, a so-called "moat" around its business. There are several examples of companies that have such a strong name brand that they seem invincible. Coca Cola has been such a company, though the challenges are relentless. Munger also uses the example of Wrigley's Chewing Gum.

"It's such a huge advantage to be by far the best-known gum company in the world. Just think of how hard it would be to replace that image. If you know you like Wrigley's Gum and you see it there for two bits, are you really going to reach for Glotz's Gum because it's 20 cents and put something you don't know in your mouth? It's not worth it for you to think about buying an alternative gum. So it's easy to understand why Wrigley's Gum has such a huge advantage."

Once you grasp the value of a company, then you have to decide how much the company is worth if you were buying it outright, or as in the case of the typical investor, simply buying a portion of the company on the stock market.

"The trouble with the Wrigley Gum-type investments is that everybody can see that they're wonderful businesses. So you look at it and you think, 'My God! The thing's at eight times book value or something. And everything else is at three times book value.' So you think, 'I know it's wonderful, but is it wonderful enough to justify that big a premium?'"

The ability to answer such questions explains why some people are successful investors and others are not.

"On the other hand, if it weren't a little difficult, everybody would be rich," Munger insisted.

Observing business over time gives an investor greater perspective on this type of thinking. Munger said he remembers when the downtown department stores in many cities seemed invincible. They offered enormous selections, had large purchasing power, and owned the highest priced real estate in town, the corners where the streetcar lines crossed. However, as time passed, private cars became the prevalent mode of transportation. The streetcar lines were taken out, customers moved to the suburbs and shopping centers became the dominant shopping venues. Some simple changes in the way we live can completely alter the long-term value of a business.

Munger is passionately opposed to certain economic theories and business practices and enjoys the freedom his status and wealth give him to express those opinions. For example, he is perpetually miffed at investors and academics who promote the harsh form of the efficient market theory of investing:

"If you think psychology is badly taught in America, you should look at corporate finance. Modern portfolio theory? It's demented!" Munger proclaimed.

The concept is taught in mainstream business schools and takes the position that all information on publicly traded companies is spread rapidly throughout the investing universe, dispelling any advantage one investor has over another. Nobody can really beat the market because adjustments to news are worked into the price of a security so quickly.[7]

Munger recalled one efficient market theorist who over the years made a career of explaining how Buffett's success was merely the result of good luck. As Buffett's performance held steady and even improved, it became more difficult to explain Buffett as a mere anomaly. ". . . this theorist finally got all the way up to six sigmas—six standard deviations—of luck. But then, people started laughing at him because six sigmas of luck is a lot. So what did he do? He changed his theory. Now, he explains, Warren has six or seven sigmas of skill."

Refuting the claims of financial writer Michael Lewis, who also seemed to portray Buffett as a greedy manipulator whose success is mainly the result of happenstance, Munger says. "He's got the idea that Warren's success for 40 years is because he flipped coins for 40 years and it has come up heads 40 times. All I can say is, if he believes that, I've got a bridge I'd like to sell him."

There is no doubt whatsoever that Berkshire attained its high level of performance, in a large part, because of the commonsense notions shared between Munger and Buffett. For example, they ignore the popular financial indicator called Beta, which measures a stock's volatility in relation to the overall market. A company with a Beta that is higher than the market average is considered by many professional investors to be a high-risk proposition.

"This great emphasis on volatility in corporate finance we regard as nonsense . . . ," said Munger. "Let me put it this way: as long as the odds are in our favor and we're not risking the whole company on one throw of the dice or anything close to it, we don't mind volatility in results. What we want are the favorable odds. We figure the volatility over time will take care of itself at Berkshire."

Both Munger and Buffett are indignant over the way the regulators allow stock options to be counted on the books so that they don't show up as an expense to the company. They mention the problem at nearly every annual meeting.

"It's fundamentally wrong not to have rational, honest accounting in big American corporations," said Munger. "And it's very important not to let little corruptions start because they become big corruptions—and then you have vested interests that fight to perpetuate them. Accounting for stock options in America is corrupt, and it's not a good idea to have corrupt accounting."

Buffett and Munger agree on most things, but they have a different opinion about who should be the decision maker when an unsolicited tender offer is made to a corporation. Buffett says his heart is with the shareholders, but Munger says there is a social interest in some cases, making it okay to make laws to govern such transactions.

"I totally agree that for the ordinary little family business that owns a theater, the shareholders ought to decide whether the theater is sold. But once you get into great big social institutions, that given certain circumstances, will go together in waves of acquisitions into huge agglomerations, that bothers me. So, I think that it's appropriate to have laws that prevent it," said Munger.[8]

If he were teaching finance, Munger said he would use the histories of 100 or so companies that did something right or something wrong.

"Finance properly taught should be taught from cases where the investment decisions are easy," said Munger. "And the one that I always cite is the early history of the National Cash Register Company. It was created by a very intelligent man who bought all the patents, had the best sales force, and the best production plants. He was a very intelligent man and a fanatic, all of whose passions were dedicated to the cash register business. And of course, the invention of the cash register was a godsend to retailing. You might even say that cash registers were the pharmaceuticals industry of a former age. If you read an early annual report when Patterson was the CEO of National Cash Register, an idiot could tell that here was a talented fanatic—very favorably located. Therefore, the investment decision was easy."

John Henry Patterson was an Ohio retailer who did not invent the cash register, but immediately saw its benefits and purchased the money-losing company. In his zealousness, Patterson became the prototype for the contemporary business innovator. He virtually invented the concept of employee benefits (the low-cost company cafeteria, for one), sales force training and motivation, and was responsible for the first house organ, "The Factory News." During the great Dayton flood of 1913, Patterson halted production and devoted the company to saving the city. He gave food, shelter, supplied electrical power, and fresh water, and his company doctors and nurses tended the injured and ill. Factory workers built boats for flooded out residents. Nevertheless, Patterson was a bulldog competitor and once lost an antitrust suit, which later was overturned by a higher court. One of Patterson's most noteworthy achievements was hiring T.J. Watson, a piano salesman, who worked at NCR for years. After Patterson fired Watson, he went to work at Computer-Tabulating-Recording Company, which Watson transformed into IBM, using many of the business skills he'd learned at NCR.

Patterson left a great business when he died, but he'd spent so much on social causes that his estate had very little money. Not that it mattered to him. Patterson was fond of saying "Shrouds don't have pockets."[9]

Though few companies last forever, all of them should be built to last a long time, says Munger. The approach to corporate control should be thought of as "financial engineering." Just as bridges and airplanes are constructed with a series of back-up systems and redundancies to meet extreme stresses, so too should corporations be built to withstand the pressures from competition, recessions, oil shocks, or other calamities. Excess leverage, or debt, makes the corporation especially vulnerable to such storms.

"It is a crime in America," stated Munger, "to build a weak bridge. How much nobler is it to build a weak company?"[10]

AMERICANS ARE OVERSOLD ON THE benefit they receive from money managers, and particularly, from mutual fund managers, and that bothers Munger enormously.

"It is, to me, just amazing what's happened in the mutual fund business," he said. "It just grows and grows and grows. And they get these fees just for maintaining shares in place—12-B-1 fees or whatever they call them. I am not charmed with the mechanics of that business."

Addressing a group of charitable foundation executives in Santa Monica, California, in 1998, Munger especially criticized Yale University for investing its endowment in the equivalent of a fund of mutual funds: "This is an amazing development. Few would have predicted that, long after Cornfeld's fall into disgrace, major universities would be leading foundations into Cornfeld's system."[11] Bernie Cornfeld in the 1970s created the ill-fated, fund-of-funds concept.

An *eminence gris* of no less stature than John Bogle, founder of the Vanguard Funds, has taken up Munger's cudgel. When Munger made his comment he was speaking to directors of nonprofit organizations and was attacking the practice of hiring consultants to hire money managers who in turn select mutual funds operated by other money managers. At each step, there is a commission to be paid, which skims off the money that can be used in the work of the charity.

"Mr. Munger goes on to point out," said Bogle, "the devastating impact of the cost of all this complexity on the return of foundations and endowments in a stock market with lower returns. Market returns—5 percent; total cost, 3 percent; net return, 2 percent."

And, said Bogle, "Please don't scoff at the use of the 5 percent return on stocks. The long-term real returns on stocks has been 7 percent, so Mr. Munger's hypothetical future figure is far from apocalyptic."[12]

Munger's recommendation to managers of the funds of not-for-profit foundations was simple: Save yourself a lot of time, money, and worry. Just put your endowments into index funds. Alternately, the foundations could follow Berkshire's lead and simply buy high quality stocks (if they are not highly overvalued in price) and hold on for the long term.[13]

It isn't even necessary to worry about diversification. "In the United States, a person or institution with almost all wealth invested, long term, in just three fine domestic corporations, is securely rich," said Munger. "And why should such an owner care if at any time most other investors are faring somewhat better or worse. And particularly so when he rationally believes, like Berkshire, that his long-term results will be superior by reason of his lower costs, required emphasis on long-term effects, and concentration in his most preferred choices."[14]

In fact, Munger went so far as to suggest that investors could have 90 percent of their wealth in a single company, if it was the right company. "Indeed, I hope the Mungers follow roughly this course. And I note that the Woodruff Foundations have, so far, proven extremely wise to retain an approximately 90 percent concentration in the founder's Coca Cola stock. It would be interesting to calculate just how all American foundations would have fared if they had never sold a share of founder's stock. Very many, I think, would now be much better off."[15]

Although Munger asserted that the vast majority of professionally managed money, after taking into account the impact of fees and transaction costs would be better off in index funds, he ended by throwing out an alternate point of view:

> Does that mean you should be in an index fund? Well, that depends on whether or not you can invest money way better than average or you can find someone who almost surely will invest money way better than average. And those are the questions that make life interesting.

If everyone put their money in index funds, Munger conceded, the prices of indexed stocks would be forced beyond intrinsic value, and the process would become meaningless.

It was this disenchantment with the management of money, in part, that led to Buffett and Munger's objection in the mid-1990s to the creation of mutual funds made up entirely of Berkshire Hathaway stock. Companies that wanted to establish the funds said it was a way to give average investors access to an exceptional investment.

Five Sigma Investment partners L.P. of Bala Cynwyd, Pennsylvania, had filed with the Securities and Exchange Commission to sell Berkshire through a vehicle called the Affordable Access Trust. The trust would require an initial deposit as small as $300. Berkshire shares at the time were trading for about $35,000 each. Another group, Nike Securities of Lisle, Illinois, planned a similar unit trust.[16]

"Frankly, what we are doing is to make Berkshire available to average people," said Sam Katz, a principal at Five Sigma. "Just because someone is not wealthy doesn't mean they don't have the aptitude or sophistication for this business."[17]

One broker involved in the deal declared, "Buffett and Munger turned out to be control freaks."[18]

Berkshire submitted a 24-page memorandum to the SEC in December 1995, saying that the securities sale would mislead investors. The memorandum, which was prepared at Munger, Tolles, also was distributed to state regulators.

"I've been in one aspect or another of investment management for what, 44 years or so, and trying not to disappoint anyone," said Buffett. "And in the process of not disappointing anyone, one of the key factors is having them have the proper expectations and being knowledgeable about what they're getting and what they're not getting. Neither Mr. Munger nor I would function as effectively if we had tens of thousands of people who were in one way or another disappointed with us. That's not Berkshire."[19]

In addition to registering a complaint with the SEC and then coming up with an alternative of their own, Munger sent a stinging letter to Five Sigma:

> Warren Buffett does not regard the current market price of Berkshire stock as a price that makes new investments in Berkshire attractive. If he were asked by a friend or family member whether he advised a new purchase of Berkshire shares at the current price, Mr. Buffett would answer, No.[20]

To make the investment trusts less attractive, Berkshire took the unusual step of creating a B-class share, which would represent one-thirtieth the value of the original shares, which now would be called A shares. The structure of the B shares, and the way in which they were presented, was unique. The deal was set up so that brokers could make very little commission money, thus discouraging them from pushing the shares onto their clients. Additionally, the underwriting syndicate for the shares included two discounter brokers, Schwab and Fidelity. By including discounters, initial shares would be more readily available to all investors.

Critics claimed that Buffett and Munger created the B shares because they could not tolerate losing control of Berkshire's shareholder policy. "This is a small problem that Mr. Buffett approached in a big way," said James K. Mulvey, an analyst with Dresdner Securities in New York.[21]

For starters Buffett and Munger planned to offer 100,000 B shares, but said they would keep adding to the offering until the public demand was met. The number of shares in the public offering increased four times, until ultimately 517,500 shares were sold at $1,110 per share, doubling Berkshire's shareholder base to 80,000 individuals. The offering added $600 million to Berkshire's capital.

Nike Securities went forward with its trust, but the Berkshire trust never became the phenomenon that the originators had hoped it would.

MICHAEL LEWIS, AMONG OTHERS, HAS accused Munger and Buffett of spouting high moral standards for the investment world, while not holding their own investments to the same requirements. They particularly point to the fact that Berkshire once invested in the stock of a company that does not serve the public good—a tobacco seller.

"We have set ourselves up, to some extent, as a moral censor of our own activities," Munger agreed, "but we have never had the attitude that when we buy a little piece of a company in an insurance portfolio, that we are a moral censor for the world."[22]

In April 1993, Berkshire took a sizable stake, approximately 5 percent, in UST, a leading maker of smokeless tobacco. The shares were trading at between $27 and $29 per share at the time. A 5 percent stake would have been worth more than $300 million. UST makes Skoal and Copenhagen, and also produces wine, including Chateau Ste. Michelle. At the same time, Berkshire sold its holdings in RJR Nabisco, which is a combined food and tobacco company.

To some it is splitting hairs, but to Munger, there is a big difference in buying stock in a corporation and owning the entire shebang. He follows different rules for each.

"If we're buying stock in major companies that are out there, (Buffett) doesn't make his judgment based on some moral overview of their whole business. We do that in judging and controlling our own behavior." [23]

Munger said that though it once held tobacco company shares, Berkshire turned down a chance to buy a tobacco company outright.

"We don't want to be in the business of selling addictive drugs, with us being the controlling owners," Munger said. "It's not the way we do the game. We'll own shares, because if we don't own them, somebody else will. But we'll never have Berkshire in a controlling interest."[24]

That said, Munger admits that he and Buffett have made many investment errors. "If I were ordaining rules for running boards of directors, I'd require that three hours be spent examining stupid blunders including quantification of effects considering opportunity costs."

Despite his criticism and his insistence that there are corrupt practices afoot in the business world, Munger feels that overall, America and its businesses usually are honorable.

"I would not agree that things are generally going to hell," said Munger. "Sure we've got some pockets of social pathology in our big cities, and we've got pockets of social pathology in the high reaches of business, but averaged out, I would say it's pretty good. If you take engineering integrity in products, when was the last time your automatic transmission went out? We've learned to do a lot of things with enormous reliability. You take a company like Boeing and all the hours that the airplanes stay in the air and the three back up systems behind every system that navigates that airplane. I would argue that there is a lot to admire in American business and a lot that's done right, And that these old-fashioned values, averaged out, are winning, not losing. It's too bad we have all that social pathology—but we have it in the high reaches of politics, why shouldn't we have it in the high reaches of business."[25]

A SHAREHOLDER ONCE ASKED BUFFETT how he spent his days. Warren said he mostly read and talked on the telephone. "That's what I do. Charlie, what do you do?"

"That [question] reminds me very much of a friend of mine in World War II in a group that had nothing to do," replied Munger. "A general once went up to my friend's boss, we'll call him Captain Glotz. He said, 'Captain Glotz, what do you do?' His boss said, 'Not a damn thing.' "

"The General got madder and madder and turned to my friend and said, 'What do you do?' "

"My friend said, 'I help Captain Glotz.' That's the best way to describe what I do at Berkshire."

A TIME TO
REAP REWARDS

Charlie talks as much as he always did, the only difference is, now people listen.

Nancy Munger

NANCY MUNGER HAS PLANNED A boat trip up to Little Rice Lake, one of the seven small lakes to which Cass Lake is connected. David Borthwick, her son from her first marriage, will drive the boat. Nancy and Charlie will be tour guides. It is an August day when the sky seems twice as wide as usual and the lake shimmers in the sun like blue lace woven with spun silver. The party motors out in the largest of Munger's boats, up the lake to examine the narrow reedy stream that is the infant Mississippi River, trickling down from its headwaters. There is a dam on the lake where the Mississippi leaves Cass Lake, but this year, 1999, the water is so high that a canoer could paddle right over the top. It's easy to imagine being a sixteenth century explorer or a French fur trapper first discovering the area. Borthwick motors up another small river, past a rustic inn, under a bridge where youngsters line up to wave at passing boats, and then jump into the river when all is clear. On and on, into more and more remote landscapes. Rice Lake lives up to its name, a pristine pond edged by wild rice paddies. The reeds ruffle in the breeze and here and there is a beaver dam.

"Let's throw out a line and fish," says Charlie, instructing David to pull the boat near the mouth of a water course that is bigger than a stream but not quite a river. "Aren't we too close to the edge," a worried Nancy asks repeatedly. "Naw," says Charlie. He urges David to pull to one side of the stream, then let the boat drift across the mouth of the inlet, and then quickly motor back when the boat nears the shallow, reed-thick edge of the lake. It doesn't take long for an extra strong gust of wind to drive the boat into the deep, thick growth of rice plants. David whips the motor on, but stalks and weeds quickly wrap around the boat's propellor, making the motor whir uselessly, throwing out the smell of something that is about to burn. Charlie, David, and a houseguest bend over the back of the boat, stripping long green shreds from the propellor, trying repeatedly to clear a spot where the motor can run long enough to push the boat into deeper water.

Rather than show her frustration, and perhaps to resist saying, "I told you so," Nancy Munger scans the sky for birds, and as luck would have it, spots an eagle hovering near a tall, distant pine. She is an avid birder and had been told there was an aerie near Rice Lake. When the bird wings away, conversation turns to her other interest, painting. "When you paint, you always notice that the dark side of clouds is on the bottom. The sky is light near the horizon, and darker as you look higher," explains Nancy.

Molly Munger cheerfully announces that, based on past experiences of boating with her father, she has worn her swimsuit underneath her slacks and is prepared to jump in the lake and push the boat out into the channel if necessary. Finally, the men prevail over the rice, and the fishless fishing party is on its way back down the string of lakes.

Getting caught in the weeds or stuck on a sandbar when boating is only one of the Munger family traditions. With long-standing commitments, friendships, and homes to visit, the Mungers' life has settled into a series of rituals. The Mungers drive from Los Angeles to their Santa Barbara home on many weekends. "We love this house," said Charlie.

The Santa Barbara "Mungerville" home sits in a wooded area, far enough from the beach that the sea view is somewhat restricted, but close enough to catch a breeze. The wood and stone house can best be described as California country French. There is a large sunroom in the center and a spacious wine cove just off the kitchen. Charlie's study has some of the same decorative elements as the Cass Lake house—a model sailing ship, carved wooden ducks, and stacks of books. Books by Somerset Maugham; biographies of Margaret Thatcher, Mark Twain, and Albert Einstein; *The Moral Animal* by Robert Wright; *Tales from the Drone's Club* by P.G. Wodehouse. And stacked on a side table, *The Ultimate Rose Book* and *The French Interior*.

"BELIEVING THAT THE SECRET OF human felicity is to aim low, I promptly did that," said Munger, adding that he wanted to be able to say what Samuel

Johnson said regarding the writing of his dictionary. "I knew very well what I was trying to do. And very well how to do it. And I have done it very well."

Of course Munger means that as a bit of a joke, and he admits he overshot his mark somewhat. Although Munger may never have expected to be a billionaire and second in command of one of the most unique and closely watched corporations in the world, he aimed at a life of quality and strove diligently to bring that about.

Buffett's life and his investment strategy seem to unfold effortlessly before him, but Munger's course has not been as easy. Both personally and professionally, he has encountered repeated obstacles and heartaches. That is what most people experience in life, Munger would say. Anyone who struggles to make the box of his life larger discovers that the box has walls that must be burst open.

"It's . . . necessary to accommodate a lot of failure, and because no matter how able you are, you're going to have headwinds and troubles," Munger told the employees at See's Candy on the company's 75th anniversary. "The Sees who created this business had failed at least once, and had seriously failed. But if a person just keeps going on the theory that life is full of vicissitudes and just does the right thinking and follows the right values it should work out well in the end. So I would say, don't be discouraged by a few reverses."[1]

By heeding basic principles and being alert for opportunities, Munger made the leap from a respectably successful lawyer to an individual investor who is known internationally for his expertise. His wealth has provided the independence he longed for as a young man.

"It was a number of ideas, not just one. A lot of ideas. In the nature of things, really wonderful ideas are virtually sure to win. You can be sure that if you master the wonderful concepts you're going to get opportunities if you look for them. . . . But you won't get an unlimited number of good ideas—so when they come along, seize them."[2]

Munger has said that accumulating the first $100,000 from a standing start, with no seed money, is the most difficult part of building wealth. Making the first million was the next big hurdle. To do that a person must consistently underspend his income. Getting wealthy, he explains, is like rolling a snowball. It helps to start on the top of a long hill—start early and try to roll that snowball for a very long time. It helps to live a long life.

Warren Buffett is known for an extremely simple lifestyle, with very few hobbies aside from reading annual reports, regular games of bridge, and a little golf. (In truth Buffett does a fair amount of travel to spend time with his wide circle of friends and to attend various business meetings.)

Charlie Munger cannot be described as a lavish person, but he lives fully and even colorfully. True, he comes running when Berkshire has a crisis and needs him, and he tends to his duties at the *Los Angeles Daily Journal,* Wesco Financial Corporation, Good Samaritan Hospital, and Harvard-Westlake School, but accompanied by Nancy, he also visits friends everywhere from Maine to Idaho, plays golf in Hawaii, and fishes on various continents and bodies of water for trout, bonefish, Atlantic Salmon, or whatever may be present and biting. He has traveled with friends Ira Marshall and Otis Booth to the Australian rain forest and with family to England, Italy, and other places. He reads voraciously about everything from dinosaurs, to black holes to psychology. With eight children who have families of their own, simply attending birthday parties, graduations, weddings, christenings, and holiday events gives him a busy social life.

As he grows older and wealthier, Munger still avoids a showy life, but he is willing to accept a little ease. "Warren kids me about flying coach,

A Munger family gathering in England.

which I used to do more often," said Munger. "Now, when traveling with Nancy, we usually go first class or business class." Finally in 2000 Munger signed up for a timeshare private jet service through the Berkshire Hathaway-owned company Executive Jet.

While shareholders come to Berkshire and Wesco annual meetings seeking financial wisdom, they also ply Munger with questions on how to properly raise a family, another subject in which he has vast experience.

"I am quite pleased with all my children in terms of morality, behavior, and such," said Munger, but he's less certain about how to make them all hunger to work hard and become even richer than he has made them.

"I've had kids in both moderate and immoderate circumstances," he said, "and to be honest, my children that were raised when we had less money have worked harder."

The Munger children, most of whom see through their father's curmudgeonly exterior, are unlikely to be ruffled by such comments. As for his gruffness, "It's very much an act, it's self-parody, it's a joke on himself," said Molly Munger. "You know people who are stiff, ponderous. He's not. He doesn't expect you to believe it. He's utilizing that particular characteristic. He has a huge range. This was the one that suited him."

The Munger children, despite their attraction to law as a career, are quite different from one another, yet each seems to have taken some characteristic from Charlie. Molly Munger is a vivacious, striking blonde whose face is shaped very much like her father's. Charles, Jr., like Charlie, Sr., is fascinated with science. Charlie, Sr. is famous for carrying a book and reading, no matter how wonderful the surrounding scenery might be. His daughter Emilie is the same. Emilie's husband once walked into their home and smelled smoke. When he checked around, he found smoke billowing from the kitchen, where food was burning in the oven. Emilie was sitting in the kitchen, so involved in a book that she was unaware of the pending disaster. On another occasion, she was waiting for a flight at an airport and went into a shop. Emilie found a book, sat on the floor and began to read. She became so engrossed that she missed her airplane. Finally, the terminal was closed and Emilie, still on the floor quietly reading, was locked in the store. She had to telephone for help to get out.

Despite the fact that some of his children have adopted religious beliefs he doesn't embrace and others spend their life in activities that probably won't be highly financially productive, Munger swells with pride when telling of Charles, Jr.'s work in science education or his wife Mandy's election to her local school board.

"He thinks I'm an ultra liberal, but part of that is for effect," said Molly, who spends an enormous amount of time on work her father would describe as left wing and who as an adult converted to Catholicism. "He likes to play the curmudgeon, but I don't think he thinks I'm a crazy person."

MUNGER HAS SAID THAT HE and Buffett don't want to go down in history as shrewd, miserable accumulators. "We didn't want to be remembered by friends and family for nothing but pieces of paper."

And so, Charlie has decided it's all right to be whimsical once in a while.

"I'm building a boat," declared Munger in the fall of 1998. "We're within 60 days of finishing. Call it Munger's folly. It's not an economic activity, but it's very creative. Nobody has built a boat exactly like it."

The 84-feet-long, 41-feet-wide catamaran was in a shipyard—of sorts—in Florida, being constructed of epoxy resin, composite materials similar to those used in aircraft, and Kevlar. Briefly it was the largest boat of its kind in the world until someone built a catamaran with a mast just a few inches higher than the Channel Cat's 102-foot pole. The Channel Cat was completed in early 1999, but not without difficulty.

King Williams—who along with Charlie designed the boat—says the story began one afternoon several years earlier when he was working on his fishing boat, which was moored at the long pier in Santa Barbara.

Williams is a former submariner and deep sea diver, first for oil companies, then on his own. He made his living diving for sea urchins in the Channel Islands, where the best specimens in the world are found. The urchins were sold in Santa Barbara and shipped overnight to Japan, where they are a culinary delicacy. Unfortunately, Williams had spent too much of his career under water and was beginning to suffer the bends when he was diving.

Williams's old East Coast lobster boat attracted a lot of attention from tourists strolling along the dock. "These two older men were looking at my boat, admiring it," said Williams. "They introduced themselves. Charlie Munger and a friend. I had no idea who they were." The two men asked all sorts of questions, and after a while Williams offered to take them out for a spin on the boat.

After that Charlie called occasionally and he and Williams went out for lunch and talked mostly about two subjects Munger finds ever-fascinating—fishing and boats. Gradually, the two became friends. As he had done before, senior financier Charlie Munger found an unlikely ally, King Williams III, a deep sea diver whose hobby is hang gliding off the Santa Barbara cliffs.

Williams is a big, easy-going fiftyish man with a ready laugh, who seems to have no fear of anything physical. Munger does not intimidate him either, but Williams has learned a lot in the relationship. "Charlie used to ask me a question, and I'd shoot back an answer," said Williams. "A couple of days later I'd think, 'why did I say that? That's not what he wanted to know.' Now I think carefully before answering him. I like to say that now I'm up to just one day behind him."

Their conversation occasionally took a philosophical turn.

"Charlie once asked me, 'King, if you could do anything in the world, what would it be?' I said I'd build the biggest catamaran I could and sail off across that ocean and you'd never see me again." Munger then quizzed him about why he would build a catamaran, and they got to talking about that type of boat and what made it good and bad. Though Williams was unprepared for what happened next, like the typical adventurer, he was game for it. "One day he said, 'go find a catamaran.'" Unfortunately the boat they discussed did not exist, and the luxury tax had pushed many yacht builders out of business, making U.S. builders difficult to find. Williams finally located a yacht manufacturer who said he could do the job in Green Cove Springs, a small town in Florida.

Three months into the project, things went off track. To be sure, Williams and Munger wanted to do some things with the boat that were outside the realm of ordinary experience. Problems at the original shipyard were such that Munger complained there were "rogues, scallywags and pirates in Florida."

"I went down, things weren't going well," said Williams. "Charlie said, 'Well, you can build a boat.' So I fired the guys."

Williams and his wife Rachel quickly packed up and went to Florida to take charge of the work. The unfinished boat was already so big that moving it would be awkward, but there was no other choice. Williams had to go into the shipyard with the sheriff, a warrant, and house movers. He arranged for a power company crew to drive down the road ahead of the boat, lowering power lines so that the boat would not snag them.

Williams rented land along the St. Johns River, not far from the original boat yard. He leased several truck tractor trailers to be used as offices. Because of the pollution created by the boat's materials, Munger and Williams were forced to build a hangar. "We made our own shipyard," Williams said.

As for the boat itself, "Charlie designed it, pretty much," said Williams. "Every week he'd send two to three drawings. I built it for him—with help from a marine engineer and 46 other guys."

Munger scrawled his notes, using a ruler and a black marker because they were easier for him to see. He drew a scale model of the main dining room, complete with tables and chairs, carefully measuring the exact space needed for comfortable seating. Williams saved all of Munger's instructions and deposited them among the ship's papers. "I cherish those drawings," he said.

Munger often called Williams on the telephone and the minute he had said what he needed to say, Munger would abruptly hang up. It has never been his habit to indulge in small talk. Williams learned not to be surprised or to take offense.

Charlie went to Florida at one point to see how the boat was progressing. He took a barrel, placed it in the upstairs room, and after sitting there for awhile looking out, insisted the windows were too high. Williams had installed relatively small windows for safety at sea. But he removed the windows and put in expansive windows that would allow people to sit in easy chairs or at tables in the main lounge and still take in a view of the water.

Because local workers were unfamiliar with the high-tech materials and equipment being utilized, Williams trained them himself. He arranged for manufacturer's representatives to come to the yard and show the workers how to do things properly. Green Cove Springs is a rural area, and many of the workers had never held a job before that paid good wages and included employee benefits. Williams (with Munger's money) arranged for unemployment, health, and workers' compensation insurance. "They all became very loyal," said Williams.

The boat construction stretched out for three years. In that time King and Rachel Williams became well-acquainted with the workers and their families, and realized how important the job was to them. When the boat was finished, Rachel, who ran the office, called the large boat builders in the region in an attempt to find employment for the construction crew.

When she called, "They'd say, well, 'send a resume.' I'd say, 'why don't you come out and see what these people can do.' We used the Channel Cat as a demo to get all of the workers jobs before we left."

Undeterred by the Titanic jinx, Williams claims the boat, which has a range of 1,500 miles, is unsinkable. The hull is composed of cells and if a puncture occurs one place, the water will not spill into other cells. The Channel Cat has motorized sails, a global positioning system, autopilot, radar, and a weather fax. The boat has a customized computer system with compact disks containing the marine charts of all the seas and harbors in the world.

In addition to the upstairs salon, below there are two state rooms, a crew bunk room and a library/lounge. The boat can carry 149 passengers and six crew. Because it was built to sea-going standards, the Channel Cat is licensed to ply waters with paying passengers from Alaska to Cabo San Lucas, at the tip of Baja California.

The boat has two 350 horsepower Cummins diesel engines, plus two generators to provide electricity. The desalination system produces 500 gallons of water per day, plenty for the crew and guests to take regular showers. There is a four-keg beer cooler in the bar, plus a 35-case cooler and an ice maker capable of producing 200 pounds per day . The boat carries a state-of-the-art audiovisual system and can pick up satellite television and telephone anywhere on the globe.

The interior is fitted out with pale bird's-eye maple, leather furniture, and a soft green carpet from an imported material that allows even motor oil to be wiped up with a paper towel.

The etched windows at the entrance can be fiber-optically lit and gently, continually change colors. At a cost of $55,000, a Florida glass artist created a story etched in the decorative glass specifically for the Channel Cat with a theme of Santa Barbara coastal life. The entry door windows depict a kelp bed, then the partition in the foyer displays various sea creatures that might be found in the kelp bed, and the story in glass progresses throughout the boat to the downstairs bathrooms. There, a mermaid wearing a seashell bra, adorns the ladies' room door and Neptune, with a great flowing beard, designates the men's room.

"I've never in my life spent money foolishly like that. I said what the hell. It was a creative thing to do," Munger insisted. Although Munger will not say how much the boat cost, it is estimated by one expert that total expenditures must have run at around $6 million.

After the three years of construction, it took another year to deliver the boat and put it into service. The Williams, along with two other crew members, sailed the Channel Cat 7,000 miles to bring it home to Santa Barbara. They started the journey during the 1999 hurricane season, which turned out to be one of the most severe seasons in recent Caribbean history. Hurricane Mitch blew through the area and the crew was forced to take emergency refuge in Havana, where they waited for 25 days at the Marina Hemingway for Mitch and other foul weather to pass. When weather permitted they sailed through the Panama Canal and started up the west coast of Central America, Mexico, and on to California.

Because of its size and passenger load, the boat must have two officers. King and his brother Rex, who once ran a charter boat service out of St. Thomas in the Virgin Islands, serve in those roles. Rachel and Rex's wife Michelle are the deck officers.

Charlie once claimed he would never spend a night on the boat, but when the Williams were bringing it around, he and Nancy flew to Cabo

San Lucas to meet the Channel Cat. They spent three days in Baja California where they went whale watching and fishing.

"Charlie wanted a dual purpose boat," said Williams. Designed as a
day-sailing party boat, Munger hopes that half the time the Channel Cat
will be rented out for corporate board meetings and the like. The other
half of the time it will be donated to organizations for fund raising events.
Munger envisions whale watching tours, lobster fishing parties, and
cruises through the Channel Islands, location of the evocative book and
movie, *Island of the Blue Dolphins.* King and Rachel hope to conduct 50
charter events each year and 50 charity events each year.

Partly because local tour boat owners objected, and partly because of
its large size, the boat has not been granted its own license to operate out
of Santa Barbara. It has, however, been used for its intended purpose in
other ports and sometimes sails under a sublicense out of Santa Barbara.
The Williams staged a Buffett Group party in Monterey, California,
attended by Buffett, Bill Gates, plus other well-known members of the corporate elite. A seven-course banquet for 65 people was served on the
boat. The dinner was catered from land, though the boat has a full-service
galley including double convection ovens. Emilie Munger held her fortieth birthday party aboard the boat in Newport Beach, California, and her
friends flew in from all around the world for the event.

After the boat was finished, King Williams and Charlie were walking
through a parking lot at a boat marina when a car backed out of a parking
space and shot toward them. Williams yelled at the driver, who slammed
on the brakes just before hitting Charlie.

Munger said to Williams, "You probably saved my life."

Williams replied, "Charlie, I'd never let anything happen to you."

Charlie snapped back, "Then you're walking on my wrong side," referring to his blind left eye.

THAT MUNGER BUILT A $6 MILLION boat for the sheer fun of it seems remark-
able, if not somewhat quirky, to his family and friends, even to King
Williams.

"Charlie is very practical," said Williams. "We were driving along
one day and Charlie said, 'I've got to show you this house I built.'"
Munger directed Williams to drive to the top of Hot Springs Road in
Montecito, where he pointed out a mansion with a sweeping view of the
Pacific, a lap pool, extensive gardens on so much land it took a golf cart to
get around. "I said, Charlie, your retirement home! Charlie replied, 'Naw,
I'd never live in a place like that.'"

"He is very distrustful of emotions." observed Molly Munger. "We heard a lot of messages about how emotions can lead you to do dumb things. I'm trying to think of a time he said, 'Go with your gut, feel the vibes. Lose yourself in the moment.' That's not where he is."

Yet Molly says there always were signs that her father could be frivolous. "At the same time, that dry of a person wouldn't have that spring in his step. After something is checked out and you can feel safe, he gets very devoted to people," said Molly. "A good argument can be made that he's a very emotional person—that it is an achievement that he brought a large psyche under control. A unique mix of an (emotional) personality under wraps."

A Postscript

When they were younger, Warren Buffett often told inquisitive shareholders that if anything happened to him, Charlie Munger would take the helm at Berkshire Hathaway. As time passed and age crept up, Munger deflected questions of corporate succession in the standard midwestern way, with humor. "They asked George Burns when he was 95, 'What does your doctor say about you smoking these big, black cigars?' And he said, 'My doctor's dead.' "

But now that Buffett is around 70 and Munger is passing his mid-70s, that reply doesn't work as well.

"In due course this corporation will have a change in management," said Munger. "There is not a way to fix that."

Both men say, however, that there is a successor (or possibly two, one for operations and one for investments) who will be revealed at the appropriate time. Furthermore, Berkshire Hathaway was built with a long tenure of effortless management in mind. "The one place a death will hurt is we're not likely to get as good an allocator of capital as Warren in the next CEO, whoever that is. But it still will be one hell of a business."[3]

Munger said he and Buffett aren't "obsessing" about their successors yet. "Fortunately, Warren plans to live almost indefinitely."

One shareholder asked, who is the next Charlie Munger? "There's not much demand," declared a matter-of-fact Munger.

Unable to resist a ghoulish joke, Munger said that when he dies people will ask, "How much did he leave?" The answer will be, "He left it all."

WHEELER, MUNGER PARTNERSHIP

Annual Percentage Change

Year	Overall Partnership	Dow Jones Industrial Average
1962	30.1	−7.6
1963	71.7	20.6
1964	49.7	18.7
1965	8.4	14.2
1966	12.4	−15.8
1967	56.2	19.0
1968	40.4	7.7
1969	28.3	−11.6
1970	−0.1	8.7
1971	25.4	9.8
1972	8.3	18.2
1973	−31.9	−13.1
1974	−31.5	−23.1
1975	73.2	44.4
Average Return	24.3	6.4

INTERVIEW LIST

Otis Booth, Bel Air, California,
November, 1999.
David and Molly Borthwick, Star
Island, Minnesota, August, 1999.
Hal Borthwick, Los Angeles,
California, May, 1999.
Warren Buffett, Omaha, Nebraska,
October, 1997.
Robert Denham, Los Angeles,
California, December, 1998.
Stephen English, Star Island,
Minnesota, August, 1999.
Carol Munger Estabrook, May, 1998,
Omaha, Nebraska.
Katharine Graham, Washington, D.C.,
November, 1998.
J.P. "Rick" Guerin, Beverly Hills,
California, October, 1998.
Lenny Gumport, Star Island,
Minnesota, August, 1999.
Roderick Hills, by telephone from
Houston, Texas, October, 1999.
Charles Huggins, South San Francisco,
California, October, 1999.
Andrew Leeka, Los Angeles,
California, November, 1999.
Stan Lipsey, Buffalo, New York,
August, 1998.
Ira and Martha Marshall, Palm Springs,
California, November, 1999.
Barry Munger, New York City,
October, 1998.
Charles T. Munger, Omaha, Nebraska,
May, 1997; Santa Barbara,

California, October, 1997;
Omaha, May, 1998; Los Angeles,
California, May 1, 1998; Omaha,
May, 1999; Star Island, August,
1999; Los Angeles, May and
November, 1999; Los Angeles,
March, 2000.
Charles T. Munger, Jr., Star Island,
Minnesota, August, 1999.
Emilie Munger, Mill Valley, California,
October, 1999.
Nancy Munger, Omaha, May, 1998 and
May, 1999; Star Island,
Minnesota, August, 1999.
Molly Munger, December, 1998, Los
Angeles, California; Star Island,
Minnesota, August, 1999.
Wendy Munger, South Pasadena,
California, December, 1998.
Chuck Rickershauser, Los Angeles,
California, December, 1998.
Ronald Olson, Los Angeles, California,
December, 1998.
Gerald Salzman, Los Angeles,
California, November 8, 1999.
Willa Davis Seemann and Lee D.
Seemann, Omaha, Nebraska,
May, 1998.
Louis Simpson, Rancho Santa Fe,
California, December, 1998.
James D. Sinegal, Issequah,
Washington, August, 1998.
King and Rachel Williams, Santa
Barbara, California, May, 1999.

TIME LINE—THE LIFE AND CAREER OF CHARLES T. MUNGER

1924	Charles Thomas Munger was born January 1 in Omaha, Nebraska.
1941–42	Munger attended the University of Michigan.
1942	Munger joined the U.S. Army Force and served as meterological officer.
1943	While serving in the Army Air Force, Munger attended the California Institute of Technology in Pasadena, California.
1948	Munger graduated from Harvard Law School, magna cum laude.
	He began practicing law in Los Angeles at Wright & Garrett, which later became Musick Peeler & Garrett.
1949	Munger was admitted to the California Bar.
1950	Munger built a relationship with Ed Hoskins and eventually joined him in ownership and operation of Transformer Engineers Co.
1959	Warren Buffett and Charles Munger met at a dinner in Omaha hosted by mutual friend Dr. Edwin Davis, Jr.
	Wesco Financial Corporation was incorporated.
1960	Munger demolished a Berry family mansion in the Hancock Park area of Los Angeles and built two homes on the lot. He sold one to finance the project and moved his family into the other.
1961	Munger and partner Ed Hoskins sold Transformer Engineers Co.
	Otis Booth and Charlie Munger began their first real estate development.
1962	On February 1, Wheeler, Munger & Co., an investment counseling firm was established in Los Angeles, with Charles Munger and Jack Wheeler as partners. The law firm of Munger, Tolles was launched with seven attorneys, including Roy Tolles, Roderick Hills, who later

became chairman of SEC and his wife, Carla Anderson Hills, who among other top government posts, became U.S. Trade Representative.

Buffett started buying shares in Berkshire Hathaway, a beleaguered New Bedford, Massachusetts, textile manufacturer.

1965   Munger stepped down as an active member of Munger, Tolles & Olson. He no longer practiced law.

Munger, Rick Guerin and Buffett began buying shares in Blue Chip Stamps.

Buffett accumulated enough shares of Berkshire Hathaway to take control of the company.

1967   Munger and Buffett went to New York to buy Associated Cotton Shops.

National Indemnity Company and National Fire and Marine Insurance Company, sister companies, were acquired for approximately $8.6 million.

1968   The first Buffett Group, including Munger, traveled to Coronado, California to meet with Benjamin Graham and discuss the flagging stock market.

Buffett started to liquidate Berkshire Hathaway's assets and restructure it as a holding company.

1969   Munger & Buffett backed the California Supreme Court appeal of Dr. Belous, a physician who referred a patient to an abortion clinic.

Munger became a trustee of Harvard School in Los Angeles, which later merged with Westlake School.

The 100-member Berkshire Partnership was terminated at end of 1969. Investors had multiple choice—take cash, take shares in Berkshire Hathaway, in Diversified Retailing, or invest in the Sequoia Fund.

In March, Buffett and Munger purchased the Illinois National Bank.

1972   Through Blue Chip Stamps, Buffett and Munger bought See's Candy for $2 million.

Rick Guerin and Munger acquired controlling interest in the Fund of Letters and changed its name to the New America Fund.

1973   *The Sun* in Omaha, under the direction of Stan Lipsey, won a Pulitzer Prize for its Boys Town exposé.

Berkshire began investing in The Washington Post Company, becoming the largest shareholder outside the family of Katharine Graham.

1974   Munger became chairman of the board of Harvard school, serving until 1979.

Buffett and Munger bought Wesco Financial, the parent company of a Pasadena savings and loan association.

1975 Munger stepped down as head of Wheeler, Munger & Co. and the partnership was liquidated in 1976. Its compounded annual growth rate from 1962 to 1975 was more than 20 percent.

1976 The Securities and Exchange Commission completed an investigation of the relationship of Blue Chip Stamps, Wesco Financial and Berkshire. Buffett and Munger settled without admitting innocence or guilt and paid $115,000 to Wesco shareholders who may have been damaged by their business practices.

Munger became chairman of Blue Chip Stamps.

1977 Through Blue Chip Stamps, Buffett and Munger purchased the *Buffalo Evening News* for $2.5 million.

Berkshire's equity interest in Blue Chip Stamps was increased to 36.5 percent at the end of the year.

Berkshire invested $10.9 million in Capital Cities Communications.

1978 Munger became Berkshire Hathaway's vice chairman and at the same time developed vision problems.

Berkshire's stake in Blue Chip Stamps increased to 58 percent, requiring that the company be fully consolidated into the balance sheet and statement of earnings of Berkshire.

1979 Wesco Financial acquired Precision Steel Warehouse.

1980 Due to failed cataract surgery, and following extremely painful complications, Munger lost the vision in his left eye. Vision in his right eye became limited, and he was forced to wear thick cataract glasses.

1983 Blue Chip Stamps was fully merged into Berkshire, a process that started several years earlier.

1984 In January, Munger became chairman and president of Wesco Financial.

1985 Wesco-Financial Insurance Co. (Wes-FIC) was incorporated with headquarters in Omaha.

Berkshire Hathaway textile mills were permanently closed.

Buffett and Munger acquired Scott & Fetzer, parent of World Book Encyclopedia, Kirby vacuum cleaners and other companies, for $315 million, virtually snatching it from the hands of Ivan Boesky.

1986 Munger and Guerin closed out the New America Fund at a large profit and distributed some of the stock to the fund investors. The Los Angeles Daily Journal Corporation was spun out and became a publicly traded, over-the-counter company with Munger as the chairman.

1987   Berkshire bought a 12 percent, $700 million stake in Salomon Bros. and Buffett and Munger were elected to the board.

1989   Munger resigned from the U.S. League of Savings in protest of the trade organization's unwillingness to support reasonable S&L reforms, despite a looming crisis in the industry.

Berkshire Hathaway invested $1.3 billion in three companies, Gillette, USAir and Champion International. Munger negotiated Berkshire's investment in Gillette. In July, Berkshire bought $600 million in preferred stock, which later was converted into 11 percent of Gillette's common.

Berkshire bought Borsheim's Jewelry Store in Omaha from the Blumkin family, who also founded the Nebraska Furniture Mart.

Munger's sister Mary died from Parkinson's Disease.

1991   A bond trader at Salomon Brothers violated federal regulations, leading to the near-bankruptcy of the company. Buffett, Munger, and the law firm of Munger, Tolles Olson struggled to save the company. Buffett took over as CEO for nine months.

1992   Mutual Savings gave up its S&L charter.

1993   Munger was listed on Forbes Four Hundred richest list.

Mutual Savings and Loan Association was liquidated.

In January, Munger and Buffett joined the board of troubled U.S. Airways.

Dexter Shoe was acquired by Berkshire for $420 million in stock.

1994   On January 1, by statutory merger, Mutual Savings became part of Wes-FIC.

1995   Berkshire Hathaway bought for $2.3 billion the 49 percent of GEICO Insurance that it didn't already own.

Munger and Buffett stepped down from U.S. Airway's board.

1996   Wes-FIC acquired Kansas Bankers Surety.

1997   Munger was named to the board of directors of Costco Companies Inc., a retailing chain based in Issequah, Washington.

Berkshire acquired FlightSafety International for $1.6 billion and International Dairy Queen for $585 million.

Salomon Brothers was sold to Travelers Group for $9 billion. Berkshire's share of the deal was about $1.7 billion.

1998   Berkshire acquired Executive Jet for $725 million.

Travelers merged with Citicorp, forming the world's largest financial service firm.

CHARLES T. MUNGER'S SPEECHES

Multidisciplinary Skills: Educational Implications*

Today I am going to engage in a game reminding us of our old professors: Socratic solitaire. I will ask and briefly answer five questions:

1. Do broadscale professionals need more multidisciplinary skill?
2. Was our education sufficiently multidisciplinary?
3. In elite broadscale soft science what is the essential nature of practicable best-form multidisciplinary education?
4. In the last fifty years, how far has elite academia progressed toward attainable best-form multidisciplinarity?
5. What educational practices would make progress faster?

We start with the question: Do broadscale professionals need more multidisciplinary skill?

To answer the first question, we must first decide whether more multidisciplinarity will improve professional cognition. And, to decide what will cure bad cognition it will help to know what causes it. One of Bernard Shaw's characters explained professional defects as follows: "In the last analysis, every profession is a conspiracy against the laity." There is a lot of truth in Shaw's diagnosis, as was early demonstrated when in the sixteenth century, the dominant profession, the clergy, burned William Tyndale at the stake for translating the bible into English.

But Shaw plainly understates the problem in implying that a conscious, self-interested malevolence is the main culprit. More important, there are frequent terrible effects in professionals from intertwined

---

*Talk by Charles T. Munger on April 24, 1998, at the 50th reunion of the Harvard Law School class that graduated in 1948

subconscious mental tendencies, two of which are exceptionally prone to cause trouble:

1. Incentive-caused bias, a natural cognitive drift toward the conclusion that what is good for the professional is good for the client and the wider civilization; and
2. "Man with a hammer" tendency, with the name taken from the proverb: "to a man with only a hammer, every problem tends to look pretty much like a nail."

One partial cure for man-with-a-hammer tendency is obvious: if a man has a vast set of skills over multiple disciplines, he, by definition, carries multiple tools and therefore will limit bad cognitive effects from "man with a hammer" tendency. Moreover, when he is multidisciplinary enough to absorb from practical psychology the idea that all his life he must fight bad effects from both the tendencies I mentioned, both within himself and from others, he has taken a constructive step on the road to worldly wisdom.

If "A" is narrow professional doctrine and "B" consists of the big, extra-useful concepts from other disciplines, then, clearly, the professional possessing "A" plus "B" will usually be better off than the poor possessor of "A" alone. How could it be otherwise? And thus the only rational excuse for not acquiring more "B" is that it is not practical to do so, given the man's need for "A" and the other urgent demands in his life. I will later try to demonstrate that this excuse for unidisciplinarity, at least for our most gifted people, is usually unsound.

My second question is so easy to answer that I won't give it much time. Our education was far too unidisciplinary. Broadscale problems, by definition, cross many academic disciplines. Accordingly, using a unidisciplinary attack on such problems is like playing a bridge hand by counting trumps while ignoring all else. This is "bonkers," sort of like the Mad Hatter's tea party. But, nonetheless, too much that is similar remains present in professional practice and, even worse, has long been encouraged in isolated departments of soft science, defined as everything less fundamental than biology.

Even in our youth, some of the best professors were horrified by bad effects from balkanization of academia into insular, turf-protecting enclaves wherein notions were maintained by leaps of faith plus exclusion of non-believers. Alfred North Whitehead, for one, long ago sounded an alarm in strong language when he spoke of "the fatal unconnectedness of academic disciplines." And, since then, elite educational institutions, agreeing more and more with Whitehead, have steadily fought unconnectedness by bringing in more multidisciplinarity, causing some awesome plaudits to be won in our time by great unconnectedness fighters at borders of academic disciplines, for instance, Harvard's E.O. Wilson and Caltech's Linus Pauling.

So, modern academia now gives more multidisciplinarity than we received, and is plainly right to do so.

The natural third question then becomes: what is now the goal? What is the essential nature of best-form multidisciplinarity in elite education? This question, too, is easy to answer. All we have to do is examine our most successful narrowscale education, identify essential elements and scale up those elements to reach the sensible solution.

To find the best educational narrowscale model, we have to look not at unthreatened schools of education and the like, too much driven by our two counterproductive psychological tendencies and other bad influences, but, instead, where incentives for effective education are strongest and results are most closely measured. This leads us to a logical place: the hugely successful education now mandatory for airline pilots. (Yes, I am suggesting today that mighty Harvard would do better if it thought more about pilot training.) In piloting, as in other professions, one great hazard is the bad effect from "man with a hammer" tendency. We don't want a pilot, ever, to respond to hazard "Y" as if it was hazard "X" just because his mind contains only a hazard "X" model. And so, for that and other reasons, we train a pilot in a strict six-element system:

1. His formal education is wide enough to cover practically everything useful in piloting.
2. His knowledge of practically everything needed by pilots is not taught just well enough to enable him to pass one test or two; instead, all his knowledge is raised to practice-based fluency, even in handling two or three intertwined hazards at once.
3. Like any good algebraist, he is made to think sometimes in a foreword fashion and sometimes in reverse; and so he learns when to concentrate mostly on what he wants to happen and also when to concentrate mostly on avoiding what he does not want to happen.
4. His training time is allocated among subjects so as to minimize damage from his later malfunctions; and so what is most important in his performance gets the most training coverage and is raised to the highest fluency levels.
5. "Check list" routines are always mandatory for him.
6. Even after original training, he is forced into a special knowledge-maintenance routine: regular use of the aircraft simulator

to prevent atrophy through long disuse of skills needed to cope with rare and important problems.

The need for this clearly correct six-element system, with its large demands in a narrowscale field where stakes are high, is rooted in the deep structure of the human mind. Therefore we must expect that the education we need for broadscale problem solving will keep all these elements but with awesomely expanded coverage for each element. How could it be otherwise?

Thus it follows, as the night the day, that in our most elite broadscale education, wherein we are trying to make silk purses out of silk, we must for best results have multidisciplinary coverage of immense amplitude, with all needed skills raised to an ever-maintained practice-based fluency, including considerable power of synthesis at boundaries between disciplines, with the highest fluency levels being achieved where they are most needed, with forward and reverse thinking techniques being employed in a manner reminding one of inversion in algebra, and with "check list" routines being a permanent part of the knowledge system. There can be no other way, no easier way, to broadscale worldly wisdom. Thus the task, when first identified in its immense breadth, seems daunting, verging on impossible.

But the task, considered in full context, is far from impossible, when we consider three factors:

First, the concept of "all *needed* skills" lets us recognize that we don't have to raise everyone's skill in celestial mechanics to that of Laplace and also ask everyone to achieve a similar skill level in all other knowledge. Instead, it turns out that the truly big ideas in each discipline, learned only in essence, carry most of the freight. And they are not so numerous, nor are their interactions so complex, that a large and multidisciplinary understanding is impossible for many, given large amounts of talent and time.

Second, in elite education, we have available the large amounts of talent and time that we need. After all, we are educating the top one percent in aptitude using teachers who, on average, have more aptitude than the students. And we have roughly thirteen long years in which to turn our most promising twelve-year-olds into starting professionals.

Third, thinking by inversion and through use of "check lists" is easily learned—in broadscale life as in piloting.

Moreover, we can believe in the attainability of broad multidisciplinary skill for the same reason the fellow from Arkansas gave for his belief in baptism: "I've seen it done." We all know of individuals, modern Ben Franklins, who have (1) achieved a massive multidisciplinary synthesis with less time in formal education than is now available to our numerous brilliant young and (2) thus become better performers in their own disciplines, not worse, despite diversion of learning time to matter outside the normal coverage of their own disciplines.

Given the time and talent available and examples of successful masters of multiple disciplines, what is shown by our present failure to minimize bad effects from "man with a hammer" tendency is only that you can't win big in multidisciplinarity in soft-science academia if you are so satisfied with the status quo, or so frightened by the difficulties of change, that you don't try hard enough to win big.

This brings us to our fourth question: Judged with reference to an optimized feasible multidisciplinary goal, how much has elite soft-science education been corrected after we left?

The answer is that many things have been tried as corrections in the direction of better multidisciplinarity. And, after allowing for some counterproductive results, there has been some considerable improvement, net. But much desirable correction is still undone and lies far ahead.

For instance, soft-science academia has increasingly found it helpful when professors from different disciplines collaborate or when a professor has been credentialed in more than one discipline. But a different sort of correction has usually worked best, namely augmentation of a "take what you wish" practice that encourages any discipline to simply assimilate whatever it chooses from other disciplines. Perhaps this worked best because it bypassed academic squabbles rooted in the tradition and territoriality that had caused the unidisciplinary folly for which correction was now sought.

In any event, through increased use of "take what you wish," many soft-science disciplines reduced folly from "man with a hammer" tendency. For instance, led by our classmate, Roger Fisher, the law schools brought in negotiation, drawing on other disciplines. Over three million copies of Roger's wise and ethical negotiation book have now been sold, and his life's achievement may well be the best, ever, from our whole class. The law schools also brought in a lot of sound and useful economics, even some good game theory to enlighten antitrust law by better explaining how competition really works.

Economics, in turn, took in from a biologist the "tragedy of the commons" model, thus correctly finding a wicked "invisible foot" in coexistence with Adam Smith's angelic "invisible hand." These days there is even some "behavioral economics," wisely seeking aid from psychology.

However, an extremely permissive practice like "take what you wish" was not destined to have 100 percent—admirable results in soft science. Indeed, in some of its worst outcomes it helped changes like (1) assimilation of Freudianism in some literature departments, (2) importation into many places of extremist political ideologies of the left or right that had, for their possessors, made regain of objectivity almost as unlikely as regain of virginity, and (3) importation into many law and business schools of hard-form efficient-market theory by misguided would-be experts in corporate finance, one of whom kept explaining Berkshire Hathaway's investing success by adding standard deviations of luck until, at six standard deviations, he encountered enough derision to force a change in explanation.

Moreover, even when it avoided such lunacies, "take what you wish" had some serious defects. For instance, takings from more fundamental disciplines were often done without attribution, sometimes under new names, with little attention given to rank in a fundamentalness order for absorbed concepts. Such practices (1) act like a lousy filing system that must impair successful use and synthesis of absorbed knowledge and (2) do not maximize in soft-science the equivalent of Linus Pauling's systematic mining of physics to improve chemistry. There must be a better way.

This brings us, finally, to our last question: in elite soft-science what practices would hasten our progress toward optimized multidisciplinarity? Here again, there are some easy answers:

First, many more courses should be mandatory, not optional. And this, in turn, requires that the people who decide what is mandatory must possess large multidisciplinary knowledge maintained in fluency. This conclusion is as obvious in the training of the would-be broadscale problem solver as it is in the training of the would-be pilot. For instance, both psychology mastery and accounting mastery should be *required* as outcomes in legal education. Yet, in many elite places, even today, there are no such requirements. Often, such is the narrowness of mind of the program designers that they neither see what is needed and missing nor are able to fix deficiencies.

Second, there should be much more problem-solving practice that crosses several disciplines, including practice that mimics the function of the aircraft simulator in preventing loss of skills through disuse. Let me give an example, roughly remembered, of this sort of teaching by a very wise but untypical Harvard Business School professor many decades ago.

This professor gave a test involving two unworldly old ladies who had just inherited a New England shoe factory making branded shoes and beset with serious business problems described in great detail. The professor then gave the students ample time to answer with written advice to the old ladies. In response to the answers, the professor next gave every student an undesirable grade except for one student who was graded at the top by a wide margin. What was the winning answer? It was very short and roughly as follows: "This business field and this particular business, in its particular location, present crucial problems that are so difficult that unworldly old ladies cannot wisely try to solve them through hired help. Given the difficulties and unavoidable agency costs, the old ladies should promptly sell the shoe factory, probably to the competitor who would enjoy the greatest marginal-utility advantage." Thus the winning answer relied not on what the students had most recently been taught in business school but, instead, on more fundamental concepts, like agency costs and marginal utility, lifted from undergraduate psychology and economics.

Ah, my fellow members of the Harvard Law Class of 1948: if only we had been much more often tested like that, just think of what more we might have accomplished!

Incidentally, many elite private schools now wisely use such multidisciplinary methods in seventh grade science, while at the same time many graduate schools have not yet seen the same light. This is one more sad example of Whitehead's "fatal unconnectedness" in education.

Third, most soft-science professional schools should increase use of the best business periodicals, like the *Wall Street Journal, Forbes, Fortune,* etc. Such periodicals are now quite good and perform the function of the aircraft simulator if used to prompt practice in relating events to multidisciplinary causes, often intertwined. And sometimes the periodicals even introduce new models for causes, instead of merely refreshing old knowledge. Also, it is not just slightly sound to have the student practice in school what he must practice, life-long after formal education is over, if he is going to maximize his good judgment. I know no person in business, respected for verified good judgment, whose wisdom-maintenance system does not include use of such periodicals. Why should academia be different?

Fourth, in filling scarce academic vacancies professors of super strong, passionate political ideology, whether on the left or right, should usually be avoided. So also for students. Best-form multidisciplinarity requires an objectivity such passionate people have lost, and a difficult synthesis is not likely to be achieved by minds in ideological fetters. In our day, some Harvard Law professors could and did point to a wonderful example of just such ideology-based folly. This, of course, was the law school at Yale which was then viewed by many at Harvard as trying to improve legal education by importing a particular political ideology as a dominant factor.

Fifth, soft-science should more intensely imitate the fundamental organizing ethos of hard science (defined as the "fundamental four-discipline combination" of math, physics, chemistry, and engineering). This ethos deserves more imitation. After all, hard science has, by a wide margin, the best record for both (1) avoiding unidisciplinary folly and (2) making user-friendly a big patch of multidisciplinary domain, with frequent good results like those of physicist Richard Feynman when he so quickly found in cold O-rings the cause of our greatest space-shuttle disaster. And previous extensions of the ethos into softer fare have worked well. For instance, biology, starting 150 years ago with a descriptive mess, not much related to deep theory, has gradually absorbed the fundamental organizing ethos with marvelous results as new generations have come to use better thinking methods containing models that answer the question: Why? And there is no clear reason why the ethos of hard science can't also help in disciplines far less fundamental than biology. Here, as I interpret it, is this fundamental organizing ethos I am talking about:

1. You must both rank and use disciplines in order of fundamentalness.

2. You must, like it or not, master to tested fluency and routinely use the truly essential parts of *all* four constituents of the fundamental four-discipline combination, with particularly intense attention given to disciplines more fundamental than your own.

3. You may never practice either crossdisciplinary absorption without attribution or departure from a "principle of economy" that forbids explaining in any other way anything readily explainable from more fundamental material in your own or any other discipline.

4. But when the step (3) approach doesn't produce much new and useful insight, you should hypothesize, and test to establishment, new principles, ordinarily by using methods similar to those that created successful old principles. But you may not use any new principle, inconsistent with an old one, unless you can now prove that the old principle is not true.

You will note that, compared with much current practice in soft-science, the fundamental organizing ethos of hard-science is more severe. This reminds one of pilot training, and this outcome is not a coincidence. Reality is talking to anyone who will listen. Like pilot training, the ethos of hard science does not say "take what you wish" but "learn it all to fluency, like it or not." And rational organization of multi-disciplinary knowledge is forced by making mandatory (1) full attribution for cross-disciplinary takings and (2) mandatory preference for the most fundamental explanation.

This simple idea may appear too obvious to be useful, but there is an old two-part rule that often works wonders in business, science, and elsewhere: (1) take a simple, basic idea and (2) take it very seriously. And as some evidence for the value of taking very seriously the fundamental organizing ethos, I offer the example of my own life.

I came to Harvard Law School very poorly educated, with desultory work habits and no college degree. I was admitted over the objection of Warren Abner Seavey through intervention of family friend Roscoe Pound. I had taken one silly course in biology in high school, briefly learning, mostly by rote, an obviously incomplete theory of evolution, portions of the anatomy of the paramecium and frog, plus a ridiculous concept of "protoplasm" that has since disappeared. To this day I have never taken any course, anywhere, in chemistry, economics, psychology or business. But I early took elementary physics, and math and paid enough attention to somehow assimilate the fundamental organizing ethos of hard science, which I thereafter pushed further and further into softer and softer fare as my organizing guide and filing system in a search for whatever multidisciplinary worldly wisdom it would be easy to get.

Thus, my life became a sort of accidental educational experiment with respect to feasibility and utility of a very gross academic extension of the fundamental organizing ethos by a man who also learned well what his own discipline had to teach.

What I found, in my extended attempts to complete by informal means my stunted education, was that, plugging along with only ordinary will but with the fundamental organizing ethos as my guide, my ability to serve everything I loved was enhanced far beyond my desserts. Large gains came in places that seemed unlikely as I started out, sometimes making me like the only one without a blindfold in a high-stake game of "pin the donkey." For instance, I was productively led into psychology, where I had no plans to go, creating large advantages that deserve a story on another day.

Today, I have no more story. I have finished my talk by answering my own questions as best I could in a brief time. What is most interesting to me in my answers is that, while everything I have said is non-original and has long been obvious to the point of banality to many sound and well educated minds, all the evils I decry remain grossly overpresent in the best of our soft-science educational domains wherein virtually every professor has a too unidisciplinary habit of mind, even while a better model exists just across the aisle in his own university. To me, this ridiculous outcome implies that the soft-science departments tolerate perverse incentives. Wrong incentives are a major cause because, as Dr. Johnson so wisely observed, truth is hard to assimilate in any mind when opposed by interest. And, if institutional incentives cause the problem, then a remedy is feasible—because incentives can be changed.

I have tried to demonstrate today, and indeed by the example of my life, that it is neither inevitable nor advantageous for soft-science educational domains to tolerate as much unidisciplinary wrongheadedness as they now do. If I could somewhat fix my many gross deficiencies, so can they. There is clearly a better way, quite feasible to trod. And, if this is so, there is an ethos, also from Dr. Johnson, that is applicable. Please remember the word Dr. Johnson used to describe maintenance of academic ignorance that is removable through diligence. To Dr. Johnson such conduct was "treachery."

And if duty will not move improvement, advantage is also available. There will be immense worldly rewards, for law schools and other academic domains as for Charlie Munger, in a more multidisciplinary approach to many problems, common or uncommon. And more fun as well as more accomplishment. The happier mental realm I recommend is one from which no one willingly returns. A return would be like cutting off one's hands.

Practical Thought about Practical Thought?*

In a long career I have assimilated various ultrasimple general notions that I find helpful in solving problems. Five of these helpful notions I will now describe. After that I will present to you a problem of extreme scale. Indeed, the problem will involve turning start-up capital of $2 million into $2 trillion, a sum large enough to represent a practical achievement. Then I will try to solve the problem, assisted by my helpful general notions. Following that, I will suggest that there are important educational implications in my demonstration. I will so finish because my objective is educational, my game today being a search for better methods of thought.

My first helpful notion is that it is usually best to simplify problems by deciding big "no-brainer" questions first.

The second helpful notion mimics Galileo's conclusion that scientific reality is often revealed only by math, as if math was the language of

---

*Informal talk by Charles T. Munger on July 20, 1996

god. Galileo's attitude also works well in messy practical life. Without numerical fluency, in the part of life most of us inhabit, you are like a one-legged man in an ass-kicking contest.

The third helpful notion is that it is not enough to think problems through forward. You must also think in reverse, much like the rustic who wanted to know where he was going to die so that he'd never go there. Indeed, many problems can't be solved forward. And that is why the great algebraist, Carl Jacobi, so often said: "invert, always invert." And why Pythagoras thought in reverse to prove that the square root of two was an irrational number.

The fourth helpful notion is that the best and most practical wisdom is elementary academic wisdom. But there is one *extremely* important qualification: you must think in a multidisciplinary manner. You must routinely use all the easy-to-learn concepts from the freshman course in every basic subject. Where elementary ideas will serve, your problem solving must not be limited, as academia and many business bureaucracies are limited, by extreme balkanization into disciplines and subdisciplines, with strong taboos against any venture outside assigned territory. Instead, you must do your multidisciplinary thinking in accord with Ben Franklin's prescription in *Poor Richard:* "if you want it done, go. If not, send."

If, in your thinking, you rely entirely on others, often through purchase of professional advice, whenever outside a small territory of your own, you will suffer much calamity. And it is not just difficulties in complex coordination that will do you in. You will also suffer from the reality evoked by the Shavian character who said: "in the last analysis, every profession is a conspiracy against the laity." Indeed, a Shavian character, for once, understated the horrors of something Shaw didn't like. It is not usually the conscious malfeasance of your narrow professional adviser that does you in. Instead, your troubles come from his subconscious bias. His cognition will often be impaired, for your purposes, by financial incentives different from yours. And he will also suffer from the psychological defect caught by the proverb: "to a man with a hammer, every problem looks like a nail."

The fifth helpful notion is that really big effects, lollapalooza effects, will often come only from large combinations of factors. For instance, tuberculosis was tamed, at least for a long time, only by routine combined use in each case of three different drugs. And other lollapalooza effects, like the flight of an airplane, follow a similar pattern.

It is now time to present my practical problem. And here is the problem:

It is 1884 in Atlanta. You are brought, along with twenty others like you, before a rich and eccentric Atlanta citizen named Glotz. Both you and Glotz share two characteristics: first, you routinely use in problem solving the five helpful notions, and, second, you know all the elementary ideas in all the basic college courses, as taught in 1996. However, all discoverers and all examples demonstrating these elementary ideas come from dates transposed back before 1884. Neither you nor Glotz knows anything about anything that has happened after 1884.

Glotz offers to invest $2 million, yet take only half the equity, for a Glotz charitable foundation, in a new corporation organized to go into the non-alcoholic beverage business and remain in that business only, forever. Glotz wants to use a name that has somehow charmed him: Coca-Cola.

The other half of the new corporation's equity will go to the man who most plausibly demonstrates that his business plan will cause Glotz's foundation to be worth a trillion dollars 150 years later, in the money of that later time, 2034, despite paying out a large part of its earnings each year as a dividend. This will make the whole new corporation worth $2 trillion, even after paying out many billions of dollars in dividends.

You have fifteen minutes to make your pitch. What do you say to Glotz?

And here is my solution, my pitch to Glotz, using only the helpful notions and what every bright college sophomore should know.

Well Glotz, the big "no-brainer" decisions that, to simplify our problem, should be made first are as follows: first, we are never going to create something worth $2 trillion by selling some generic beverage. Therefore we must make your name, "Coca-Cola," into a strong, legally protected trademark. Second, we can get to $2 trillion only by starting in Atlanta, then succeeding in the rest of the United States, then rapidly succeeding with our new beverage all over the world. This will require developing a product having universal appeal because it harnesses powerful elemental forces. And the right place to find such powerful elemental forces is in the subject matter of elementary academic courses.

We will next use numerical fluency to ascertain what our target implies. We can guess reasonably that by 2034 there will be about eight billion beverage consumers in the world. On average, each of these consumers will be much more prosperous in real terms than the average consumer of 1884. Each consumer is composed mostly of water and must ingest about 64 ounces of water per day. This is eight eight-ounce servings. Thus, if our new beverage, and other imitative beverages in our new market, can flavor and otherwise improve only 25 percent of ingested water worldwide, and we can occupy half of the new world market, we can sell 2.92 trillion eight-ounce servings in 2034. And if we can then net four cents per serving, we will earn $117 billion. This will be enough, if our business is still growing at a good rate, to make it easily worth two trillion dollars.

A big question, of course, is whether four cents per serving is a reasonable profit target for 2034. And the answer is yes, if we can create a beverage with strong universal appeal. One hundred fifty years is a long time. The dollar, like the roman drachma, will almost surely suffer monetary depreciation. Concurrently, real purchasing power of the average beverage consumer in the world will go way up. His proclivity to inexpensively improve his experience while ingesting water will go up considerably faster. Meanwhile, as technology improves, the cost of our simple product, in units of constant purchasing power, will go down. All four factors will work together in favor of our four-cents-per-serving profit target. Worldwide beverage-purchasing power in dollars will probably multiply by a factor of at least forty over 150 years. Thinking in reverse, this makes our profit-per-serving target, under 1884 conditions, a mere one fortieth of four cents or one tenth of a cent per serving. This is an easy-to-exceed target as we start out if our new product has universal appeal.

That decided, we must next solve the problem of invention to create universal appeal. There are two intertwined challenges of large scale: first, over 150 years we must cause a new-beverage market to assimilate about one fourth of the world's water ingestion. Second, we must so operate that half the new market is ours, while all our competitors combined are left to share the remaining half. These results are lollapalooza results. Accordingly, we must attack our problem by causing every favorable factor we can think of to work for us. Plainly, only a powerful combination of many factors is likely to cause the lollapalooza consequences we desire. Fortunately, the solution to these intertwined problems turns out to be fairly easy, if one has stayed awake in all the freshman courses.

Let us start by exploring the consequences of our simplifying "no-brainer" decision that we must rely on a strong trademark. This conclusion automatically leads to an understanding of the essence of our business in proper elementary academic terms. We can see from the introductory course in psychology that, in essence, we are going into the business of creating and maintaining conditioned reflexes. The "Coca-Cola" trade name and trade dress will act as the stimuli, and the purchase and ingestion of our beverage will be the desired responses.

And how does one create and maintain conditioned reflexes? Well, the psychology text gives two answers: (1) by operant conditioning, and (2) by classical conditioning, often called Pavlovian conditioning to honor the great Russian scientist. And, since we want a lollapalooza result, we must use both conditioning techniques—and all we can invent to enhance effects from each technique.

The operant-conditioning part of our problem is easy to solve. We need only (1) maximize rewards of our beverage's ingestion, and (2) minimize possibilities that desired reflexes, once created by us, will be extinguished through operant conditioning by proprietors of competing products.

For operant conditioning rewards, there are only a few categories we will find practical:

1. Food value in calories or other inputs;
2. Flavor, texture, and aroma acting as stimuli to consumption under neural preprogramming of a man through Darwinian natural selection;
3. Stimulus, as by sugar or caffeine;
4. Cooling effect when man is too hot or warming effect when man is too cool.

Wanting a lollapalooza result, we will naturally include rewards in all the categories.

To start out, it is easy to decide to design our beverage for consumption cold. There is much less opportunity, without ingesting beverage, to counteract excessive heat, compared with excessive cold. Moreover, with excessive heat, much liquid must be consumed, and the reverse is not true. It is also easy to decide to include both sugar and caffeine. After all, tea, coffee, and lemonade are already widely consumed. And it is also clear that we must be fanatic about determining, through trial and error, flavor and other characteristics that will maximize human pleasure while taking in the sugared water and caffeine we will provide. And, to counteract possibilities that desired operant-conditioned reflexes, once created by us, will be extinguished by operant conditioning employing competing products, there is also an obvious answer: we will make it a permanent obsession in our company that our beverage, as fast as practicable, will at all times be available everywhere throughout the world. After all, a competing product, if it is never tried, can't act as a reward creating a conflicting habit. Every spouse knows that.

We must next consider the Pavlovian conditioning we must also use. In Pavlovian conditioning powerful effects come from mere association. The neural system of Pavlov's dog causes it to salivate at the bell it can't eat. And the brain of man yearns for the type of beverage held by the pretty woman he can't have. And so, Glotz, we must use every sort of decent, honorable Pavlovian conditioning we can think of. For as long as we are in business, our beverage and its promotion must be associated in consumer minds with all other things consumers like or admire.

Such extensive Pavlovian conditioning will cost a lot of money, particularly for advertising. We will spend big money as far ahead as we can imagine. But the money will be effectively spent. As we expand fast in our new-beverage market, our competitors will face gross disadvantages of scale in buying advertising to create the Pavlovian conditioning they need. And this outcome, along with other volume-creates-power effects, should help us gain and hold at least 50 percent of the new market everywhere. Indeed, provided buyers are scattered, our higher volumes will give us very extreme cost advantages in distribution.

Moreover, Pavlovian effects from mere association will help us choose the flavor, texture, and color of our new beverage. Considering Pavlovian effects, we will have wisely chosen the exotic and expensive-sounding name "Coca-Cola," instead of a pedestrian name like "Glotz's sugared, caffeinated water." For similar Pavlovian reasons, it will be wise to have our beverage look pretty much like wine, instead of sugared water. And so we will artificially color our beverage if it comes out clear. And we will carbonate our water, making our product seem like champagne, or some other expensive beverage, while also making its flavor better and imitation harder to arrange for competing products. And, because we are going to attach so many expensive psychological effects to our flavor, that flavor should be different from any other standard flavor so that we maximize difficulties for competitors and give no accidental same-flavor benefit to any existing product.

What else, from the psychology textbook, can help our new business? Well, there is that powerful "monkey-see, monkey-do" aspect of human nature that psychologists often call "social proof." Social proof, imitative consumption triggered by mere sight of consumption, will not only help induce trial of our beverage. It will also bolster perceived rewards from consumption. We will always take this powerful social-proof factor into account as we design advertising and sales promotion and as we forego present profit to enhance present and future consumption. More than with most other products, increased selling power will come from each increase in sales.

We can now see, Glotz, that by combining (1) much Pavlovian conditioning, (2) powerful social-proof effects, and (3) a wonderful-tasting, energy-giving, stimulating and desirably-cold beverage that causes much operant conditioning, we are going to get sales that speed up for a long time by reason of the huge mixture of factors we have chosen. Therefore, we are going to start something like an autocatalytic reaction in chemistry, precisely the sort of multi-factor-triggered lollapalooza effect we need.

The logistics and the distribution strategy of our business will be simple. There are only two practical ways to sell our beverage: (1) as a syrup to fountains and restaurants, and (2) as a complete carbonated-water product in containers. Wanting lollapalooza results, we will naturally do it both ways. And, wanting huge Pavlovian and social-proof effects, we will always spend on advertising and sales promotion, per serving, over 40 percent of the fountain price for syrup needed to make the serving.

A few syrup-making plants can serve the world. However, to avoid needless shipping of mere space and water, we will need many bottling plants scattered over the world. We will maximize profits if (like early General Electric with light bulbs) we always set the first-sale price, either (1) for fountain syrup, or (2) for any container of our complete product. The best way to arrange this desirable profit-maximizing control is to make any independent bottler we need a subcontractor, not a vendee of syrup, and certainly not a vendee of syrup under a perpetual franchise specifying a syrup price frozen forever at its starting level.

Being unable to get a patent or copyright on our super important flavor, we will work obsessively to keep our formula secret. We will make a big hoopla over our secrecy, which will enhance Pavlovian effects. Eventually food-chemical engineering will advance so that our flavor can be copied with near exactitude. But, by that time, we will be so far ahead, with such strong trademarks and complete, "always available" worldwide distribution, that good flavor copying won't bar us from our objective. Moreover, the advances in food chemistry that help competitors will almost surely be accompanied by technological advances that will help us, including refrigeration, better transportation, and, for dieters, ability to insert a sugar taste without inserting sugar's calories. Also, there will be related beverage opportunities we will seize.

This brings us to a final reality check for our business plan. We will, once more, think in reverse like Jacobi. What must we avoid because we don't want it? Four answers seem clear:

> *First,* we must avoid the protective, cloying, stop-consumption effects of aftertaste that are a standard part of physiology, developed through Darwinian evolution to enhance the replication of man's genes by forcing a generally helpful moderation on the gene carrier. To serve our ends, on hot days a consumer must be able to drink container after container of our product with almost no impediment from aftertaste. We will find a wonderful no-aftertaste flavor by trial and error and will thereby solve this problem.

Second, we must avoid ever losing even half of our powerful trade-marked name. It will cost us mightily, for instance, if our sloppiness should ever allow sale of any other kind of "cola," for instance, a "peppy cola." If there is ever a "peppy cola," we will be the proprietor of the brand.

Third, with so much success coming, we must avoid bad effects from envy, given a prominent place in the Ten Commandments because envy is so much a part of human nature. The best way to avoid envy, recognized by Aristotle, is to plainly deserve the success we get. We will be fanatic about product quality, quality of product presentation, and reasonableness of prices, considering the harmless pleasure we will provide.

Fourth, after our trademarked flavor dominates our new market, we must avoid making any huge and sudden change in our flavor. Even if a new flavor performs better in blind taste tests, changing to that new flavor would be a foolish thing to do. This follows because, under such conditions, our old flavor will be so entrenched in consumer preference by psychological effects that a big flavor change would do us little good. And it would do immense harm by triggering in consumers the standard deprival super-reaction syndrome that makes "take-aways" so hard to get in any type of negotiation and helps make most gamblers so irrational. Moreover, such a large flavor change would allow a competitor, by copying our old flavor, to take advantage of both (1) the hostile consumer super-reaction to deprival and (2) the huge love of our original flavor created by our previous work.

Well, that is my solution to my own problem of turning $2 million into $2 trillion, even after paying out billions of dollars in dividends. I think it would have won with Glotz in 1884 and should convince you more than you expected at the outset. After all, the correct strategies are clear after being related to elementary academic ideas brought into play by the helpful notions.

How consistent is my solution with the history of the real Coca-Cola company? Well, as late as 1896, twelve years after the fictional Glotz was to start vigorously with $2 million, the real Coca-Cola company had a net worth under $150 thousand and earnings of about zero. And thereafter the real Coca-Cola company did lose half its trademark and did grant perpetual bottling franchises at fixed syrup prices. And some of the bottlers were not very effective and couldn't easily be changed. And the real

Coca-Cola company, with this system, did lose much pricing control that would have improved results, had it been retained. Yet, even so, the real Coca-Cola company followed so much of the plan given to Glotz that it is now worth about $125 billion and will have to increase its value at only 8 percent per year until 2034 to reach a value of $2 trillion. And it can hit an annual physical volume target of 2.92 trillion servings if servings grow until 2034 at only 6 percent per year, a result consistent with much past experience and leaving plenty of plain-water ingestion for Coca-Cola to replace after 2034. So I would guess that the fictional Glotz, starting earlier and stronger and avoiding the worst errors, would have easily hit his $2 trillion target. And he would have done it well before 2034.

This brings me, at last, to the main purpose of my talk. Large educational implications exist, if my answer to Glotz's problem is roughly right and you make one more assumption I believe true—that most Ph.D. educators, even psychology professors and business school deans, would not have given the same simple answer I did. And, if I am right in these two ways, this would indicate that our civilization now keeps in place a great many educators who can't satisfactorily explain Coca-Cola, even in retrospect, and even after watching it closely all their lives. This is not a satisfactory state of affairs.

Moreover—and this result is even more extreme—the brilliant and effective executives who, surrounded by business school and law school graduates, have run the Coca-Cola company with glorious success in recent years, also did not understand elementary psychology well enough to predict and avoid the "New Coke" fiasco, which dangerously threatened their company. That people so talented, surrounded by professional advisers from the best universities, should thus demonstrate a huge gap in their education is also not a satisfactory state of affairs.

Such extreme ignorance, in both the high reaches of academia and the high reaches of business, is a lollapalooza effect of a negative sort, demonstrating grave defects in academia. Because the bad effect is a lollapalooza, we should expect to find intertwined, multiple academic causes. I suspect at least two such causes.

First, academic psychology, while it is admirable and useful as a list of ingenious and important experiments, lacks intradisciplinary synthesis. In particular, not enough attention is given to lollapalooza effects coming from combinations of psychological tendencies. This creates a situation reminding one of a rustic teacher who tries to simplify school work by rounding pi to an even three. And it violates Einstein's injunction that "everything should be made as simple as possible—but no more simple." In general, psychology is laid out and misunderstood as electromagnetism would now be misunderstood if physics had produced many brilliant experimenters like Michael Faraday and no grand synthesizer like James Clerk Maxwell.

And, second, there is a truly horrible lack of synthesis blending psychology and other academic subjects. But only an interdisciplinary approach will correctly deal with reality—in academia as with the Coca-Cola company.

In short, academic psychology departments are immensely more important and useful than other academic departments think. And, at the same time, the psychology departments are immensely worse than most of their inhabitants think. It is, of course, normal for self-appraisal to be more positive than external appraisal. Indeed, a problem of this sort may have given you your speaker today. But the size of this psychology-department gap is preposterously large. In fact, the gap is so enormous that one very eminent university (Chicago) simply abolished its psychology department, perhaps with an undisclosed hope of later creating a better version.

In such a state of affairs, many years ago and with much that was plainly wrong already present, the "New Coke" fiasco occurred, wherein Coke's executives came to the brink of destroying the most valuable trademark in the world. The academically correct reaction to this immense and well-publicized fiasco would have been the sort of reaction Boeing would display if three of its new airplanes crashed in a single week. After all, product integrity is involved in each case, and the plain educational failure was immense.

But almost no such responsible, Boeing-like reaction has come from academia. Instead academia, by and large, continues in its balkanized way to tolerate psychology professors who mis-teach psychology, non-psychology professors who fail to consider psychological effects obviously crucial in their subject matter, and professional schools that carefully preserve psychological ignorance coming in with each entering class and are proud of their inadequacies.

Even though this regrettable blindness and lassitude is now the normal academic result, are there exceptions providing hope that disgraceful shortcomings of the educational establishment will eventually be corrected? Here, my answer is a very optimistic yes.

For instance, consider the recent behavior of the economics department of the University of Chicago. Over the last decade, this department has enjoyed a near monopoly of the Nobel prizes in economics, largely by getting good predictions out of "free market" models postulating man's rationality. And what is the reaction of this department, after winning so steadily with its rational-man approach?

Well, it has just invited into a precious slot amid its company of greats a wise and witty Cornell economist, Richard Thaler. And it has done this because Thaler pokes fun at much that is holy at the University of Chicago. Indeed, Thaler believes, with me, that people are often massively irrational in ways, predicted by psychology that must be taken into account in microeconomics.

In so behaving, the University of Chicago is imitating Darwin, who spent much of his long life thinking in reverse as he tried to disprove his own hardest won and best loved ideas. And so long as there are parts of academia that keep alive its best values by thinking in reverse like Darwin, we can confidently expect that silly educational practices will eventually be replaced by better ones, exactly as Carl Jacobi might have predicted.

This will happen because the Darwinian approach, with its habitual objectivity taken on as a sort of hair shirt, is a mighty approach. Indeed, no less a figure than Einstein said that one of the four causes of his achievement was "self criticism," ranking right up there alongside curiosity, concentration, and perseverance.

And, to further appreciate the power of self-criticism, consider where lies the grave of that very ungifted undergraduate, Charles Darwin. It is in Westminister Abbey, right next to the headstone of Isaac Newton, perhaps the most gifted student who ever lived, honored on that headstone in five Latin words constituting the most eloquent praise in all graveyard print: *hic iacet quod mortale fuet*—"here lie the remains of what was mortal."

A civilization that so places a dead Darwin will eventually develop and integrate psychology in a proper and practical fashion that greatly increases skills of all sorts. But all of us who have dollops of power and see the light should help the process along. There is a lot at stake. If, in many high places, a universal product as successful as Coca-Cola is not properly understood and explained, it can't bode well for our competency in dealing with much else that is important.

Of course, those of you with 50 percent of net worth in Coca-Cola stock, occurring because you tried to so invest 10 percent after thinking like I did in making my pitch to Glotz, can ignore my message about psychology as too elementary for useful transmission to you. But I am not so sure that this reaction is wise for the rest of you. The situation reminds me of the old-time Warner & Swasey ad that was a favorite of mine: "The company that needs a new machine tool, and hasn't bought it, is already paying for it."

NOTES

Chapter One   An Extraordinary Combination of Minds

1. "The Forbes Four Hundred," *Forbes*, October 18, 1993.
2. Linda Grant, *Los Angeles Times*, April 1991.
3. Carol J. Loomis, "The Inside Story of Warren Buffett," *Fortune*, April 11, 1988. p. 26.
4. Robert Dorr, "Buffett's Right Hand Man . . " *Omaha World Herald*, August 10, 1986.
5. Roger Lowenstein, *Buffett· Making of an American Capitalist* (New York: Random House, 1995), p. 75.
6. "Richest List has Gates at No. 1, plus 83 Californians," *Los Angeles Times*, September 29, 1997, p. D-2.
7. See note 5, p. 162.
8. Judith H. Dobrzynski, "Warren's World," *Business Week*, May 10, 1993, p. 32.
9. "The Forbes 400," *Forbes*, October 14, 1996, p. 240.
10. Roger M. Grace, "Prospectives," *Metropolitan-News Enterprise*, June 1, 1999, p. 10.
11. Phil Swigard, "Main Street Journal," self-published newsletter, May 1999.
12. Carmen Moran and Margaret Massam, "An Evaluation of Humour in Emergency Work," *The Australasian Journal of Disaster and Trauma Studies, Volume· 1997-3*.

Chapter Two   The Lake—A Place That Defines Munger

1. Charles Munger, Berkshire Hathaway annual meeting, Omaha, Nebraska, May 1999.
2. Charles Munger, letter to J D. Ramsey, June 17, 1999. Used with the permission of the author.
3. "News Trends: Now Hear This," *Fortune*, May 31, 1993, p. 22.
4. Robert Dorr, "Buffett's Right Hand Man . ." *Omaha World Herald*, August 10, 1986.

Chapter Three   The Nebraskans

1. "Interesting Facts about the Cornhusker State," University of Nebraska, College of Independent Study, 1998–99 Bulletin.
2. *This Fabulous Century: Sixty Years of American Life, 1920-1930* (New York: Time-Life Books, 1970), p. 25.
3. J.B. Munger, *The Munger Family*, self-published in 1915, part of the genealogy collection, Los Angeles Public Library.
4. "33 years . . . A Federal Judge," *World Herald*, March 2, 1939.
5. Ibid.
6. Ibid.

7. *This Fabulous Century: Sixty Years of American Life, 1920-1930* (New York: Time-Life Books, 1970), p. 27.

8. Charles Munger, See's Seventy-Fifth Anniversary Lunch, Los Angeles, California, March 1998.

9. *This Fabulous Century: Sixty Years of American Life, 1920-1930* (New York: Time-Life Books, 1970), p. 128

10. Ibid

11. Carol Loomis, "Mr Buffett on the Stock Market," *Fortune,* November 22, 1999, p 212.

12. From a letter by Charles Munger, as reported: Robert Dorr, "Ex-Omahan Traded Law for Board Room," *Omaha World Herald,* August 31, 1977.

13. Roger Lowenstein, *Buffett: Making of an American Capitalist* (New York: Random House, 1995), p. 20.

14. Ibid.

15. From a letter by Charles Munger, as reported: Robert Dorr, "Ex-Omahan Traded Law for Board Room," *Omaha World Herald,* August 31, 1977.

Chapter Four   Surviving the Wars

1 Nicholas Lemann, *The Big Test: The Secret History of the American Meritrocracy* (New York: Ferrar Straus & Giroux, 1999), p. 189.

2 Ibid.

3. Charles Munger, "The Need for more Multidisciplinary Skill from Professionals: Educational Implications." Address to the fiftieth reunion of the Harvard Law School Class of 1948. April 4, 1999

4. Charles Munger, See's Candy, Seventy-Fifth Anniversary Lunch, Los Angeles, California, March 1998.

5. Ibid.

6. Charles Munger, Harvard School Commencement Speech, Los Angeles, California, June 13, 1996.

7. Interview with Roy Tolles, Roger Lowenstein, *Buffett: Making of an American Capitalist* (New York· Random House, 1995), p. 20.

8 Superior Court of the State of California for the County of Los Angeles, *Metropolitan News Company v. Daily Journal Corporation and Charles T. Munger,* July 1, 1999, Vol. 12, p. 1810.

9. Nicholas Lemann, *The Big Test: The Secret History of the American Meritrocracy* (New York: Farrar, Straus & Giroux, 1999), p. 192.

Chapter Five   Putting Together a New Life

1 *Outstanding Investor Digest,* March 13, 1998.

2. From a letter by Charles Munger, reported: Robert Dorr, "Ex-Omahan Traded Law for Board Room," *Omaha World Herald,* August 31, 1977.

Chapter Six   Munger Makes His First Million

1. Richard Dawkins, *The Selfish Gene* (Oxford, UK, Oxford University Press, 1976), p. 250.

2. Kelly Barron, "Charlie's Pal, Otis," *Forbes,* October 12, 1998.

3. Andrew Kilpatrick, *Of Permanent Value: The Story of Warren Buffett* (Birmingham, Alabama. AKPE, 1998), p. 684

4. Charles Munger, Chairman's letter, Wesco Financial Corp., March 5, 1990.

5. Ibid.

Chapter Seven   A Combination of Big Ideas

1. From a letter by Charles Munger, as reported: Robert Dorr, "Ex-Omahan Traded Law for Board Room," *Omaha World Herald*, August 31, 1977.

2. Warren E. Buffett, "The Superinvestors of Graham and Doddsville," Speech, Columbia Business School, May 17, 1984.

3. David Elsner, "It Works: Buying $1 for 40 cents," *Chicago Tribune*, December 8, 1985, Section 7, p. 1.

4. Robert Dorr, "Buffett's Right Hand Man. . ." *Omaha World Herald*, August 10, 1986.

5. Charles Munger, Wesco Annual Meeting, Pasadena, California, May 1991.

6. L.J. Davis, "Buffett Takes Stock," *New York Times Magazine*, April 1, 1990, p. 61.

7. *Forbes*, January 22, 1996

8. Ibid.

9. L.J. Davis, "Buffett Takes Stock," *New York Times Magazine*, April 1, 1990, p. 61.

10. Carol J. Loomis, "The Inside Story of Warren Buffett," *Fortune*, April 11, 1988, p. 26.

11. L.J. Davis, "Buffett Takes Stock," *New York Times Magazine*, April 1, 1990, p. 61.

12. Andrew Kilpatrick, *Of Permanent Value: The Story of Warren Buffett* (Birmingham, Alabama: AKPE, 1998), p. 728.

Chapter Eight   Pound-for-Pound, the Best Law Firm

1. Carol Loomis, "Mr. Buffett on the Stock Market," *Fortune*, November 22, 1999, p. 216.

2. "The Top," *California Law Business*, September 28, 1998, p. 21.

3. Nicholas Lemann, *The Big Test: The Secret History of the American Meritrocracy* (New York: Ferrar, Straus & Giroux, 1999), p. 214.

4. www.vault.com/vstore/snapshots/SnapShotHome.

5. Ibid.

6. Jaclyn Fierman, "The Perilous New World of Fair Pay," *Fortune*, June 13, 1994, p. 57.

7. Ibid.

8. Michael Parrish, "Buffett Finds Aide at L.A. Law Office That Reflects His Style," *Los Angeles Times*, August 27, 1991.

Chapter Nine   Operating Wheeler, Munger Out of a Utility Room

1. Warren E. Buffett, "The Superinvestors of Graham and Doddsville," Speech, Columbia Business School, May 17, 1984.

2. Ibid.

3. Nicholas Lemann, *The Big Test: The Secret History of the American Meritrocracy* (New York: Ferrar Straus & Giroux, 1999), p. 214.

4. David Santry, "Shareholder Heaven at New America Fund," *Business Week*, December 3, 1979, p. 103.

5. Ibid.

6. Dolly Setton and Robert Lenzner, "The Berkshire Bunch," *Forbes*, October 12, 1998.

7. Kelly Barron, "Charlie's Pal Otis," *Forbes*, October 12, 1998.

Chapter Ten   Blue Chip Stamps

1   Roger Lowenstein, *Buffett: Making of an American Capitalist* (New York: Random House, 1995), p. 170.

2. Ibid.

3. Ibid., p. 179.

4. SEC File No. HO-784, *Blue Chip Stamps et al.* Charles Munger, letter to Charles E. Rickershauser, Jr., October 22, 1974.

5   Ibid., Order directing private investigation, December 10, 1974.

6. Robert Dorr, "Five Assigned to Corporate Staff," *Omaha World Herald*, July 10, 1983

7. Warren Buffett, Letter to Shareholders, Berkshire Hathaway Inc., February 26, 1982.

8. Robert Dorr, "Five Assigned to Corporate Staff," *Omaha World Herald*, July 10, 1983.

9. Superior Court of the State of California for the County of Los Angeles, *Metropolitan News Company v. Daily Journal Corporation and Charles T. Munger*, July 1, 1999, Vol. 12, p. 1815.

10. *Outstanding Investor Digest*, June 30, 1993.

11. *Smith et al. v. Berkshire Hathaway, Inc. et al.* California Superior Court, Los Angeles County, Case No. BC170173[4/29/97].

12. "Blue Chip Stamp Investors Sue Berkshire Hathaway," Bloomberg News Service, *Omaha World Herald*, May 2, 1997, p. 18.

13. Andrew Kilpatrick, *Of Permanent Value: The Story of Warren Buffett* (Birmingham, Alabama: AKPE, 1998), p 308.

Chapter Eleven   See's Candy Teaches a Lesson

1   Charles Munger, See's Seventy-Fifth Anniversary Luncheon, Los Angeles, California, March 1998.

2. Mary McNamara, "In Their Capable Hands," *Los Angeles Times*, July 19, 1999, p. E1

3. Angeli, Michael, "Live, from D.C., Sonny Bono," *Esquire*, November 1, 1994, p 66.

4. Roger Lowenstein, *Buffett: The Making of an American Capitalist* (New York: Random House, 1995), p. 164.

5. Ibid.

6. Ibid.

7. Charles Munger, lecture at the University of Southern California, 1994.

8. Andrew Kilpatrick, *Of Permanent Value: The Story of Warren Buffett* (Birmingham, Alabama: AKPE, 1998), p. 679.

9. Charles Munger, Wesco Financial Corporation annual meeting, Pasadena, California, May 1998.

10. Charles Munger, Omaha, Nebraska, Berkshire Hathaway annual meeting, May 2, 1997.

11. Ibid.

12. Haywood Kelly, "A Quick Q&A with Warren Buffett," http://www.bcpl.net /~rclayton/buffett1.htm.

13. Charles Munger, Berkshire Hathaway annual meeting, Omaha, Nebraska, May 1997

14. Charles Munger, See's Seventy-Fifth Anniversary Luncheon, Los Angeles, California, March, 1998.

Chapter Twelve   The Belous Case

1.   Sarah Booth Conroy, "Taking Inventory of Ben Franklin," *Washington Post,* October 19, 1998, p. D02.

2.   Ibid.

3.   Ibid.

4.   Charles Munger, See's Candy Seventy-Fifth Anniversary Lunch, Los Angeles, California, March, 1998.

5   From a speech Charles T. Munger made at the Rotary Club, Santa Barbara, California, October 1997.

6.   Jim Rasmussen, "Buffett's Fans Fill Events," *Omaha World Herald,* May 4, 1998, p. A1.

7.   Roger Lowenstein, *Buffett: The Making of an American Capitalist* (New York: Random House, 1995), p. 117

8.   Ibid., p. 346.

9.   Charles Munger, Letter to Fortune, *Fortune,* June 18, 1990, p. 44.

10.   Stephen Buttry, "Buffett Hails Planned Parenthood," *Omaha World Herald,* April 28, 1994.

Chapter Thirteen   *The* Buffalo Evening News

1.   Roger Lowenstein, *Warren Buffett: The Making of an American Capitalist* (New York: Random House, 1995), p. 205.

2.   Ibid., p. 218.

3   Carol J. Loomis, "The Inside Story of Warren Buffett," *Fortune,* April 11, 1988, p. 26.

4.   Blue Chip Stamps, 1981 Annual Report, as reprinted in Berkshire Hathaway Inc. 1981 Annual Report, p. 46.

Chapter Fourteen   *Charlie Munger Goes to War with the Savings and Loan Industry*

1.   Superior Court of the State of California for the County of Los Angeles, *Metropolitan News Company v. Daily Journal Corporation and Charles T. Munger,* July 1, 1999, Vol. 12, p. 1818.

2.   Charles Munger, Chairman's Letter, Wesco Financial Corporation Annual Report, March 1983.

3.   Charles Munger, Wesco Financial Corporation Annual Report, 1989.

4.   Charles T. Munger, Chairman's Letter, Wesco Financial Corporation Annual Report, March 8, 1999.

5.   Charles Munger, Wesco Financial Corporation Annual Report to Shareholders, 1998.

6.   Charles Munger, Wesco Financial Corporation Annual Report, 1999.

7.   Charles Munger, Chairman's letter, Wesco Financial Corporation, March 5, 1990.

8   Kathleen Day, "Buffett S&L Pulls out of U.S. League," *Washington Post,* May 31, 1989, p. F1.

9.   Brett Duval Fromson, "Money & Markets: Will the FCIC run out of Money," *Fortune,* October 8, 1990.

10.   Charles Munger, Chairman's letter, Wesco Financial Corporation, March 5, 1990.

11.   Charles Munger, Wesco Financial Corporation Annual Report, 1990.

12.   Kathleen Day, *S&L Hell* (New York: W.W. Norton, 1993).

13.   Charles Munger, Wesco Financial Corporation Annual Report, 1989.

14. Jim Rasmussen, "Berkshire Unit to Shed Mutual S&L," *Omaha World Herald,* April 22, 1993, p. 18.

15. Charles Munger, Wesco Financial Corporation Annual Report, 1989.

16. Ibid.

17. Charles T. Munger, Chairman's Letter, Wesco Financial Corporation Annual Report, 1999.

18. Charles T. Munger, Chairman's Letter, Wesco Financial Corporation Annual Report, 1996.

19. "Conversations from the Warren Buffett Symposium," edited by Lawrence A. Cunningham, *Cardozo Law Review,* Vol. 19, Numbers 1 & 2, September–November 1997, p. 773.

20. Ibid.

21. "Wesco Sold Part of Travelers Stake in 2nd Quarter," *Bloomberg News,* August 19, 1998.

22. Charles T. Munger, Chairman's Letter, Wesco Financial Corporation Annual Report, 1999.

23. Ibid.

24. Brett D. Fromson, "Sharing in a Piece of Buffett's Pie," *Washington Post,* November 26, 1993, p. B12.

Chapter Fifteen The Blossoming of Berkshire Hathaway

1. Charles Munger, See's Candy Seventy-Fifth Anniversary Lunch, Los Angeles, California, March 1998.

2. Superior Court of the State of California for the County of Los Angeles, *Metropolitan News Company v. Daily Journal Corporation and Charles T. Munger,* July 1, 1999, Vol. 12, pp. 1819-20.

3. *Worth,* April 1997.

4 Andrew Kilpatrick, *Of Permanent Value: The Story of Warren Buffett* (Birmingham, Alabama: AKPE, 1998), p. 158.

5. Charles Munger, Wesco Financial annual meeting, Pasadena, California, May 21, 1997.

6. *Forbes,* January 22, 1996.

7 Roger Lowenstein, *Buffett: The Making of an American Capitalist* (New York: Random House, 1995), p. 223.

8. Alan Bersten, "Buffett Tells Shareholders What He Seeks in Firms," *Omaha World Herald,* May 21, 1986.

9. Berkshire Hathaway Annual Report, March 14, 1978.

10. Charles Munger, Berkshire Hathaway annual meeting, Omaha, Nebraska, May 1995.

11. John Nauss, CPCU, *Best's Review,* June 1999.

12. Charles Munger, Berkshire Hathaway annual meeting, Omaha, Nebraska, May 1993.

13. Charles Munger, Berkshire Hathaway annual meeting, Omaha, Nebraska, May 1991.

14. Jim Rasmussen, "Warren Buffett Is Selling Omaha," *Omaha World Herald,* May 2, 1998, p. A1.

15. Judith H. Dobrzynski, "Warren's World," *Business Week,* May 10, 1993.

16. Charles T. Munger, Omaha, Nebraska, Berkshire Hathaway annual meeting, 1992.

17. Charles Munger, Omaha, Nebraska, Berkshire Hathaway annual meeting, 1994.

18. John Taylor, "Berkshire Shareholders Quiz Boss," *Omaha World Herald,* May 2, 1995, p. 14.

19. Andrew Kilpatrick, *Of Permanent Value: The Story of Warren Buffett* (Birmingham, Alabama: AKPE, 1998), p. 679.

Chapter Sixteen   Berkshire in the 1990s—Power Building

1. Brett D. Fromson, "How Do You Think Big?" *Washington Post,* January 9, 1994, p. H1.

2. *Forbes,* October 18, 1993.

3. Laurie P. Cohen, "Warren Buffett: His Folksy Image Belies a Killer Instinct," *Wall Street Journal,* November 8, 1991, p. A6.

4. Anthony Bianco, "The Warren Buffett You Don't Know," *Business Week,* July 5, 1999, p. 54.

5. Alice Schroeder and Gregory Lapin, "Berkshire Hathaway: The Ultimate Conglomerate Discount," Paine-Webber Equity Research, January 1999.

6. Berkshire Hathaway Annual Report, March 26, 1979.

7. Steve Jordan, "Berkshire Report Notes Insurance, USAir Downside," *Omaha World Herald,* March 20, 1995, Business Section, p. 12.

8. Gary Weiss and David Greising, "Poof! Wall Street's Sorcerers Lose Their Magic," *Business Week,* January 27, 1992, p. 74.

9. Stan Hindon, "The Geico Deal: How Billionaire Buffett Bit at $70," *Washington Post,* November 6, 1995, p 29.

10. Greg Burns, "This Sage Isn't from Omaha," *Business Week,* April 1, 1996.

11. Alice Schroeder and Gregory Lapin, "Berkshire Hathaway: The Ultimate Conglomerate Discount," Paine-Webber Equity Research, January 1999.

12. www.ntsb.gov/publictn/1999/AAAR9901.htm.

13. Steve Jordan, "Berkshire Report Notes Insurance, USAir Downside," *Omaha World Herald,* March 20, 1995, Business Section, p. 12.

14. Warren Buffett, Omaha, Nebraska, Berkshire Hathaway Annual Meeting, May 1997.

15. Associated Press, "Airplane Firm Attracts Stake by Buffett Firm," *Omaha World Herald,* May 5, 1990.

16. UPI, "Berkshire to Buy More of Firm," *Omaha World Herald,* September 17, 1990.

17. Dolly Setton and Robert Lenzner, "The Berkshire Bunch," *Forbes,* October 12, 1998.

18. Don Bauder, "PS Group Board Member Steps Down with a Parting Shot," *San Diego Union-Tribune,* April 13, 1999, p. C-1.

19. John Taylor, "Buffett Dazzles 7,700 with Humor," *Omaha World Herald,* May 6, 1997, p. 1.

20. Lawrence A. Cunningham, ed., "Conversations from the Warren Buffett Symposium," Cardozo Law Review, Volume 19, Nos. 1 and 2, September–November, 1997, p. 813.

21. Tim W Ferguson, "A Revolution that has a long way to go," *Forbes,* August 11, 1997.

22. Ibid.

23. The Motley Fool, http://www.fool.com, May 5, 1999.

24. Dean Calbreath, "Munger Group Buys Chunk of Price REIT," *San Diego Union-Tribune,* February 11, 1999, p. C-2.

25. "Berkshire Hathaway Earnings Fall," The Associated Press, March 11, 1998.

26. *Forbes,* October 18, 1993.

27. John Taylor and Jim Rasmussen, "Buffett Takes Center Stage for Upbeat Berkshire Bash," *Omaha World Herald,* May 5, 1998, p. 18.

Chapter Seventeen   Salomon Brothers

1. Laurie P. Cohen, "Buffett Shows Tough Side to Salomon—and Gutfruend," *Wall Street Journal*, November 8, 1991, p. A6.

2. Carol J. Loomis, "Warren Buffett's Wild Ride at Salomon," *Fortune*, October 27, 1997, p. 114.

3. Ibid.

4. Laurie P. Cohen, "Buffett Shows Tough Side to Salomon—and Gutfruend," *Wall Street Journal*, November 8, 1991, p. A6.

5. Kurt Eichenwald, "Salomon's 2 Top Officers to Resign Amid Scandal," *New York Times*, August 17, 1991, p. A1.

6. Carol J. Loomis, "Warren Buffett's Wild Ride at Salomon," *Fortune*, October 27, 1997, p. 114.

7. Steve Coll, "Buffett to Buy Stake in Salomon Brothers, Inc." *Washington Post*, September 28, 1987.

8. Sarah Bartlett, "Changing of the Guard at Salomon," *New York Times*, August 17, 1997, p. L33.

9. Carol J. Loomis, "The Inside Story of Warren Buffett," *Fortune*, April 11, 1988, p. 26.

10. Ibid., p. 114.

11. Warren Buffett, Chairman's Letter, Berkshire Hathaway Annual Report, 1987.

12. Sarah Bartlett, "Changing of the Guard at Salomon," *New York Times*, August 17, 1991, p. L33

13. Ibid.

14. Roger Lowenstein, *Buffett: The Making of an American Capitalist* (New York: Random House, 1995), p. 374.

15. Daniel Hertzberg and Laurie P. Cohen, "Scandal Is Fading Away for Salomon, but Not for Trader Paul Mozer," *Wall Street Journal*, August 7, 1992, p. A1.

16. Sarah Bartlett, "Fate of One Top Officer Still Appears Uncertain," *New York Times*, August 17, 1991, p. 44.

17. Roger Lowenstein, *Buffett: The Making of an American Capitalist* (New York: Random House, 1995), p. 297.

18. Leah Nathans Spiro, "The Lion in Winter," *Business Week*, May 1, 1995, p. 152.

19. Laurie P. Cohen, "Buffett Shows Tough Side to Salomon—and Gutfruend," *Wall Street Journal*, November 8, 1991, p. A6.

20. Carol J. Loomis, "Warren Buffett's Wild Ride at Salomon," *Fortune*, October 27, 1997, p. 114.

21. Laurie P. Cohen, "Buffett Shows Tough Side to Salomon—and Gutfruend," *Wall Street Journal*, November 8, 1991, p. A6.

22. Warren Buffett, Chairman's Letter, Salomon Bros. Annual Report, 1992.

23. Roger Lowenstein, *Buffett: The Making of an American Capitalist* (New York: Random House, 1995), p. 388.

24 Carol J. Loomis, "Warren Buffett's Wild Ride at Salomon," *Fortune*, October 27, 1997, p. 114

25. Jaclyn Fierman, "The Perilous New World of Fair Pay," *Fortune*, June 13, 1994, p. 57.

26. Andrew Kilpatrick, *Of Permanent Value: The Story of Warren Buffett* (Birmingham, Alabama: AKPE, 1998), p. 676.

27. "Salomon's New Look May Seem Familiar," *Business Week*, June 15, 1992.

28. Thomas S. Mulligan, "California: News and Insight on Business," *Los Angeles Times*, June 10, 1998.

29. Thomas S. Mulligan, "California: News and Insight on Business," *Los Angeles Times,* June 10, 1998.

30. Leah Nathans Spiro, "The Lion in Winter," *Business Week,* May 1, 1995, p. 152.

31. Roger Lowenstein, *Buffett: The Making of an American Capitalist* (New York: Random House, 1995), p. 409.

32. Leah Nathans Spiro, "The Lion in Winter," *Business Week,* May 1, 1995, p. 152.

33. Ibid.

34 Ibid.

35. James Sterngold, "Two More Quit in Turmoil at Salomon," *New York Times,* February 12, 1998, p. D1.

36. Leah Nathans Spiro, "Turmoil at Salomon," *Business Week,* May 1, 1995, p. 144.

37. "The Trillion Dollar Bet," *Nova,* PBS Television, February 8, 2000.

38. David Sherreff, "Lessons from the Collapse of Hedge Fund, Long Term Capital Management," http://risk.ifci.ch/146520.htm.

39. Charles Munger, "Investment Practices of Leading Charitable Foundations," Speech to the Foundation Financial Officers Group, Santa Monica, California, October 14, 1998.

40. Laurie P. Cohen, "Buffett Shows Tough Side to Salomon—and Gutfruend," *Wall Street Journal,* November 8, 1991, p. A6.

41. "How Buffett Cleaned Up Salomon," *U.S. News and World Report,* June 20, 1994, p. 64.

Chapter Eighteen   The Daily Journal Corporation—A Modest Media Empire

1. Charles T. Munger, Berkshire Hathaway Annual Meeting, Omaha, Nebraska, May 1987.

2 Superior Court of the State of California for the County of Los Angeles, *Metropolitan News Company v. Daily Journal Corporation and Charles T. Munger,* July 1, 1999, Vol. 12, p. 1823.

3. Ibid., p. 1844

4. Ibid., p. 1890.

5. Ibid

6. Ibid., p. 1827.

7. Ann Davis, "Meet Mr. Munger: Shrewd Investor with Odd Investment," *Wall Street Journal,* November 19, 1997, B1.

8. Ibid.

9. Ron Russell, "Raking Muck," *New Times Los Angeles,* August 1999

10. Jack Epstein and James Evans, "Brill's Blitz," *California Business,* June 1987.

11. Ibid.

12. Ibid.

13. Ibid.

14. Ibid.

15. Ibid.

16. Ann Davis, "Meet Mr. Munger: Shrewd Investor with Odd Investment," *Wall Street Journal,* November 19, 1997, B1.

17. Ibid.

18. Roger M. Grace, "Perspectives," *Metropolitan-News Enterprise,* June 1, 1999.

19. "Brash 'Brill's Content' Makes a Splash," clin403.htmatwww.usatoday.com.

20. Roger M. Grace, "Perspectives," *Metropolitan-News Enterprise,* June 1, 1999.

21. Ann Davis, "Meet Mr. Munger: Shrewd Investor with Odd Investment," *Wall Street Journal*, November 19, 1997, B1.

22. Ibid.

23. Gail Diane Cox, "Munger, Grace spar over retrial," *The National Law Journal*, May 24, 1999.

24. Ibid.

25. Roger M. Grace, "Perspectives," *Metropolitan-News Enterprise*, June 1, 1999.

26. Ron Russell, "Raking Muck," *New Times Los Angeles*, August 1999.

27. Ann Davis, "Meet Mr. Munger: Shrewd Investor with Odd Investment," *Wall Street Journal*, November 19, 1997, B1

28. Superior Court of the State of California for the County of Los Angeles, *Metropolitan News Company v. Daily Journal Corporation and Charles T. Munger*, July 1, 1999, Vol 12, p 1832

29. Charles Munger, Speech, Santa Barbara, California, November 1998.

Chapter Nineteen   Doing Good at Good Samaritan Hospital

1. Charles Munger, "Investment practices of Leading Charitable Foundations," Speech to the Foundation Financial Officers Group, Santa Monica, California, October 14, 1998.

2. *Forbes*, January 22, 1996

3. Mary Lou Loper, "RSVP/The Social City," *Los Angeles Times*, October 12, 1997, p. E-10.

4. Harvard-Westlake school newsletter, Spring, 1995.

5. Charles Munger, "The Need for More Multidisciplinary Skill from Professionals: Educational Implications." Address to the 50th reunion of the Harvard Law School Class of 1948. April 4, 1999.

6. Ibid.

7. Ibid.

8. Ibid.

9. Ibid.

10. *Forbes*, January 22, 1996

Chapter Twenty   Elder Statesman and Conscience of the Investment World

1 Lawrence A. Cunningham, ed., "Conversations from the Warren Buffett Symposium," Cardozo Law Review, Volume 19, Nos. 1 and 2, September-November 1997, pp. 769–770.

2. Ibid.

3. Ibid., p. 774.

4. *Outstanding Investor Digest*, March 13, 1998.

5. Charles T. Munger, Harvard School Commencement Speech, Los Angeles, California, June 13, 1986.

6. *Outstanding Investor Digest*, March 13, 1998.

7. Ibid

8. Lawrence A. Cunningham, ed , "Conversations from the Warren Buffett Symposium," Cardozo Law Review, Volume 19, Nos. 1 and 2, September-November 1997.

9. "John Henry Patterson," http://www3.ncr.com/history/jhp/jhp.htm.

10. Louis Lowenstein, "Stockholders, Humbug!" *Washington Post*, January 14, 1990, p. B1.

11. Charles Munger, "Investment practices of Leading Charitable Foundations," Speech to the Foundation Financial Officers Group, Santa Monica, California, October 14, 1998.

12. Charles Munger, as quoted by John C. Bogle, "The Money Show," Disney Coronado Springs Resort, Florida, February 3, 1999.

13. Charles Munger, "Investment practices of Leading Charitable Foundations," Speech to the Foundation Financial Officers Group, Santa Monica, California, October 14, 1998.

14. Ibid.

15. Ibid.

16. Frank Lalli, "Buffett's New Stock: Looks Great but it's less filling," *Money,* April 1996.

17. "Billionaire Buffett Asks SEC to Stop Sale of Cheap Shares," *St. Louis Post-Dispatch,* February 24, 1996, p. 8A.

18. Frank Lalli, "Buffett's New Stock: Looks Great but it's less filling," *Money,* April 1996

19. Steve Jordan, "Buffett's Stock Issue a Missile at 'Miniature Berkshires,'" *Omaha World Herald,* February 14, 1996, p. 20.

20. "Billionaire Buffett Asks SEC to Stop Sale of Cheap Shares," *St. Louis Post-Dispatch,* February 24, 1996, p. 8A.

21. Frank Lalli, "Buffett's New Stock: Looks Great but it's less filling," *Money,* April 1996

22. Steve Jordan, "Berkshire's No. 2: Warren Buffett Is No Fallen Angel," *Omaha World Herald,* February 12, 1992, p. 10.

23. Ibid

24. Ibid.

25. Charles Munger, See's Candy Seventy-Fifth Anniversary Lunch, Los Angeles, California, March 1998.

Chapter Twenty-One   A Time to Reap Rewards

1. Charles Munger, See's Candy Seventy-Fifth Anniversary Lunch, Los Angeles, California, March, 1998.

2. Kenneth Kaufman, "Who Manages, Who Leads?" *Hospitals & Health Networks,* November 5, 1995, p. 62.

3. Anthony Bianco, "The Warren Buffett You Don't Know," *Business Week,* July 5, 1999, p. 66.

INDEX

294 INDEX